Crime and Delinquency in Britain

Sociological Readings edited by
W. G. CARSON and PAUL WILES

Martin Robertson & Company Ltd

First published 1971 by
Martin Robertson & Company Ltd
17 Quick Street London N1 8HL
Reprinted 1974

SBN 85520 003 0 (paper)
SBN 85520 002 2 (case)

Printed by
Robert MacLehose & Company Ltd Glasgow

Contents
Preface

Preface

The idea of compiling this collection of readings developed out of our experience as teachers of the sociology of crime and out of a growing awareness of the need to make British criminological material more easily available. In setting about this task, we were conscious of British criminology's heavy indebtedness to American theorisation and we have therefore attempted to make this connection a salient feature of our introductions to the modern material comprising the bulk of the book. At the same time however, we acknowledge and try to trace the development of a distinctively British perspective against which the partial assimilation of American ideas has taken place.

In presenting a relatively small number of readings, we hope that the fragmentation which can so easily occur in undertakings of this kind has been avoided. We are only too aware, however, that this approach inevitably leaves gaps in our coverage of the sociological perspective on crime and delinquency in this country. In respect of these, we can only hope that this collection may provide both an introduction and some encouragement for a wider reading of the available literature. The decisions about what should be included in this collection and about how the readings should be edited were taken jointly and we therefore share responsibility for any anomalies which may have occurred. The task of writing the introductions was undertaken by W. G. Carson but was accompanied by full discussion and exchange of ideas at all stages.

We are indebted to both authors and publishers for permission to reproduce material and we are particularly grateful to those writers who have prepared papers specifically for this volume. Our thanks are due to Veronica Fairhead for typing assistance and we acknowledge a wider debt to our students at Bedford College, Sir John Cass College and the London School of Economics who provided the impetus for us to undertake this venture.

W. G. Carson
Bedford College
University of London

Paul Wiles
Faculty of Law
University of Sheffield

October 1970

A: The Development of a Sociological Perspective on Crime in Britain

Introduction

While this book is about the sociological study of crime and delinquency in Britain, much of the material which it contains is heavily indebted to theoretical perspectives developed in the United States. This is not to say, however, that Britain lacks her own tradition with regard to the study of crime. Since the process of industrialisation and urbanisation began to alter the parameters of crime in Britain, the social problem of lawlessness has frequently occupied the minds of British thinkers, with the result that a distinct and essentially pragmatic approach to the subject has indeed developed in this country. Today, British criminology in general owes little to any source other than this indigenous tradition, while the distinctly sociological approach to crime in this country, at its best, represents a fusion between British social pragmatism and American theorisation. Thus, as subsequent sections will be concentrating upon this more recent development, this section is concerned with the growth of the earlier British tradition.

It begins with an extract from 'The Condition of the Working Class in England', published in 1848 when the process of industrialisation had already gathered considerable momentum. To the author, Frederick Engels, the apparent increase in crime over the preceding years was neither surprising nor difficult to explain: it was the logical outcome of 'the extension of the proletariat' concomitant upon industrialisation, and as he saw it, of the exploitation of this class by an emergent bourgeoisie prospering under the principles of untrammelled competition. Brutalised and demoralised, the new workers had become 'a race wholly apart' and one for which all freedom in the sense of volition ceased when exploitation became particularly severe. Its crimes were only symptomatic of a more basic conflict between the classes, a conflict which would inevitably erupt one day in undisguised warfare to surprise a bourgeoisie which had failed to comprehend the true significance of increased criminal activity.

Whatever the true symbolic meaning of criminal behaviour, Engels' prediction remains as yet unfulfilled. But this was not the only count upon which he was wrong even in the short term. For those who either held or aspired to hold power in England during the first half of the nineteenth

7

century were not nearly so oblivious of the dangers as he seemed to believe. The marked sensitivity to crime and to its potential political implications at the beginning of the century has been aptly described by Radzinowicz:

'The concept of the dangerous classes as the main source of crime and disorder was very much to the fore at the beginning of the nineteenth century. They were made up of those who had so miserable a share in the accumulating wealth of the industrial revolution that they might at any time break out in political revolt as in France. At their lowest level was the hard core of parasites to be found in any society, ancient or modern. And closely related to this, often indistinguishable from it were the "criminal classes". . . . It served the interests and relieved the conscience of those at the top to look upon the dangerous classes as an independent category, detached from the prevailing social conditions.' (1)

By the time at which Engels was writing, this particular brand of moral paranoia was indeed changing; but the outlook appeared, if anything, even more frightening. Successive reports and enquiries carried out by men such as Chadwick, as often as not at the instigation of governments anxious to disarm political opponents, were exposing another apparently sinister possibility − a breakdown in law and order that pervaded the new working class as a whole. Crowded together in ghetto-like areas of towns and cities which were expanding on a scale unprecedented, enduring physical conditions of extreme hardship all the more apparent for being concentrated, England's emergent class of industrial wage labourers seemed ripe for sedition and crime. In the words of one commentator quoted by Allan Silver in his excellent study, 'The Demand for Order in Civil Society', the situation in 1844 was one in which

'destitution, profligacy, sensuality and crime advance with unheard-of-rapidity in the manufacturing districts and the dangerous classes there massed together combine every three or four years in some general strike or alarming insurrection which, while it lasts, excites universal terrors.' (2)

And to make things worse, while the traditional machinery of control inherited from an agrarian society was proving increasingly ineffectual in the face of urbanisation, the new propertied class was showing itself unwilling to shoulder the burden involved in the traditional system of policing. Probably no better evidence exists for the inaccuracy of Engels' interpretation than this shrewd reluctance on the part of the new entrepreneurs to become embroiled in a task likely to exacerbate their already strained relations with the working class (3).

8

The increasing heterogeneity of thinking on the subject of crime in mid-nineteenth century England was mirrored in the work of Henry Mayhew, a journalist whose social and moral topographies of London began to appear in the eighteen fifties. On the one hand, his descriptions of the non-workers of the metropolis and more specifically of those unwilling to work, urban successors to the sturdy but idle vagabonds who had so excited Tudor legislators, revealed a lingering preoccupation with a morally exogenous class of criminals; on the other, his ability to empathise with the impoverished and underprivileged reflected a growing realisation that a substantial proportion of criminals could no longer be viewed as 'detached from prevailing social conditions'. When he conceded the importance of pressure from 'a variety of circumstances' as a causal factor behind the criminality of *involuntary* non-workers, when he wrote of shirt-workers and slop-tailors being 'impelled' towards crime by the impact of illness or mishap upon their economic predicament of barest subsistence, he was writing about factors beyond the individual's control (4). He was writing, in effect, about a form of social determinism which had also relentlessly impressed itself upon the minds of those who investigated conditions in other and more highly industrialised cities than London.

The sociological significance of Mayhew's work constitutes the central theme of the second extract in this section. Taken from a comparatively recent review of early English criminology, it emphasises his awareness of the need for a system of classification augmenting that provided in official returns, his painstaking ecological method and, above all, his recognition of the part played by social factors in the etiology of crime. In this latter context, the review also illustrates the way in which some other commentators were beginning to acknowledge the existence of a Gordian knot between criminal behaviour and the processes of industrialisation and urbanisation (5).

It is important, however, that these changing perspectives should not be misinterpreted. Certainly Mayhew and those who tended to view crime within the context of a working rather than a dangerous class did make a substantial contribution to the growth of the idea that the phenomenon was a product of society. But they did not pursue the logic of this determinism into the formulation of macro-sociological theories about the nature of the social system and its role in generating criminal behaviour. Rather, their more practical bent led them to follow its logic in another direction, namely, towards the discovery and implementation of appropriate measures for dealing with the problem. To suggest that their contribution helped to pave the way for 'an interpretation of crime in terms of the whole economic structure of society' or, for that matter, in terms of any theory of society on a grand scale is to misunderstand the essential pragmatism of this nascent determinism (6). Then as now British criminology's impact upon social policy far surpassed its contribution to social theory.

Another equally erroneous impression which might be gained from this increased emphasis upon the social context in which crime occurred is that nineteenth century England now unequivocally accepted its own responsibility for what appeared to be an alarming increase in lawlessness and disorder (7). Old ideas die hard and even if the idea of a dangerous class of 'moral outsiders' was becoming palpably untenable, this did not by any means exhaust the supply of potential scapegoats. According to Engels, for example, the impact of urbanisation itself, was not necessarily immune from such an interpretation. The growth of the cities was, he claimed, attractively easy to present as spontaneous and might therefore be held to account without any agonised self-appraisal on the part of the propertied class (8). Even easier to cast in the scapegoat-role was another development, namely the influx of Irish immigrants, which was approaching a peak in the two decades following the famine of 1846-47 in that country. Here was a different kind of outsider and one whose presence had already been noted in connection with both political radicalism (9) and poor urban conditions (10). The social rationale behind his early selection for the part has been described in words not so different from those employed by Radzinowicz to describe attitudes towards the dangerous classes:

'The fact that the Irish areas were singled out for special mention by the numerous commissions concerned to inquire into conditions in the large industrial towns led to the assumption that the Irish were responsible for these conditions. . . . It was perhaps easier for contemporaries to lay the blame at the point that the evil was most evident rather than at its source.' (11)

Both of the above questions are critically examined at some length in our excerpt from Luke O. Pike's 'History of Crime in England' which was published between 1873 and 1876. Interesting rather than particularly influential, this discussion relies heavily upon official statistics and is distinguished by a marked reluctance to reach categorical conclusions on either subject. Migrants may indeed possess 'a natural disposition which leads them into a prison more frequently than the native inhabitants' but, at the same time, it is 'quite demonstrable that causes apart from the character of the immigrants affect the number of committals'. So too of the towns. They may indeed concentrate 'the modern temptations to commit crime in all its newest and most attractive forms', but they do not 'make' criminals of any save those 'of the fitting material'.

The same year that saw the appearance of Pike's final volume saw also the publication in Italy of Cesare Lombroso's famous book, 'L'Uomo delinquente'. Sometimes mistakenly credited with having founded modern criminology (12), this writer was indeed one of the leading exponents of the positivist approach to crime with its emphasis upon scientific method, determinism and invariable social laws (13). But even though his anthropological variant on the theme of social outsiders was critically discussed in late nineteenth century England, the more general theoretical issues raised by this specifically criminological brand of positivism remained relatively neglected (14). As Hermann Mannheim has observed of British criminology in that and subsequent periods,

'the English mind, with its practical rather than theoretical bias, has been more interested in penological questions of treatment than in the criminological and philosophical issues of causation and responsibility.' (15)

This is not to say, of course, that in a wider sociological context the Positivist Movement, based on the teachings of Comte, was totally without influence in this country. As Mary Farmer has shown, during the last quarter of the century there was a thriving congerie of extremely able Englishmen who espoused this doctrine (16). But once again, although they translated and promulgated Comte's philosophy, these scholars did little to develop sociological theory. Rather, the main thrust of their effort was directed toward the 'scientific' investigation of social conditions and, following the Comtean ideal of progress, toward the use of such investigations as guides to social action (17). It was in the field of social reform that they made their most significant contribution (18), and it is to this more indigenous version of the philosophy rather than to its distinctively criminological counterpart that the greater part of any debt to positivism is owed by the sociological investigators of crime in this country.

In opting for the promotion of progress through conciliatory reform rather than full-scale social upheaval (19), the English Positivists were at one with other major trends in social thinking during this period. According to O. R. McGregor, just as in the earlier part of the century social research and social policy 'derived essentially from middle-class anxieties to maintain the stability of institutions by correcting the measured costs and inefficiencies of social wastage', so in its dying years they were increasingly dominated by anxieties about competitive economic efficiency, the consequences of a widened franchise, the spread of socialism and, perhaps most of all, about threats of imminent war. Beset by such problems within and without, 'how could the confidence and support of the whole nation be secured when there was a canker of poverty at the heart of the Empire?' (20). In the new century this preoccupation was destined to become even more central as Britain approached the age of 'demostrategy' in which civilian morale became an integral part of war itself, and a politically inescapable consideration for the maintenance of stability in its aftermath (21).

Poverty had, of course, been a recurrent theme in social commentaries for many years before the close of the nineteenth century. In the eighteen nineties and early nineteen hundreds, however, its investigation reached

11

new peaks of systematisation with the surveys conducted by Charles Booth and B. S. Rowntree (22), which stood out in sharp contrast against what one biographer has seen as the deductive method and propagandist zeal of the earlier writings (23). In the decades which followed, and particularly in the wake of the First World War and the subsequent economic crisis, a number of studies aimed at a similarly systematic investigation of the connection between poverty and crime were instituted (24). We conclude this selection of historical readings with two examples of such studies.

The first is taken from Sir Cyril Burt's much wider study of delinquency which was published in 1925, its appearance in such an eclectic context reflecting the extent to which poverty had become an accepted part of British criminology's standard explanatory repertoire despite the parallel development of other and non-sociological orientations. In Burt's discussion we see, too, his obvious indebtedness to Booth and Rowntree and his self-confessed derivation of the poverty hypothesis from social reformers rather than from social or criminological theorists.

The second and final example comes from Mannheim's 'Social Aspects of Crime in England between the Wars' which did not appear until early in the Second World War. By this time the economic collapse of the thirties and a marked increase in recorded crime had added a new urgency to social investigation and a new dimension to the concept of poverty. The 'successive contrast' in economic prosperity which Burt had conceded as important in relation to a few (25), had become for some time a characteristic of the many. It is thus not surprising to find Mannheim at this time concerning himself with the dynamic rather than the static aspects of poverty (26) and analysing the relationship between crime and unemployment; by then all too many people had good cause to recognise the latter as a major reason for 'sudden changes in the economic position of the masses'.

1. L. Radzinowicz Ideology and Crime London, Heinemann (1966) p. 38
2. A. Silver 'The Demand for Order in Civil Society: A Review of Some Themes in the History of Urban Crime, Police and Riot' in D. Bordua (ed) The Police New York, Wiley (1967)
3. Ibid. p. 3
4. Henry Mayhew London Labour and the London Poor Vol. 4 'Those that will not work' London, Charles Griffin (1894)
5. Another good review of ecological studies in the nineteenth century may be found in T. Morris The Criminal Area London, Routledge & Kegan Paul (1957) Chap. 3
6. As, for example, does Radzinowicz op. cit. p. 42. Much more than time and distance separates early English criminological empiricism from the low twentieth century Marxism of the Dutchman Wilhelm Bonger. See W. E. Bonger Crime and Economic Conditions Boston, Little, Brown & Co. (1916)

7. See J. J. Tobias Crime and Industrial Society in the early 19th Century London, Batsford (1967)
8. See below p. 16
9. E. P. Thompson The Making of the English Working Class London, Penguin (1968) p. 409 ff.
10. J. A. Jackson The Irish in Britain London, Routledge & Kegan Paul (1963) Chap. 3
11. Ibid. p. 41
12 A. Lindesmith and Y. Levin 'The Lombrosian Myth in Criminology' American Journal of Sociology XLII, (March 1937) pp. 653-71
13. See M. E. Wolfgang 'Cesare Lombroso' in H. Mannheim (ed) Pioneers in Criminology London, Stevens (1960)
14. H. Mannheim (ed) Pioneers in Criminology London, Stevens (1960) p. 18
15. Ibid.
16. M. E. Farmer 'The Positivist Movement and the Development of English Sociology' The Sociological Review 15 (1), (March 1967) pp. 5-20
17. See J. E. McGee A Crusade for Humanity: The History of Organised Positivism in England London, Watts & Co. (1931)
18. See L. Sklair The Sociology of Progress London, Routledge & Kegan Paul (1970)
19. Ibid.
20. O. R. McGregor 'Social Research and Social Policy in the Nineteenth Century' British Journal of Sociology VIII (2), (June 1957) pp. 146-57
21. See R. M. Titmuss Essays on the Welfare State London, Allen & Unwin (1963) Chap. 4
22. Charles Booth Life and Labour of the People in London 9 vols. 2nd ed. London, Macmillan (1892-97). B. S. Rowntree Poverty: A Study of Town Life London, Macmillan (1901)
23. T. S. Simey and M. B. Simey Charles Booth: Social Scientist London, Oxford University Press (1960)
24. For a review of such studies see B. Wootton Social Science and Social Pathology London, Allen & Unwin (1959) Chap. 3
25. C. Burt The Young Delinquent 2nd ed. London, University of London Press (1927) p. 84
26. See also D. S. Thomas Social Aspects of the Business Cycle London, Routledge & Kegan Paul (1925)

Crime and the Condition of the Working-Class

by Frederick Engels
Reprinted from 'The Condition of the Working-Class in England' in Karl Marx and Frederick Engels on Britain
. Moscow, Foreign Languages Publishing House (1953) Chap. 5

A town, such as London, where a man may wander for hours together without reaching the beginning of the end, without meeting the slightest hint which could lead to the inference that there is open country within reach, is a strange thing. This colossal centralisation, this heaping together of two and a half millions of human beings at one point, has multiplied the power of this two and a half millions a hundredfold; has raised London to

13

the commercial capital of the world, created the giant docks and assembled the thousand vessels that continually cover the Thames. I know nothing more imposing than the view which the Thames offers during the ascent from the sea to London Bridge. The masses of buildings, the wharves on both sides, especially from Woolwich upwards, the countless ships along both shores, crowding ever closer and closer together, until, at last, only a narrow passage remains in the middle of the river, a passage through which hundreds of steamers shoot by one another; all this is so vast, so impressive, that a man cannot collect himself, but is lost in the marvel of England's greatness before he sets foot upon English soil.

But the sacrifices which all this has cost become apparent later. After roaming the streets of the capital a day or two, making headway with difficulty through the human turmoil and the endless lines of vehicles, after visiting the slums of the metropolis, one realises for the first time that these Londoners have been forced to sacrifice the best qualities of their human nature, to bring to pass all the marvels of civilisation which crowd their city; that a hundred powers which slumbered within them have remained inactive, have been suppressed in order that a few might be developed more fully and multiply through union with those of others. The very turmoil of the streets has something repulsive, something against which human nature rebels. The hundreds of thousands of all classes and ranks crowding past each other, are they not all human beings with the same qualities and powers, and with the same interest in being happy? And have they not, in the end, to seek happiness in the same way, by the same means? And still they crowd by one another as though they had nothing in common, nothing to do with one another, and their only agreement is the tacit one, that each keep to his own side of the pavement, so as not to delay the opposing streams of the crowd, while it occurs to no man to honour another with so much as a glance. The brutal indifference, the unfeeling isolation of each in his private interest becomes the more repellant and offensive, the more these individuals are crowded together, within a limited space. And, however much one may be aware that this isolation of the individual, this narrow self-seeking is the fundamental principle of our society everywhere, it is nowhere so shamelessly bare-faced, so self-conscious as just here in the crowding of the great city. The dissolution of mankind into monads, of which each one has a separate principle and a separate purpose, the world of atoms, is here carried out to its utmost extreme.

Hence it comes, too, that the social war, the war of each against all, is here openly declared. Just as in Stirner's recent book, people regard each other only as useful objects; each exploits the other, and the end of it all is, that the stronger treads the weaker under foot, and that the powerful few, the capitalists, seize everything for themselves, while to the weak many, the poor, scarcely a bare existence remains.

What is true of London, is true of Manchester, Birmingham, Leeds, is

14

true of all great towns. Everywhere barbarous indifference, hard egotism on one hand, and nameless misery on the other, everywhere social warfare, every man's house in a state of siege, everywhere reciprocal plundering under the protection of the law, and all so shameless, so openly avowed that one shrinks before the consequences of our social state as they manifest themselves here undisguised, and can only wonder that the whole crazy fabric still hangs together.

Since capital, the direct or indirect control of the means of subsistence and production, is the weapon with which this social warfare is carried on, it is clear that all the disadvantages of such a state must fall upon the poor. For him no man has the slightest concern. Cast into the whirlpool, he must struggle through as well as he can. If he is so happy as to find work *i.e.*, if the bourgeoisie does him the favour to enrich itself by means of him, wages await him which scarcely suffice to keep body and soul together; if he can get no work he may steal, if he is not afraid of the police, or starve, in which case the police will take care that he does so in a quiet and inoffensive manner. During my residence in England, at least twenty or thirty persons have died of simple starvation under the most revolting circumstances, and a jury has rarely been found possessed of the courage to speak the plain truth in the matter. Let the testimony of the witnesses be never so clear and unequivocal, the bourgeoisie, from which the jury is selected, always finds some backdoor through which to escape the frightful verdict, death from starvation. The bourgeoisie dare not speak the truth in these cases, for it would speak its own condemnation. But indirectly, far more than directly, many have died of starvation, where long continued want of proper nourishment has called forth fatal illness, when it has produced such debility that causes which might otherwise have remained inoperative, brought on severe illness and death. The English working-men call this "social murder," and accuse our whole society of perpetrating this crime perpetually. Are they wrong?

The manner in which the great multitude of the poor is treated by society to-day is revolting. They are drawn into the large cities where they breathe a poorer atmosphere than in the country; they are relegated to districts which, by reason of the method of construction, are worse ventilated than any others; they are deprived of all means of cleanliness, of water itself, since pipes are laid only when paid for, and the rivers so polluted that they are useless for such purposes; they are obliged to throw all offal and garbage, all dirty water, often all disgusting drainage and excrement into the streets, being without other means of disposing of them; they are thus compelled to infect the region of their own dwellings. Nor is this enough. All conceivable evils are heaped upon the heads of the poor. If the population of great cities is too dense in general, it is they in particular who are packed into the least space. As though the vitiated atmosphere of the streets were not enough, they are penned in dozens into single rooms, so that the air which they breathe at night is enough in itself

15

to stifle them. They are given damp dwellings, cellar dens that are not waterproof from below, or garrets that leak from above. Their houses are so built that the clammy air cannot escape. They are supplied bad, tattered, or rotten clothing, adulterated and indigestible food. They are exposed to the most exciting changes of mental condition, the most violent vibrations between hope and fear; they are hunted like game, and not permitted to attain peace of mind and quiet enjoyment of life. They are deprived of all enjoyments except that of sexual indulgence and drunkenness, are worked every day to the point of complete exhaustion of their mental and physical energies, and are thus constantly spurred on to the maddest excess in the only two enjoyments at their command. And if they surmount all this, they fall victims to want of work in a crisis when all the little is taken from them that had hitherto been vouchsafed them.

Thus are the workers cast out and ignored by the class in power, morally as well as physically and mentally. The only provision made for them is the law, which fastens upon them when they become obnoxious to the bourgeoisie. Like the dullest of the brutes, they are treated to but one form of education, the whip, in the shape of force, not convincing but intimidating. There is, therefore, no cause for surprise if the workers, treated as brutes, actually become such; or if they can maintain their consciousness of manhood only by cherishing the most glowing hatred, the most unbroken inward rebellion against the bourgeoisie in power. They are men so long only as they burn with wrath against the reigning class. They become brutes the moment they bend in patience under the yoke, and merely strive to make life endurable while abandoning the effort to break the yoke.

And when all these conditions have engendered vast demoralisation among the workers, a new influence is added to the old, to spread this degradation more widely and carry it to the extremest point. This influence is the centralisation of the population. The writers of the English bourgeoisie are crying murder at the demoralising tendency of the great cities; like perverted Jeremiahs, they sing dirges, not over the destruction, but the growth of the cities. Sheriff Alison attributes almost everything, and Dr. Vaughan, author of "The Age of Great Cities," still more to this influence. And this is natural, for the propertied class has too direct an interest in the other conditions which tend to destroy the worker body and soul. If they should admit that "poverty, insecurity, overwork, forced work, are the chief ruinous influences," they would have to draw the conclusion, "then let us give the poor property, guarantee their subsistence, make laws against overwork," and this the bourgeoisie dare not formulate. But the great cities have grown up so spontaneously, the population has moved into them so wholly of its own motion, and the inference that manufacture and the middle-class which profits from it alone have created the cities is so remote, that it is extremely convenient for the ruling class to ascribe all the evil to this apparently unavoidable source; whereas the great cities really only secure a more rapid and certáin development for evils already existing in the germ.

In view of all this, it is not surprising that the working-class has gradually become a race wholly apart from the English bourgeoisie. The bourgeoisie has more in common with every other nation of the earth than with the workers in whose midst it lives. The workers speak other dialects, have other thoughts and ideals, other customs and moral principles, a different religion and other politics than those of the bourgeoisie. Thus they are two radically dissimilar nations, as unlike as difference of race could make them, of whom we on the Continent have known but one, the bourgeoisie. Yet it is precisely the other, the people, the proletariat, which is by far the more important for the future of England.

The contempt for the existing social order is most conspicuous in its extreme form — that of offences against the law. If the influences demoralising to the working-man act more powerfully, more concentratedly than usual, he becomes an offender as certainly as water abandons the fluid for the vaporous state at 80 degrees, Réaumur. Under the brutal and brutalising treatment of the bourgeoisie, the working-man becomes precisely as much a thing without volition as water, and is subject to the laws of Nature with precisely the same necessity; at a certain point all freedom ceases. Hence with the extension of the proletariat, crime has increased in England, and the British nation has become the most criminal in the world. From the annual criminal tables of the Home Secretary, it is evident that the increase of crime in England has proceeded with incomprehensible rapidity. The numbers of arrests for *criminal* offences reached in the years: 1805, 4,605; 1810, 5,146; 1815, 7,898; 1820, 13,710; 1825, 14,437; 1830, 18,107; 1835, 20,731; 1840, 27,187; 1841, 27,760; 1842, 31,309 in England and Wales alone. That is to say, they increased sevenfold in thirty-seven years. Of these arrests, in 1842, 4,497 were made in Lancashire alone, or more than 14 per cent. of the whole; and 4,094 in Middlesex, including London, or more than 13 per cent. So that two districts which include great cities with large proletarian populations, produced one-fourth of the total amount of crime, though their population is far from forming one-fourth of the whole. Moreover, the criminal tables prove directly that nearly all crime arises within the proletariat; for, in 1842, taking the average, out of 100 criminals, 32.35 could neither read nor write; 58.32 read and wrote imperfectly; 6.77 could read and write well; 0.22 had enjoyed a higher education, while the degree of education of 2.34 could not be ascertained. In Scotland, crime has increased yet more rapidly. There were but 89 arrests for criminal offences in 1819, and as early as 1837 the number had risen to 3,176, and in 1842 to 4,189. In Lanarkshire, where Sheriff Alison himself made out the official report, population has doubled once in thirty years, and crime once in five and a half, or six times more rapidly than the population. The offences, as in all civilised countries, are, in the great majority of cases, against property, and have, therefore, arisen from want in some form; for what a man has, he does not steal. The proportion of offences against property to the population, which in the Netherlands is as 1: 7,140, and in France, as 1: 1,804, was in England, when Gaskell wrote, as 1: 799. The proportion of offences against persons to the population is, in the Netherlands, 1: 28,904; in France, 1: 17,573; in England, 1: 23,395; that of crimes in general to the population in the agricultural districts, as 1: 1,043; in the manufacturing districts as 1: 840. In the whole of England to-day the proportion is 1: 660; though it is scarcely ten years since Gaskell's book appeared!

These facts are certainly more than sufficient to bring any one, even a bourgeois, to pause and reflect upon the consequences of such a state of things. If demoralisation and crime multiply twenty years longer in this proportion (and if English manufacture in these twenty years should be less prosperous than heretofore, the progressive multiplication of crime can only continue the more rapidly), what will the result be? Society is already in a state of visible dissolution; it is impossible to pick up a newspaper without seeing the most striking evidence of the giving way of all social ties. I look at random into a heap of English journals lying before me; there is the *Manchester Guardian* for October 30, 1844, which reports for three days. It no longer takes the trouble to give exact details as to Manchester, and merely relates the most interesting cases: that the workers in a mill have struck for higher wages without giving notice, and been condemned by a Justice of the Peace to resume work; that in Salford a couple of boys had been caught stealing, and a bankrupt tradesman tried to cheat his creditors. From the neighbouring towns the reports are more detailed: in Ashton, two thefts, one burglary, one suicide; in Bury, one theft; in Bolton, two thefts, one revenue fraud; in Leigh, one theft; in Oldham, one strike for wages, one theft, one fight between Irish women, one non-Union hatter assaulted by Union men, one mother beaten by her son, one attack upon the police, one robbery of a church; in Stockport, discontent of working-men with wages, one theft, one fraud, one fight, one wife beaten by her husband; in Warrington, one theft, one fight; in Wigan, one theft, and one robbery of a church. The reports of the London papers are much worse; frauds, thefts, assaults, family quarrels crowd one another. A *Times* of September 12, 1844, falls into my hand, which gives a report of a single day, including a theft, an attack upon the police, a sentence upon a father requiring him to support his illegitimate son, the abandonment of a child by its parents, and the poisoning of a man by his wife. Similar reports are to be found in all the English papers. In this country, social war is under full headway, every one stands for himself, and fights for himself against all comers, and whether or not he shall injure all the others who are his declared foes, depends upon a cynical calculation as to what is most advantageous for himself. It no longer occurs to any one to come to a peaceful understanding with his fellow-man; all differences are settled by threats, violence, or in a law-court. In short, every one sees in his neighbour an enemy to be got out of the way, or, at best, a tool to be used for his own advantage. And this war grows from year to year, as the criminal tables show, more violent, passionate, irreconcilable. The enemies are dividing gradually into two great camps — the bourgeoisie on the one hand, the workers on the other. This war of each against all, of the bourgeoisie against the proletariat, need cause us no surprise, for it is only the logical sequel of the principle involved in free competition. But it may very well surprise us that the bourgeoisie remains so quiet and composed in the face of the rapidly gathering storm-clouds, that it can read all these things daily in the papers without, we will not say indignation at such a social condition, but fear of its consequences, of a universal outburst of that which manifests itself symptomatically from day to day in the form of crime. But then it is the bourgeoisie, and from its standpoint cannot even see the facts, much less perceive their consequences. One thing only is astounding, that class prejudice and preconceived opinions can hold a whole class of human beings in such perfect, I might almost say, such mad blindness. Meanwhile, the development of the nation goes its way whether the bourgeoisie has eyes for it or not, and will surprise the property-holding class one day with things not dreamed of in its philosophy.

English Ecology and Criminology of the Past Century

by L. Lindesmith and Y. Levin
Reprinted from Journal of Criminal Law, Criminology and Police Science North Western University School of Law (1937) Vol. 27 No. 6 pp. 801-16

The emphasis that has been placed in recent years upon what is known as the "ecological approach" to the study of crime makes it appropriate to pay attention to a period in English history when ecological studies of this subject appear to have been as much in fashion as they are today. Roughly between the years 1830 and 1860, a considerable interest in territorial or regional studies of crime was manifested in England. Over a period of several decades there were accumulated a mass of data and a body of knowledge which were never really discredited or displaced by work of superior scientific merit along the same lines, but were simply relegated to the background in favor of the psychiatric, biological and other types of theories of the later 19th century, and eventually forgotten or disregarded. Although present day criminologists who adopt the ecological approach do not refer to their English predecessors for guidance and corroboration, it is surprising to find that the emphasis which is being placed upon social factors in the causation of crime is closely paralleled in these earlier studies of what might be called the Pre-Lombrosian era. The recent revival of some of these old points of view and techniques suggests the comparison of the older studies with contemporary ones in order to evaluate more precisely the progress criminology has made in the last hundred years. The enthusiasm of social scientists often leads them to attribute greater originality to contemporary studies and less value to the old than is actually warranted by the facts in the case. In the descriptions of some of these older studies which follow, we have attempted to keep in mind contemporary work along the same lines so as to facilitate comparison. Limitations of space prevent more than passing reference to many maps, tables, or discussion which deserve far more extended treatment than we shall attempt in the present article.

Before analyzing the statistical data in these earlier studies, it should be noticed that numerous general observations regarding the concentration of crime in 'low' neighbourhoods were made by writers and officials dealing with criminals. Thus, on the basis of his observations, and not with the aid of statistics, Walter Buchanan, one of Her Majesty's Justices of the Peace for the County of Middlesex, writing in 1846, noted that

'The great recesses of juvenile crime in the metropolitan districts to the north of the Thames are Spitalfields, Bethnal-Green, Shoreditch, Hoxton, Wapping, Ratcliffe, White Chapel, Shaffron-Hill, Almonry, Tothill Fields, Gray's Inn Lane, St. Giles, Seven Dials, Drury Lane, Field Lane, and Lisson Grove; and although in some parts of Maryle-Bone, St. Pancras, Chelsea, Islington, Clerkenwell, Limehouse, Padding-ton, Kensington and elsewhere in and about the metropolis, young thieves resort, they are not to be compared in number to those who are to be found issuing from the above named places. In the densely crowded lanes and alleys of these areas, wretched tenements are found, containing in every cellar and on every floor, men and women, children both male and female, all huddled together, sometimes with strangers, and too frequently standing in very doubtful consanguinity to each other. In these abodes decency and shame have fied; depravity reigns in all its horrors.' (1)

That juvenile delinquents and adult criminals were concentrated in the deteriorated areas of the large towns and cities was a matter of common observation. Not only those whose work brought them in direct contact with criminals and youthful delinquents, but others, notably writers on social and political economy, observed the effects of deterior-ated housing conditions. Allison observes that

'If any person will walk thru St. Giles, the crowded alleys of Dublin, or the poorer quarters of Glasgow at night, he will no longer worry at the disorderly habits and profligate enjoyments of the lower order; his astonishment will be, that there is so little crime in the world. . . . The great cause of human corruption in these crowded situations is the contagious nature of bad example. . . . A family is compelled by circumstances or induced by interest to leave the country. The extravagant price of lodgings compels them to take refuge in one of the crowded districts of the town, in the midst of thousands in similar necessitous circumstances with themselves. Under the same roof they probably find a nest of prostitutes, in the next door a den of thieves. In the room which they occupy they hear incessantly the revel of intoxication or are compelled to witness the riot of licentiousness.' (2)

The author relates of this family that one of the sons becomes a member of one of the numerous bands of thieves, commits a house-breaking, and is sentenced to be transported. The daughters become prostitutes and the children of a once happy and virtuous family are thrown upon the streets to pick up a precarious subsistence. He concludes that this unhappy history of a family proceeds not from any extraordinary depravity in their character, but from the almost irresistible nature of the temptations to which the poor are exposed.

Contemporary observers of what we now call the Industrial Revolution carefully noted the growth of large towns, which was one of the marked features of the transformation of England from an agricultural country to an industrial one. In the early decades of the nineteenth century, students of political economy began to assess the growth of the factory towns, a growth which was apparent to every one. In a volume published in 1843, a writer discusses the growth of manufacturing in England and its attendant good effects on the population, such as the growth of large and princely fortunes, the encouragement given to the arts, the enterprise and energy created by the establishment of factories. At the same time he declares that

'Among the numerous causes which appear inseparable from manufactories, producing crime and immorality, the following deserve particular notice. The crowding together of the working classes in narrow streets, filthy lanes, alleys and yards, is a serious evil and one which has hitherto increased in all manufacturing towns. The poor are not resident in these places from choice, but from necessity. Families are not huddled together into dark ill-ventilated rooms from any peculiar pleasure it affords. They may indeed have become insensible of the inconvenience and wretchedness of such situations, but slender and uncertain means do not enable them to command more comfortable abodes. They are fixed there by circumstances.' (3)

In his evidence before a Select Committee of Crime in 1830, the Governor of Coldbath Prison stated that:

'In my opinion the crowning cause of crime in the metropolis is to be found in the shocking state of the habitations of the poor, their confined and fetid localities, the consequent necessity for consigning children to the streets for requisite air and exercise. These causes combine to product a state of frightful demoralization. The absence of cleanliness, of decency, and of all decorum; the disregard of any heedful separation between the sexes; the polluting language; and the scenes of profligacy, hourly occurring, all tend to foster idleness and vicious abandonment.' (4)

When the reformatories were established in the 1850 decade, the Chief Inspector, Sydney Turner, noted in his annual report for 1856 that the juvenile delinquents committed from the deteriorated districts of London presented a special problem because of their association in gangs. He advocated that these delinquents be committed to various reformatories instead of being permitted to concentrate in any one reformatory. (5)

The following quotation from M. D. Hill, Recorder of Birmingham, will serve to illustrate how the effects of city life upon personal conduct were analyzed in the middle of the nineteenth century:

'A century and a half ago, as far as I have been able to ascertain, there was scarcely a large town in the island except London. When I use the term 'large town' I mean where an inhabitant of the humbler classes is unknown to the majority of the inhabitants of that town. By a small town, I mean a town where, 'a converso' every inhabitant is more or less known to the mass of people of that town. I think it will not require any long train of reflection to show that in small towns there must be a sort of natural police, of a very wholesome kind, operating upon the conduct of every individual, who lives, as it were, under the public eye. But in a large town, he lives, as it were, in absolute obscurity; and we know that large towns are sought by way of refuge, because of that obscurity, which, to a certain extent, gives impunity. Again, there is another cause which I have never seen much noticed, but which, having observed its operation for many years, I am disposed to consider it very important, and that is the gradual separation of classes which takes place in towns by a custom which has gradually grown up, that every person who can afford it lives out of town, and at a spot distant from his place of business. Now this was not formerly so; it is a habit which has, practically speaking, grown up within the last half century. The result of the old habit was that rich and poor lived in proximity; and the superior classes exercised that species of silent but very efficient control over their neighbors, to which I have already referred. They are now gone, and the consequence is, that large masses of the population are gathered together without those wholesome influences which operated upon them when their congregation was more mixed, when they were divided, so to speak, by having persons of a different class of life, better educated, amongst them. These two causes, namely, the magnitude of towns and the separation of classes, have acted so concurrently, and the effect has been that we find in very large towns, which I am acquainted with, that in some quarters there is a public opinion and a public standard of morals very different from what we should desire to see. Then the children who are born amongst these masses grow up under that opinion, and make that standard of morals their very own; and with them the best lad, or the best man, is he who can obtain subsistence, or satisfy the wants of life, with the least labour, by begging or by stealing, and who shows the greatest dexterity in accomplishing his object, and the greatest wariness in escaping the penalties of the law; and lastly the greatest power of endurance and defiance, when he comes under the lash of the law.' (6)

We have selected for examination the work of Henry Mayhew (7) who utilized official statistics in investigating the problems of crime in their wider aspects. Mayhew's volume, *The Criminal Prisons of London*, in addition to containing a detailed description of the prisons of London, as the title indicates, includes also a wealth of statistics and illuminating observations on such subjects as: juvenile delinquency, the evolution of the juvenile offender into the habitual criminal, recidivism, female crime, the concentration of various types of crime in certain localities within London and in certain counties of England and Wales, classifications of crime and criminals, the evaluation of police statistics, the history of the 'delinquency areas' of London, methods of prison administration and prison discipline, and the role of early family and community conditions in producing criminals. Many of the statistical tables cover all of England and Wales by counties; some give data by police districts within London, other tables compare cities and other territorial divisions. It is interesting in connection with the general problem of the relation of crime to the social life of the period that Mayhew introduces his study with a general topographical description of London and London streets, giving population and other general descriptive data for the city as a whole. He has a section entitled "Some Idea of the Size and Population of London" and a "Table Showing the Area, Number of Houses, and proportion of Houses to Each Acre in London, 1851" by districts — 36 of them. In a similar manner he notes the "Distribution and Density of the Population of London in 1851" in terms of the same 36 districts and, on the page facing this table, represents the same data on a shaded ecological map of the city. He does the same for the average income tax assessments and poor rate assessments per house in these districts, and gives us an idea of "mobility" by listing the number of vehicles passing through each of the principal London streets in 24 hours.

Perhaps of even greater interest in this volume is the ecological study of the residences of the members of the various branches of the legal profession in London, in which Mayhew shows the concentration in what he calls the "legal capital," Chancery Lane, which he describes in detail. He traces the ramifications radiating out from this legal capital and describes the legal "suburbs" of the city, listing more than a hundred "legal localities." In order to place this material in its proper setting, he precedes it with the statistics showing the proportion of the population included in the professional classes of each of the counties of England and Wales and in London.

The other volume, "Those Who Will Not Work," is remarkable in revealing the full extent and detailed character of Mayhew's ecological description of London crime. In it he classifies London "beggars, thieves, prostitutes, cheats and swindlers" into a total of more than one hundred specific groups. He and his collaborators discuss and describe the habitat and mode of making a living of each of these groups and specify quite exactly the districts in which they commit their depredations as well as the streets and localities where they live. This volume abounds in graphic descriptions of the various crime areas and in personal testimony obtained by interviews with persons in the walks of life and areas under consideration, in the manner of the "participant observer" of contemporary sociology. There are recorded in this volume more than a dozen narratives of professional criminals, written in the first person in the criminal's own words, telling his life history, describing the natural evolution of the professional from the juvenile criminal, and giving vivid descriptions of the modus operandi in the various "rackets," as we would call them. (8)

In the appendix of Mayhew's "Those Who Will not Work" there is a series of fifteen maps with accompanying tables showing the distribution (by rates whenever appropriate) of the following, in each of the counties of England and Wales:

Map No. 1 — Density of Population
2 — Intensity of Criminality
3 — Intensity of Ignorance
4 — Number of Illegitimate Children
5 — Number of Early Marriages
6 — Number of Females
7 — Committals for Rape
8 — Committals for Carnally Abusing Girls
9 — Committals for Disorderly Houses
10 — Concealment of Births
11 — Attempts at Miscarriage
12 — Assaults with Intent
13 — Committals for Bigamy
14 — Committals for Abduction
15 — Criminality of Females

The tables usually cover a ten year period (1841-1850). In arriving at correlations without the use of the coefficient, which was not known at that time, Mayhew lists the counties above and below the average according to their respective deviations from the average, and then juxtaposes two such series and analyzes their differences and similarities. (9)

Perhaps one of the major points made in recent ecological studies of crime, and one that has received a great deal of attention and been heralded as a landmark in the scientific study of crime, is that crime rates, juvenile and adult, vary from one community to another within cities; and that crime is concentrated in certain areas and not distributed uniformly. This fact was well known to Mayhew, who, in addition to working out rates by counties and cities, also computed rates for police districts within London, and went a step farther in specifying what particular kinds of crimes were to be found in particular areas within the city. He calls attention to the fact that London's "rookeries" of crime have long histories, some of which extend back more than five hundred years. He made personal investigations of these areas, which have been "nests of London's beggars, prostitutes and thieves" continuously for centuries. His masterly descriptions of such districts as St. Giles, Spitalfields, Westminster, and the Borough are precise delimitations of characteristic areas of London vice and crime. The following excerpt is typical:

'There is no quarter of the Metropolis impressed with such strongly-marked features as the episcopal city of Westminster. We do not speak of that vague and straggling electoral Westminster, which stretches as far as Kensington and Chelsea to the west, and even Temple Bar to the east; but of that Westminster proper — that triangular snip of the Metropolis which is bounded by the Vauxhall Road on one side, St. James Park on another, and by the Thames on the third — that Westminster which can boast of some of the noblest and some of the meanest buildings to be found throughout London (the grand and picturesque old Abbey, and the filthy and squalid Duck Lane — the brand new and orate Houses of Parliament, and the half-dilapidated and dingy old Almonry) which is the seat at once of the great mass of law makers and law-breakers — where there are more almshouses, and more prisons and more schools — more old noblemen's mansions and more costermonger's hovels — more narrow lanes, and courts, and more broad unfinished highways — whose Hall is frequented by more lawyers, and whose purlieus are infested by more thieves — whose public houses are resorted to by more paviors — whose streets are thronged by more soldiers — on whose doorsteps sit more bare-headed wantons — and whose dry arches shelter more vagabond urchins than are to be noted in any other part of the Metropolis — ay, and perhaps in any other part of the world.' (10)

In his analysis of juvenile crime Mayhew compares rates in the various counties and notes that the rates of juvenile delinquency are highest in those counties which have large cities in them. He takes note of the difference in age distribution from one locality to another when he makes these comparisons. (11) In the county containing London he shows that 41% of the juvenile offenders came from one of the seven police districts and 24% from another. The other districts contributed an average of between 5% and 8% and the country only 5½% of the total. He further splits up the rural returns to show that most of the rural offenders came from one district — Hammersmith. He lists areas and streets of London which particularly abound in gangs of juvenile delinquents. The following excerpts taken from *"Those Who Will Not Work"* show clearly an amazing ecological knowledge of London crime of that day:

'In order to find these houses it is necessary to journey eastwards, and leave the artificial glitter of the West-end, where vice is pampered and caressed. Whitechapel, Wapping, Ratcliff Highway, and analogous districts are prolific in the production of these infamies. St. Georges in-the-east abounds with them." . . . "Whitechapel has always been looked upon as a suspicious unhealthy locality. To begin with, its population is a strange amalgamation of Jews, English, French, Germans and other antagonistic elements." . . . "Ship alley is full of foreign lodging houses." . . . "Tiger Bay like Frederick Street is full of brothels and thieves lodging houses." . . . "The most of those engaged in this kind of robbery in Oxford Street come from the neighborhood of St. Giles and Lisson Grove." . . . "The most accomplished pickpockets reside at Islington, Hoxton, Kingsland Road, St. Lukes, The Borough, Camberwell and Lambeth in quiet respectable streets, and occasionally change their lodging if watched by the police." . . . "Some Londoners are in the habit of stealing horses. These often frequent the Old Kent Road, and are dressed as grooms or stableman." . . . "Dog stealing is very prevalent, particularly in the West-end of the Metropolis, and is a rather profitable class of felony. These thieves reside at the Seven Dials, the neighborhood of Belgravia, Chelsea, Knightsbridge, and low neighborhoods, some of them men of mature age." . . . "There are great numbers of expert cracksmen known to the police in the different parts of the Metropolis. Many of these reside on the Surrey side, about Waterloo Road and Kent Road, the Borough, Hackney and Kingsland Road and other localities.'

It is no doubt true that many of the facts having to do with the concentration of crime in particular areas were noted long before the time of Mayhew, inasmuch as London's crime areas had acquired histories of several centuries when he wrote. What is particularly noteworthy about Mayhew, as well as the other students of his day was that they used these facts definitely and consciously for the purposes of what was known as "moral" or "social science." Thus Mayhew remarks:

'Surely even the weakest-minded must see that our theories of crime, to be other than mere visionary hypotheses, must explain roguery and vagabondage *all over the world*, and not merely be framed with reference to that little clique among human society which we happen to call our State.' (12)

Students of today who are in the habit of considering Lombroso the first scientific student of crime will be surprised to Find Mayhew anticipating in the middle of the 19th century the criticisms of the early Lombrosian viewpoint which were advanced near the end of the 19th and in the first part of the 20th century. He states:

'But crime, we repeat, is an effect with which the shape of the head and the form of the features appear to have no connection whatever.... Again we say that the great mass of crime in this country is committed by those who have been bred and born to the business, and who make a regular trade of it, living as systematically by robbery or cheating as others do by commerce or the exercise of intellectual or manual labour.' (13)

He thus definitely rejects the view of the criminal as a distinct physical type in favor of what might be called an environmental or sociological view. In fact, if we were to select the main theme of his books we should say that it was the point that habitual crime is the result of a natural evolution of juvenile crime in response to the impact of social factors.

1. Buchanan, Walter, Remarks on the Causes and State of Juvenile Crime in the Metropolis With Hints for Preventing Its Increase (1846) pp. 6-7
2. Allison, A., Principles of Population (1840) p. 76
3. Holland, G. C., Vital Statistics of Sheffield (1843) p. 138
4. Quoted in "The Causes of Crime in the Metropolis," Taits Edinburgh Magazine, Vol. 17 (1830) p. 332
5. On the formation and habits of juvenile gangs and the prevention of juvenile delinquency, see Report of the Select Committee on Criminal and Destitute Juveniles (1852); "The Garrett, The Cabin, and the Goal," Irish Quarterly Review, Vol. 3 (1853) pp. 229-381; "Reformatory Schools in France and England," ibid. Vol. 4 (1854) pp. 691-792; "Our Juvenile Criminals – The Schoolmaster or the Gaoler," ibid. Vol. 4 (1854) pp. 1-71; "Juvenile Delinquents and Their Management," ibid. Vol.5 (1855) pp.773-822. Report of the Special Committee Appointed by the: National Assembly of France to Consider the Treatment of Juvenile Offenders, Dec. 14th, 1849. (Trans. 1850.) Mary Carpenter, Juvenile Delinquents: Their Condition and Treatment (1853); "Juvenile Criminals," North British Review, Vol. 10 (1848) pp. 1-38. First Report

of the Commissioners Appointed to Inquire as to the Best Means of Establishing an Efficient Constabularly Force in the Counties of England and Wales (1839)

6. Evidence before Select Committee on Criminal and Destitute Juveniles, op. cit., p. 33. Nearly a century later, another student of urban life observed: "The mobility of the city has broken down the isolation of the local community, admitting divergent elements of experience, divergent standards and values, divergent definitions of social situations. At the same time it has resulted in a rate of movement that makes strangers of neighbors. A large part of the city's population lives much as do people in a great hotel, meeting but not knowing one another. The result is a dissolution of social solidarity and public opinion. Face to face and intimate relationships in local areas are replaced by casual, transitory, disinterested contacts. There arises an extreme individuation of personal behaviour that makes of the local area within the city something vastly different from the town or village community. There is no common body of experience and tradition, no unanimity of interest, sentiment and attitude which can serve as a basis of collective action." See H. W. Zorbaugh, The Gold Coast and the Slum (1929) pp. 250-251

7. The careers of Henry Mayhew (1812-1887) and two of six brothers, Horace and Augustus, are separately recorded in the Dictionary of National Biography. All three brothers devoted themselves to literature, drama and journalism, at early ages. Abandoning the study of law, Henry Mayhew's first venture was the publication, with Gilbert a Beckett of 'Figaro in London,' a weekly periodical 1831-1839; later he wrote several dramas. He is best known, however, as one of the originators, and for a short time, one of the editors of 'Punch,' and as the first one to mark out a new path in philanthropic journalism which takes the poor of London as its theme. His principal work, in which he was assisted by John Binny and others, was London Labour and the London Poor, a series of articles, anecdotic and statistical, on the petty trades of London, originally appearing in the 'Morning Chronicle.' Two volumes were published in 1851; but their circulation was interrupted by litigation in Chancery. In 1856 a continuation of it appeared in monthly parts as the "The Great World of London" which was ultimately completed and published as the Criminal Prisons of London and Scenes of Prison Life (1862). A portion of this volume was written by John Binny. Mayhew's London Labour and the London Poor (4 vols.) appeared in its final form in 1864 and again in 1865. The title page of each volume is as follows: London Labour and the London Poor: a cyclopedia of the Condition and Earnings of Those That Will Work, Those That Cannot Work, and Those That Will Not Work. The fourth volume acknowledging the assistance of John Binny and other contributors, is devoted to thieves, swindlers, beggars, and prostitutes. In his preface of London Labour and the London Poor, Mayhew writes that his volume is "The first attempt to publish the history of a people, from the lips of the people themselves — giving a literal description of their labour, their earnings, and their sufferings, in their own 'unvarnished' language. It is the first commission of inquiry into the state of the people undertaken by a private individual and the first 'blue book' ever published in twopenny numbers."

8. The importance of a direct personal study of criminals outside of institutions in order to gain understanding of their attitudes and motives and techniques was emphasized by many writers in addition to Mayhew and Binny. A reviewer, commenting on a book by Mary Carpenter, stated: "Miss Carpenter has at last supplied us with the material needed to qualify us so to understand the conditions of a life altogether unlike our own, as to enable us to perceive what sort of minds we have to deal with. . . . The main object of Miss Carpenter's book is to establish the principles on which our treatment of criminals should proceed. . . . She has perhaps rendered a greater service in disclosing to us the entire natural history of the lawless classes. She supplies us with the material essentially

necessary as the basis of action on any theory of judgment and punishment of offenders. ... But the first requisite to action under any of these views is to understand the peculiar character of criminal life, in its origin and progress." Edinburgh Review, Vol. 122 (1865) p. 337-371. In an article on "Professional Thieves" another writer remarked, "Thieving, considered as an art, is only just beginning to be understood in this country; it is scarcely thirty years since honest men turned their attention to the subject with a determination to master it. ... But obviously, crime will never be cured until its origin and career are thoroughly understood. ... Would that the professional thieves would be induced to come forward and candidly tell us all about it. We will never fully understand them until they explain themselves. Police, prison discipline, fence masters, penal servitude, on each of these subjects a conference of old thieves, earnest and out-spoken, would speedily teach the public more than they can ever learn from associations for the promotion of social science, parliamentary committees, government commissioners, prison inspectors and police reports. Believing that we cannot understand people of any class or character unless we go among them, see them in their open hours of unreserved communication, and hear what they have to say for themselves, I have for some time past made the most of every opportunity of becoming, as a clergyman, acquainted with the origin, character, acts and habits of professional thieves." Cornhill Magazine, Vol. 6 (1862) p. 640-653

9. Mayhew points out that the official system of classification of crimes fails to divide criminals into two main types, habitual and casual. "It is impossible to arrive at any accurate knowledge of the subject of crime and criminals generally, without first making this analysis of the several species of offenses according to their causes; or, in other words, without arranging them into distinct groups or classes, according as they arise, either from an habitual indisposition to labour on the part of some of the offenders, or from the temporary pressure of circumstances upon others. The official returns on this subject are as unphilosophic as the generality of such documents, and consist of a crude mass of incongruous facts, being a statistical illustration of the "rudis indigestaque moles" in connection with a criminal chaos, and where a murderer is classed in the same category with the bigamist, a sheep-stealer with the embezzler, and the Irish rebel or traitor grouped with the keeper of a disorderly house, and he, again, with the poacher and perjurer." The Criminal Prisons of London (1862) p. 87

10. The Criminal Prisons of London, p. 353

11. See also Neison, F. G. P., "Statistics of Crime in England and Wales for the Years 1842, 1843, 1844." Journal of the Statistical Society vol. 9 (1846) p. 223-276

12. Mayhew, H., The Criminal Prisons of London, p. 383

13. ibid., p. 413

Migration and Urban Crime *by Luke Owen Pike*
  *Reprinted from A History of Crime in England London,
  Smith Elder and Co. (1876) Chap. 13*

The migrations of British subjects from one part of the United Kingdom to another have an effect upon crime which is most clearly perceptible in the annual returns. It may be laid down as a general principle that in the counties into which there is most immigration there is most crime, and in the counties into which there is least immigration there is least crime. A most striking contrast, for example, is presented by the north-western counties (Cheshire and Lancashire) on the one hand, and the south-western group (including Cornwall, Devonshire, Dorsetshire, Somersetshire, and Wiltshire) on the other. In the former there are 3,224 immigrants aged twenty years and upwards in every 10,000 of the population aged twenty years and upwards, and there are about 115 persons annually committed to prison in every 10,000 of the total population. In the latter the immigrants are in the proportion of only 1,103 in 10,000 of the same ages, and the number of persons annually committed to prison amounts to no more than 30 in 10,000 of the total population.

It would be unphilosophical to attribute this coincidence of numbers to one cause alone − to forget that a higher rate of immigration is associated with a denser population, in which the temptations to petty theft are greater, drink is, perhaps, more accessible, crowds are more readily drawn together, brawls are more easily excited, and police are near at hand to arrest the offenders. It is, indeed, quite demonstrable that causes apart from the character of the immigrants affect the number of committals, and aid in producing the marked difference which exists between the districts of greater and less attractiveness to strangers. Not only are there fewer persons committed in equal numbers of the population in the south-western than in the north-western counties − not only is the relative proportion maintained when the population under twenty years of age is disregarded, but in one section at least of the immigrant population itself the tendency to commit crime is reduced when that section constitutes a smaller fraction of the whole. Of the Irish-born population in the north-western counties about 454 in 10,000 are annually committed to prison; of the Irish-born population in the south-western counties about 158 in 10,000. It may, therefore, be said that the Irish in the north-western counties are more than twice as criminal as the Irish in the south-western counties, and the sum of the causes independent of immigration must bring about this result.

While, however, the power of other causes must be admitted, the very figures which prove it prove also the powerful influence of migration upon crime. In the north-western counties the whole of the existing causes, including immigration, make the total number of committals for every 10,000 inhabitants almost four times as great as in the south-western counties; but the number of Irish committed in the north-western counties is (in the 10,000 Irish) considerably less than three times the number committed in the south-western. So far as the Irish immigrants are concerned, therefore, one or both of the following propositions must be true: − the incentives to crime act less powerfully upon the Irish than upon the rest of the population in the crowded north-western counties; or the conditions tending towards the diminution of crime in the south-western counties have less effect upon them. But in any case this particular section of the immigrant population must have a stronger tendency than the native population to break the existing laws — a fact very clearly established by the proportion of Irish-born persons committed to prison to the whole of the persons so committed. In the north-western counties the Irish inhabitants are 6.6 per cent. of the whole, and the committals of Irish 25.6 per cent. of the total committals; in the south-western counties the Irish inhabitants are 0.6 per cent. of the whole, and the committals of Irish 3.6.

The Irish incomers into our towns and counties, if not the English, Scotch, and foreign incomers also, possess, therefore, a natural disposition which leads them into a prison more frequently than the native inhabitants. Nor, when the past history and present condition of Ireland are borne in mind, is there any reason to be surprised at the fact, or to cast it as a reproach against the Irish people. That reckless spirit of indignation which prompts the agrarian outrage was once as common in England as it has ever been in Ireland; and if Ireland has been longer in effecting a reconciliation with her conquerors than England, she has had fewer opportunities and more difficulties both political and religious. The number of committals to prison is, in proportion to the population, greater in Ireland than in England, just as the number of Irish committed to prison in England is proportionately greater than that of the English. The number of the crimes regarded by the law as most serious — the indictable offences — is, it is true, proportionately less in Ireland than in England. But this rule does not hold good with respect to murder, to offences against the person in general, or to malicious offences against property, towards which the Irish in their own country display a greater tendency than the English on the average in England. Though, too, the proportionate excess of Irish committals in England appears greatly reduced if attention be restricted to the indictable offences which are not determined summarily, it does not from any point of view cease to be an excess. Of these graver crimes more than eight per cent. are committed in England by the Irish. The Irish are less than two and a half per cent. of the total population of England, and they barely exceed four per cent. of the population of our largest towns. If it be argued that most of the greater offenders are above twenty years of age, that there are few Irish immigrants who are below that age, and who do not reside in the great towns, and that no comparison is fair to the Irish which is not limited to the town population aged twenty and upwards, the argument, when admitted as correct, does not reduce Irish crime to the level of English. There is but one of our large towns in which the population above twenty years of age is not considerably more than half of the whole population. In equal numbers of Irish and English inhabitants the committals of Irish for the greater crimes are more than double the committals of the English. It follows, therefore, that even could it be conceded (and it certainly cannot) that a person under twenty years of age is incapable of a grave offence, there would be an excess of Irish criminality proportionate to the excess of inhabitants twenty years old and upwards (as compared with the

31

number below that age) which, even in the large towns, is often more than five per cent., and rarely less than three.

With certain exceptions, of which, however, the importance is not to be forgotten, our largest and most representative towns exhibit a remarkable coincidence in the number of Irish immigrants and the number of indictable offences. Out of nine selected towns Bristol has in proportion to its population the smallest number of Irish-born residents and the smallest number of indictable offences, and Sheffield the next smallest number of both. In respect of both, Durham stands fourth on the list; and the metropolis, Birmingham, Newcastle-on-Tyne, and Wolverhampton, though they do not show a complete agreement between the number of criminals and the number of Irish inhabitants, do not show a very great divergence. But Liverpool and Manchester, though they are the two towns in which there is the largest proportion of Irish and the largest proportion of indictable offences, present a very marked contrast one to the other. In Liverpool there are, more than fifteen per cent. of Irish, and there are one hundred and twenty-eight inhabitants to every indictable offence. In Manchester there are considerably less than nine per cent of Irish; and there are to every indictable offence only eighty-four inhabitants. In Liverpool, too, the natives of England and Wales are only seventy-seven and a half per cent. of the whole population; in Manchester they are more than eighty-seven and a half per cent., while in the north-western counties, on the average, they barely exceed seventy-eight per cent.

The inference may, therefore, justly be drawn that whatever the effect of immigration in general into any town, the immigration of Irish in particular cannot be regarded as the chief cause of the most serious crime in that town. The Irish have, not only in England but in Ireland, a tendency to commit crime (including the minor offences) greater than that of the English in England. It may, therefore, reasonably be assumed that as immigrants into English towns they are punished for all offences (including those which are indictable) more frequently than the English immigrants. There is, however, no evidence that Irish immigrants are much, if at all, more guilty of indictable offences (considered separately) than English immigrants, though more guilty than Englishmen in general. It would be illogical to expect, from the comparatively small number of indictable offences committed by the Irish in Ireland, that a proportionately small number should be committed by the Irish in England. The Irish are, above all others, an emigrating people, and those among them who do not leave their homes must include a smaller proportion than is to be found among the emigrants, of persons at the criminal age, and of the enterprising disposition which, in new and difficult circumstances, sometimes leads men into crime. According to all probability, therefore, more crimes should be committed in proportion to their numbers by the Irish who leave their native place to seek their fortunes, than by their less active or less confident fellow-countrymen whom they leave behind. This,

32

however, is an argument which is not less applicable to the English than to the Irish, and the statistics of England and Ireland afford a striking illustration of its truth.

The crimes to which the Irish in Ireland are specially prone are murder and malicious offences against property. The crimes to which the non-emigrant rural population of England is specially prone are precisely the same. The explanation of this remarkable coincidence appears to be simple, and is in the main supplied by history. The peasant who remains where his forefathers have remained for generations naturally commits (when he becomes criminal at all) crimes of the same kind as were committed by his ancestors. The inclination to kill, to burn, and to destroy, as the records of the past assure us, has been handed down by tradition and inherited association to the rustic both in England and in Ireland. In 1871 the rural population of England and Wales was about 38 per cent. of the whole, the urban population (including, however, some towns of less than 1,000 inhabitants) about 62 per cent. The county constabularly renders the yearly accounts for the rural districts, and for a portion of the urban districts (as defined in the census returns), or, in other words, for about 56 per cent. of the whole population. The larger towns have their own police; and a marked excess of any one crime in the returns of the county constabulary must almost necessarily be caused by the excess of that crime in the rural districts, and would probably be still more marked if the police divisions were identical with the census divisions of rural and urban. In the three years ending in 1873, the murders (as proved upon trial) in the districts under the county constabulary were, on the average, nearly 62 per cent. of the whole, the attempts to murder more than 53 per cent., and the burglaries more than 40 per cent. It may, indeed, be conceded on the other side that the cases of manslaughter were only 35 per cent., and the cases of robbery with violence little over 30 per cent. But the exceptions do not really affect the point under consideration. Culpable carelessness in driving through the overcrowded streets of a large town is regarded as manslaughter when it causes death, but it is not in any way dependent on impulse prompting the offender to kill or maim. Want of opportunity seems also the explanation of the comparatively small number of rustic robberies with violence. In a country road or lane a robber may wait long before he sees a wayfarer whose purse or watch would be worth the risk of an attack. The streets of a large city or its suburbs are good hunting-grounds at almost any hour of the day or night. In the metropolis the temptation is counteracted by the efficiency of the police. The percentage is there a little below what it might be expected to be from the number of inhabitants; but even in the less carefully watched towns the percentage of robberies from the person with violence is very much below the percentage of murders in the rural districts.

Among all the greater offences, however, that which most distinguishes the country from the towns is arson. More than 88 per cent. of the cases reported occur in the rural districts. It may be argued, of course, that it is easier and less dangerous for one man to set another man's rick on fire in the country than for one man to burn down another man's house in London; but the explanation is altogether insufficient to meet the facts of the case. The motive for setting light to another man's hay stack is pure malice; but there is a motive which might prompt a man to burn his own house — the desire to make a profit out of an Insurance Office. Such an act of dishonesty is equally easy in town or country; but as the number of houses is greater in the towns than in the country the number of attempts to defraud Insurance Companies should be proportionately greater also. As a matter of fact, however, the number of cases of arson, from all motives combined, in the whole of the towns, is less than twelve per cent. of the total in England and Wales. The inevitable conclusion seems to be that there is some instinct in the rustic which prompts him to commit wanton and malicious destruction out of sheer vindictiveness. But this, like the desire to shed blood, is the instinct of the savage, of the uncivilised warrior, and even of some warriors who call themselves civilised. It is, in fact, one among many illustrations of the survival of barbarism in the midst of civilisation.

It has often been alleged that crime is chiefly the growth of the towns, and that rural simplicity is invariably accompanied by rural innocence. The small percentage, in the English rural districts, of most crimes except murder, arson, and the allied offences, appears at first sight to form some basis for the opinion, which is also in some degree confirmed by the great excess of crime in Dublin as compared with the rural districts of Ireland. It is not, however, an inference which can fairly be drawn from statistics, though the recent statistics of all towns and all rural districts may seem to warrant it. It is disproved by all past history as clearly as any conclusion can be disproved by any historical facts. Our town population is now both absolutely and relatively greater than at any previous time. It is indisputable that, as we look back along preceding ages, we find the town population less and less, until, in the reign of Edward II., we see the rural population constituting the whole numerical strength of the country excepting only a small fraction. It is no less indisputable that law-breaking has, on the whole, diminished as towns have grown. The fact, therefore, that towns-people are more criminal in proportion to their numbers than country-people, cannot be explained by any trite platitudes on rustic purity and city corruption.

The truth is, that the modern temptations to commit crime in all its newest and most attractive forms, are crowded together in the towns and cities with multitudes of persons of the criminal age who have shown some energy and enterprise in leaving their homes to seek their fortunes. By the very same process, too, by which a throng of possible criminals is added every year to the inhabitants of the towns, the villages and hamlets are relieved of that portion of their population from which most danger might

34

be apprehended. Every young rustic who leaves his native cottage, and afterwards has the misfortune to become the inmate of a borough gaol, not only adds one to the actual number of borough commitments, but possibly subtracts one from the number of county commitments, and so causes a difference of two in the respective totals. In the whole of a population so migratory as that of modern England, the effect thus produced must obviously be very great; and the marvel is, not that the towns should exhibit in most offences some excess of crime in proportion to the number of inhabitants, but that there should be an excess of any form of crime in the rural districts. The towns make no criminals but such as were of the fitting material before they committed a crime; but the country was for ages the scene of every deed of violence perpetrated under every pretext. The towns offer a field of enterprise for all human ingenuity; the remote provinces contribute to them a supply of inhabitants among whom the instincts of violence and rapine are apt to re-appear upon the smallest provocation.

Poverty and Delinquency *by Sir Cyril Burt*
Reprinted from The Young Delinquent *London,*
University of London Press (1925) pp. 66-78

Definition. – Of the conditions obtaining within the delinquent's home the first and most obvious are the material. How far is poverty – economic stress, with all its various concomitants – productive of juvenile crime? Many writers upon social reform have proclaimed that the root of human evil is the want of money. But money may be wanting in different degrees. Once more the need for definition is plain. What is meant by being poor?

Poverty may be most conveniently defined to mean earnings insufficient for the maintenance of bodily health. By taking the expenditure needed for food, rent, clothing, and fuel, with a family of a stated size, it is possible to calculate, for any given year, a minimum standard for the cost of living. This minimum standard may be termed the poverty-line; it marks the margin of a bare subsistence. I find, in my delinquent cases, that, where full particulars were obtainable, 16 per cent. fell definitely below this line of poverty; one child in six was thus in want of the common necessities of life. Of these necessitous offenders by far the majority had been reported for theft. In households below the poverty-line, as many as 81 per cent. of the offences belonged to this category; in households above the poverty line, only 63 per cent.

In classifying these and the remainder of my cases, I have adopted the broad economic categories suggested by Charles Booth in his study of *Life and Labour in London.* The entire population he divides into eight social classes or strata, as follows:

A. *Very poor.* Occasional labourers; loafers; street-sellers; the destitute, the criminal, and the semi-criminal. (Among my delinquent cases, 7.3 per cent. of the boys, and 5.4 per cent. of the girls, were from homes of this type.)

B. *Very Poor.* Irregular earnings; casual labour. (This class and the preceding approximately include all those below the poverty-line, as just laid down; and live in 'primary poverty.')

C. *Poor.* Intermittent earnings; seasonal labour.

D. *Poor.* Small, but constant earnings; unskilled, but regular labour. (Most of this class, and all of the preceding, may be described as living in 'secondary poverty': their earnings do not suffice to maintain a constant level of physical health, because, though theoretically above the minimal standard for necessities, much of it is absorbed by other expenditure, useful, needless, or unintelligent.)

E. *Comfortable.* Regular standard earnings: artisans, small shopkeepers (with no assistants).

F. *Comfortable.* High class labour, well paid: foremen, best-paid artisans.

G. *Well-to-do.* Lower middle class: larger shopkeepers, tradesmen, small employers, clerks.

H. *Well-to-do.* Upper middle and upper classes: servant-keeping families, and professional men.

Of my delinquent children, 19 per cent. – one in five – come from classes A and B, that is, from homes that were 'very poor' in the sense above defined. Of the general population of London only 8 per cent., less than half the former figure, come from such homes. 37 per cent. of the delinquents come from the next two classes (C and D) – 'moderately poor'; and of the general population, 22 per cent. The biggest of my batches, 42 per cent., come from classes E and F – those designated by Booth as 'comfortable.' (1)

Thus, *over one-half of the total amount of juvenile delinquency is found in homes that are poor or very poor;* and the figures show very trenchantly, were figures needed for the purpose, that poverty makes an added spur to dishonesty and wrong.

Yet our attention will not be confined to the poorer classes alone. Since of the total inhabitants of London no more than 30 per cent. belong to the lowest social strata (classes A, B, C, and D), the amount of delinquency coming from those lowest social strata is, beyond question, disproportionate; nevertheless, in the higher and more prosperous ranks, its frequency is still unexpectedly large. And, when nearly half the offenders come from homes that are far from destitute, poverty can hardly be the sole or the most influential cause.

Local Distribution of Juvenile Delinquency. – The broad association between crime in the young and poverty in the home and its surroundings, is at once impressed upon the eye, if a chart be made of the distribution of juvenile delinquency in the different parts of London. With this aim in view, I have secured the address of every boy or girl reported as an industrial school case during the last two years, namely, 1922 and 1923; and have calculated, for each electoral area in the county, what is the ratio of reported cases to the total number of children on the rolls of the Council's schools. The percentages so obtained have been made the basis of a map of juvenile crime.

The streets where the incidence of childish crime is greatest are located in zones or areas of half a dozen types:

(i) Highest of all are the figures in the three small boroughs adjacent to the City on its northern edge — Holborn, Finsbury, and Shoreditch. These districts, after the City itself, are the oldest regions of London. The opprobrious title of 'the darkest spot for crime' has usually been applied to Hoxton; but, in actual fact, it would be a label more fittingly affixed to the eastern portion of Finsbury. In Finsbury the annual percentage of juvenile offenders rises to more than 4 per thousand. Here are by far the most densely populated parts; here the death-rate is all but the highest; and here, too, is one of the highest of the birth-rates. Poverty is not extreme: yet not one family in a hundred is sufficiently well-to-do to pay for the education of its children. Shoreditch follows Finsbury very closely in each of these respects. Of my own cases coming from this quarter, a large proportion, larger than anywhere else in the county, belong to families whose only trade is crime — coiners, burglars, house-breakers, and pick-pockets. It is a region made familiar, even to those who do not know their London, by the adventures of Oliver Twist, and his various villainous companions; and the first impression which the visitor receives is still very much the same as Oliver's, as he picked his way hither at nightfall, with the experienced Mr. Dawkins as his guide: the side-streets seem 'lined with foul and frowsy dens, where vice is closely packed, and lacks the room to turn — the haunts of hunger and disease, and shabby rags that scarcely hold together.'

Those more intimate with this neighbourhood — with the purlieus of St. Luke's, and the contiguous parishes of Clerkenwell, where Irish, Jews, and Italians mingle with the lowest type of English loafer — will realize how suitably these places lie, and how centrally disposed the whole quarter is, as a strategic base for nefarious designs. The professional criminal likes to fix his headquarters, not in the heart of hard-working penury, but on the edge of the richer haunts of business, pleasure, or residential comfort; at the same time, he feels safer with a wide slum-district at his rear, where he can lose himself upon occasion, much as Fagin and Bill Sikes retreated into Whitechapel when the hue and cry was raised.

(ii) A little farther north, there is a second and a broader zone where delinquency is almost as common, though not quite so thickly packed. It is formed by the southern portions of St. Marylebone, of St. Pancras, and of Islington; and extends across Haggerston into South Hackney. Of these

37

more scattered districts, though poor back-alleys are common enough, many parts are vicious rather than poor; St. Marylebone has one of the highest illegitimate birth-rates. But the haunts that appear most criminal, those of St. Marylebone and St. Pancras, are located in the rookeries that have grown up near the termini of the four big railways. Farther north still, directly the line of the Regent's Canal is crossed, moral and material conditions seem to improve together.

(iii) Immediately south of the Thames, the long line of slums lying by the northern shores of Battersea, Lambeth, and Southwark, and stretching through Bermondsey, Rotherhithe, and Deptford, into the riverside parts of Greenwich and Woolwich, form a region fairly prolific in juvenile offenders. But except in the district immediately south of the city (North Southwark and the parts adjacent), the figures nowhere approach those obtaining on the other side.

(iv) To the north of the river, a similar slum-quarter, very mixed in racial character, is to be found in the nearer parts of the East End — Whitechapel and St. George's, Mile End and Limehouse, and the south-west corner of Bethnal Green. These two broad areas, north and south of the river respectively, are alike exceedingly poor — more uniformly poor, indeed, than any we have mentioned: once more, both the death-rate and birth-rate are high; the dwellings are overpacked; and there is little open space.

(v) Towards the west, the ring round the City is completed by the nearer portion of the West End, namely, the Abbey division of Westminster, the chief amusement-district of London. Here again, however, are the resorts of vice rather than of crime, of indulgence more than of indigence: Westminster, indeed, though more salubrious and less congested, shares with Holborn and St. Marylebone the highest proportion of illegitimate births. Around Victoria Station, as around Waterloo Station on the opposite side of the Thames, the streets and alleys are often of a criminal type — resembling those near the big railway termini farther north.

(vi) Finally, in the outlying districts to the north of Islington, Paddington, Kensington, and Hammersmith, and in those to the south of Tooting, Norwood, and Dulwich, in the low-lying portions of Lewisham, and in similar parts of West Woolwich, there are small and isolated patches of crime. In neighbourhoods such as these the lawless population is often limited to a few narrow and notorious side-streets that startle the stranger as he picks a cross-cut from one main highway to another. It is said that the families that have made such streets a by-word were in many instances removed to these regions on the circumference from the central London slums, when the large clearances were made at the end of last century. A few groups seem to have sprung up near the big suburban places of amusement, Earl's Court, the White City, and the Crystal Palace, at the time when these exhibitions were first opened or built.

38

The more reputable regions, comparatively free from juvenile delinquency, are, first of all, in the centre, the City of London itself, and, secondly, on the margin, the residential suburbs, such as Hampstead and Stoke Newington in the extreme north, and, in the extreme south, the various divisions of Wandsworth and the greater part of Lewisham: these marginal districts, judged by every social index, are well towards the top of the list.

Over a large extent of London, then, the poorer districts seem the more criminal. Yet a close acquaintance with the poorest parts themselves will show that the correspondence is anything but absolute. Hence, it becomes of interest to gauge the correlation more exactly, and to give it some measure of statistical precision. To this end I have taken, not electoral divisions, but boroughs: for the separate electoral divisions no comparable figures upon social conditions are available.

The correlations between the figures for juvenile delinquency and several statistical assessments of other social conditions are sufficient to show that the connexion of childish offences with poverty and its concomitants is significantly high, though not so high, perhaps, as previous inquirers, trusting mainly to experience and general impression, have, as a rule, implied. With the amount of poverty in each borough, as assessed by Charles Booth's survey, the amount of juvenile delinquency is correlated to the extent of .67; with the relative amount of poor relief, to the extent of nearly .50; with the number of children scheduled for school purposes (probably the best single index of the present social character of each borough as a whole), to the extent of .63. The highest coefficient of all is that for the correlation between juvenile delinquency and overcrowding, namely, .77. The correlation with the death-rate is nearly as high. Allowing for the gross shortcomings, inevitable in estimates so crude, so vague, and in some cases so largely out of date, these several figures are remarkably consistent one with another. They indicate plainly that it is in the poor, overcrowded, insanitary households, where families are huge, where the children are dependent solely on the State for their education, and where the parents are largely dependent on charity and relief for their own maintenance, that juvenile delinquency is most rife.

1. This figure will probably surprise those familiar with none but the industrial school type. The explanation is clear. In the better kind of home, the parents and interested friends more often desire – and more successfully attempt – to debar their children's petty misdemeanours from becoming a subject of official inquiry and action; the official agency in its turn, when apprised of all the facts, is more reluctant to banish a child from a good home to an industrial school.

   It is, I may add, my general experience that, in well-to-do homes (and, I fancy, in comfortable homes – though the present figures hardly bear this out), delinquent girls are fewer in proportion to their total number than delinquent boys.

Crime and Unemployment *by Hermann Mannheim*
Reprinted from <u>Social Aspects of Crime in England</u>
<u>between the Wars</u> *London, Allen and Unwin (1940) Chap. 5*

I. Though the significance of economic factors in the causation of crime is fairly generally accepted, there may still be some room for doubt as to the methods best suited to their scientific investigation. It may, for instance, appear questionable whether a set of figures could be obtained that might be regarded as sufficiently representative of the economic position to be usefully compared with the corresponding figures of the *Criminal Statistics*. Well-founded objections could probably be raised against the choice of any single economic factor as well as against any combination of various such factors for purposes of comparison. This is no place for a discussion of the methodological difficulties involved. (1) In view of the unparalleled prominence which unemployment has gained in this country during the interval between the Wars, the author has regarded it as justifiable to single out this factor for a more detailed comparison with the simultaneous currents of crime, particularly so as no such investigation, based upon English material, seems as yet to have been published. Generally speaking, the unemployment index should represent a more reliable factor for the measurement of the economic position in a given country and its criminological implications than indices of wages, cost of living, export trade, and similar sets of figures. We have come to realize that it is more the dynamic than the static aspect of poverty that has to be considered in criminological research. Sudden changes in the economic position of the masses of the population, however, are more frequently due to unemployment than to any other economic factor. A hundred or more years ago there was hardly any serious enquiry into the causes of crime in this country that would not have stressed, in general terms, the ruinous consequences of lack of work, though there existed at that time no exact methods of measuring the extent of this evil. Now, in spite of the improved technique of unemployment statistics, they have lost much of their value for criminological research because of the various steps taken by the State to alleviate the worst hardships caused by lack of work.

Theoretically, the relationship between unemployment and crime can be measured in two ways: either by comparing the fluctuations of unemployment figures and of Criminal Statistics (statistical method), or by examining individual criminal cases with the view to finding out the percentage of persons who had been unemployed whilst committing crime and to study the effect which unemployment had upon them (individual case method). Both methods have to struggle against great odds.

(a) In the first place, unemployment statistics do not tell the whole story, particularly those of former years when the system of unemployment insurance was still incomplete. As late as 1932 it was stated in a

40

Sheffield enquiry that "about 43 per cent of the boys and about 50 per cent of the girls engaged in or available for occupations in the city are outside the scope of the statistics." Even if we could regard the statistics of unemployment and of crime as representing the actual amount of both, it cannot be overlooked, however, that there are, besides unemployment, many other factors involved of an economic, social or psychological character, which may counterbalance the effect of unemployment as a crime-producing agency. Moreover, it is not so much occasional short-term unemployment, but rather enforced idleness of long duration that adversely affects the worker's power of resistance. The duration of unemployment, however, is a factor which is not always clearly shown in ordinary statistics. Though figures concerning the length of unemployment are regularly published, the criticism has been made that they consider even very brief intervals of employment as a complete break. Finally, long-term unemployment may show its effect even many years after being brought to an end, and it is capable of changing permanently the whole attitude of a family towards society. Such a change may express itself in actions at a time when its external cause has already disappeared. We should not, therefore, adopt a too rationalistic attitude in investigations of this kind by treating the fact that an improvement in employment figures may occasionally be accompanied by a rise in crime as conclusive evidence against any causal connection between unemployment and crime. Other difficulties may be caused by the not infrequent phenomenon that the extent of unemployment shows opposite tendencies in different areas and different industries. Two examples of this kind may be given. Whilst a general improvement took place between December 1935 and December 1937, the unemployment percentage in the building industry went up from 17.9 to 20.7; and in spite of a considerable decline in unemployment in the Special Areas as a whole and also in South Wales, the position of Merthyr Tydfil deteriorated from 57.7 to 60.6 per cent unemployment between November 26, 1934, and September 21, 1936. It may therefore sometimes be misleading to operate with figures covering all industries and the country as a whole.

The further question arises whether fluctuations of crime in general or only those of certain categories of crime ought to be made the object of a comparison with unemployment statistics. Obvious as it may be that our primary concern must be the specifically economic type of offence, it cannot be denied that certain crimes against the State have no less economic relevance than larceny and fraud. Especially coining is one of those crimes to which skilled craftsmen turn in periods of unemployment; the local figures are, however, too scanty to offer sufficient material for comparisons. Even the commission of certain sexual crimes may be encouraged by idleness. (2) Bearing in mind the smallness of the remaining groups of indictable offence, we may be justified in using for our comparison chiefly the figures for indictable offences as a whole with occasional sidelights on the figures for larceny, breakings, etc. Statistics of attempted suicide, illuminating as they would otherwise be, are not sufficiently reliable, since they are completely dependent upon the changing attitude of the local Police.

(b) The individual case method, on the other hand, has to face the problem of how to obtain reliable evidence with regard to the employment situation of individual criminals. Prisoners are not altogether trustworthy in their statements on this point, and it is only in more important cases that Courts will take the trouble to check their allegations. One of the principal rules in the "Handbook of Crime" which circulated among Mark Benney's Borstal colleagues was: "Always try to keep an Unemployment Book stamped up to date. In case of trouble it halves your sentence." (3) Sometimes, however, it may be wiser to follow the opposite course. Professional lawbreakers who have reason to fear a sentence of Preventive Detention may be anxious to show continuously some sort of fictitious employment in order to disprove any contention that they are leading "persistently a dishonest or criminal life." (4)

It may be advisable to show the development of both sets of figures since the beginning of the present century. This, of course, has to be done with some caution. Not only that the War years have to be excluded in any case — there are also considerable objections against any uniform treatment of pre-war and post-war unemployment figures. (5)

The parallelism between the movement of unemployment and that of persons tried for indictable offences in general is not particularly close before the War, except for the striking upward trend in 1908-9 and the more gradual, but equally distinct, decline between 1909 and 1911. Whilst the fall in unemployment begins already after 1904 and continues throughout 1906 and 1907, the decline on the criminal side concerns the year 1906 only; moreover, there is no equivalent in unemployment figures for the sudden rise in convictions in 1912 which may — at least partly — rather have been caused by the strike wave of that year. Hardly more significant becomes the parallelism if we compare unemployment with the movement of crimes reported to the Police, whether they be indictable offences in general or special types of them.

When considering the early post-War figures we are somewhat struck by the fact that, in spite of the stability of the unemployment percentages, there was a sharp rise in crime from 1919 to 1920 — much more than from 1920 to 1921 in spite of the amazing jump in unemployment in the latter year. The explanation may be, first, that the unemployment wave of 1921 did in fact already begin in the last quarter of 1920 and that real wages were never after the War so low as in the first half of that year; moreover, that the year 1919 is still too atypical to be treated as an appropriate starting-point for comparisons. Remarkable is the fact, nevertheless, that in 1921 there was a decline in crimes against property with violence, a category which is generally supposed to be the most sensitive towards

42

economic influences. Begging offences, on the other hand, show the expected upward trend. Another noticeable feature is that between 1923 and 1929 "Crimes Known to the Police" jumped from 110,000 to 134,000 in spite of the comparative stability of the unemployment figures. This fact has justly been stressed by Professor A. M. Carr-Saunders who regarded it as proving that some cause other than unemployment must account for the rise in crime. By analysing the age distribution of offenders he found that the highest increase had occurred in the age group under 14 which cannot be directly affected by unemployment. Children may, of course, have to suffer when their parents are out of work. Even this explanation, however, does not hold good for the period in question where there was no rise in unemployment. Considering that — except for the year of the General Strike — the increase refers mainly to the Police Returns (the Court Statistics show hardly any changes), we may therefore be tempted to think that it was partly due to changes in methods of reporting, recording and prosecuting, whilst the economic and social aftermath of the Strike requires a special examination.

Similar divergencies between unemployment percentages and the movement of crime are to be found in the period after 1932 when a continuous fall in unemployment has entirely failed to bring about a decrease in crime. For this period it is equally true as it was for the years dealt with by Professor Carr-Saunders that the increase in crime concerned exclusively the age groups under 21. For those over 21 the movement of crime corresponds fairly accurately to the fluctuations of unemployment.

Year	Unemploy-ment per-centages	Number of male offenders found guilty of indictable offences per 100,000 of population in each age group					
		10 years but under 14 years	14 years but under 16 years	16 years but under 21 years	21 years but under 30 years	30 years and over	All ages (10 years and over)
1929	10.3	516	628	536	402	166	299
1930	15.8	518	708	622	409	169	314
1931	21.1	540	740	647	431	175	326
1932	21.9	592	767	748	485	180	354
1933	19.8	615	807	678	454	171	337
1934	16.6	788	855	686	444	171	351
1935	15.3	983	1,006	720	439	163	370
1936	12.9	1,051	1,053	767	446	168	383
1937	10.6	1,222	1,125	800	463	172	404
1938	12.6	1,183	1,143	841	487	173	407

Criminal Statistics, 1938, p. xxix; Ministry of Labour Gazette.

The elimination of the age groups under 21 thus has the effect of demonstrating the close conformity between the two sets of figures for the remainder of the population. The big jump in offences known to the Police which occurred in 1932 is, as we know, again partly due to changed methods in Police registration.

II. Recent investigators who have made comparisons between the fluctuations of unemployment and the numbers of *prison inmates* have stressed the close similarity shown by these movements. Prison Statistics, dependent as they are upon the policy of the Courts, are no safe guide for investigations of this kind. Of the greatest importance, however, are the results of the systematic observations of prison inmates by Prison Commissioners, Prison Governors, Chaplains, and other officials, as published in their Annual Reports. Hardly anywhere has the overwhelming force of unemployment as a crime-producing agency been more clearly recognized than in these documents.

The Report for the year ending March 31, 1921 — a year which only in its second half had seen a sharp rise in unemployment (6) — comments on the fact that receptions on conviction had risen only by 8,477, from 35,439 to 43,916 (i.e. from 98.4 to 116.7 per 100,000 of population) in spite of the much greater deterioration in industrial life. The explanation offered is, besides improved education and changed Court methods, the beneficial effect of Unemployment Pay which prevented acute distress. (7) The Report for the following year (April 1921 — April 1922), which included the worst industrial depression before 1929, again makes it clear that the increase in receptions, though substantial (from 43,916 to 47,126 = from 116.7 to 124.4 per 100,000), would have been far greater but for the effect of Unemployment Benefit. (8) Nevertheless, it is added, "it is probably right to say that unemployment is one of the chief contributory factors to the prison population of to-day, and, further, that its effect is cumulative, that is to say, a man becomes gradually demoralized by prolonged idleness and is more likely to drift into prison, either through debt or through committing some offence, after two years' unemployment, than he is after one." With regard to Unemployment Benefit, it may be remembered that the rate of payment for adult men, which had been raised from 15s. to 20s. in March 1921, was reduced to 15s. in July 1921 and only in August 1924 raised again to 18s. (9)

In the following years it is chiefly the young prisoner who claims the attention of the prison authorities, because ". . . of all aspects of the unemployment problem, this is the saddest and the one fraught with the gravest danger to the nation." (10) The consequences of the "blind alley" system make themselves felt within the prison gates.

The Governor of Preston Prison, in the centre of the Lancashire industrial district, writes: (11)

"The question of unemployment seriously affects the lads in this area. The majority of the lads leave school at the age of 14 years and are straightway employed as errand or messenger boys in the towns, minor jobs in the mines, or scalers and rivet boys in the shipyards in Barrow. The wage is small but satisfies the schoolboy. However, when they reach the age of 16 they want more money, plenty of young boys from school are found to take their places and consequently the idle period arrives and the career of crime commences."

This Report may be read in conjunction with the following account of employment conditions in Barrow-in-Furness: (12)

"That town has experienced the most extraordinary vicissitudes since 1914.... The town is geographically isolated, after enormous expansion during the Great War it suffered severly in 1921 and 1922, when about one-half the population was out of work."

The Governor of Wandsworth Prison reports that of young prisoners over 18 years of age, 55 per cent, and of prisoners under 18 years 70 per cent, were out of work at the time of the offence. (13) Most outspoken in his comment is the Governor of Durham Prison. (14)

"Three years ago I drew attention to the young prisoner who had earned wages during the days of war out of all proportion to his market value, and who, when the slump in trade came, resented the changed economic conditions and took to crime. This type is now evanescent as a young prisoner and has become merged in the ranks of the adult prison population. The young prisoner who is succeeding him is a bird of quite a different feather. He has never done any work at all — he does not know what work is, and sees no connection between it and daily bread. Two or three years ago he left school and has loafed about the streets ever since. His father, mother, brothers, sisters and he are all living on the 'dole.' All his companions are in like condition with himself and through sheer idleness and ennui he lapses into serious crime. The boy problem of to-day seems to me more difficult of solution than it ever was. The country is raising a population of unemployables, loafers and thieves, and lads cannot be blamed — they are the victims of the trade conditions that have prevailed for the last three years. To suggest an antidote is not easy. Compulsory attendance at school to (say) 16 years of age unless work was assured meantime would keep many a lad and girl out of mischief and prison."

In subsequent years, with improving trade conditions, this note is no longer struck so forcibly, until in 1931, after the beginning of the new unemployment wave, the outlook again becomes one of despair.

"For almost 50 per cent of these young men the future is difficult, or even hopeless. They have no homes to which they can return, no decent friends and no stability of character essential to face life in these circumstances ... less than 50 per cent have jobs to go to or even unemployment benefit to draw and it is difficult for them not to return to prison." (15)

The prison authorities are by no means the only ones who have expressed, in one form or other, their conviction that a very considerable part of the total crime rate in this country has been due to unemployment. In 1932, Sir Herbert Samuel (as he then was) drew the attention of the House of Commons to the fact that the graph of crime was, year after year, moving up and down in a course almost exactly parallel to the unemployment graph. (16)

The Cardiff Probation Committee, in its Annual Reports for 1933 and following years, states that most persons of employable age, placed under Probation in that area, were at the time of the offence either wholly or partly unemployed.

Even for a type of crime which can count on very little sympathy from any side — living on the earnings of prostitution — it was claimed in the *Report on Corporal Punishment* (17) that the sharp rise between 1930 and 1935 (from an annual average of 102 between 1925 and 1929 to the peak figure of 265 in 1933) was partly due to unemployment.

1. The literature on the subject is too vast to be given in full. Three recent contributions to it may, however, be mentioned; Thorsten Sellin, Research Memorandum on Crime in the Depression (1937); Herbert Schwartz, "Kriminalitat und Konjunktur," International Review for Social History (edited by the International Institute for Social History, Amsterdam), vol. iii, 1938; L. Radzinowicz, "A note on Methods of Establishing the Connexion between Economic Conditions and Crime," Sociological Review, vol. xxxi, July 1939.
2. See, however, Chapter 4, p. 122.
3. Mark Benney, Low Company, p. 239.
4. Prevention of Crime Act, 1908, section 10 (2) (a).
5. See Sir William Beveridge, Unemployment (1903), Longmans, Green & Co., pp. 348-9.
6. See the quarterly figures given by Sir William Beveridge, op. cit., p. 460.
7. Report 1921, p. 5 et seq. See also Criminal Statistics, 1921, p. 5.
8. Report 1922, p. 6. See also Hugh Massingham's account of life in the East End of London I Took off my Tie, p. 160): "The really tragic and pitiful cases were those who for one reason or another had never been able to draw the dole, and who were scraping together an existence by stealing and begging, and doing any odd jobs that came their way."
9. Sir W. Beveridge, op. cit., p. 275.
10. Report 1924, p. 6.
11. Report 1924, p. 58.
12. John and Sylvia Jewkes, The Juvenile Labour Market (1938), p. 101.
13. Report 1924, p. 63. See also Report 1923, p. 55 (Cardiff) and p. 63 (Maidstone).

14. Report 1924, p. 46.
15. Prison Commissioners' Report, 1931, p. 54 (Nottingham Prison).
16. See Howard Journal (1932), p. 3.
17. Report 1938, pp. 76, 87.

B: The Sociology of Delinquency in Contemporary Britain

Introduction

This section draws together a representative sample of post-war writing on the subject of juvenile delinquency in this country. As the longest section in the book it reflects the fact that contemporary British sociologists have attended more assiduously to the theoretical and practical questions posed by delinquency than they have to those raised by any other genre of criminal behaviour. This is not surprising. As we have seen in the historical section, our sociological perspective on crime has long taken its major cues from the preoccupations prevailing among social policy-makers, and there can be little doubt that, whatever the ambiguities of the official statistics, public concern about juvenile delinquency has been steadily mounting since the Second World War. The concern bolstered by bewilderment that characterises the reaction of many adults to what is so frequently portrayed as the increasing waywardness of youth has served to focus sociological attention on delinquency as a pressing 'social problem' (1). Added to this, the sociologist has not completely broken free from the traditional belief that the juvenile delinquent of today is the hardened and persistent adult criminal of tomorrow. Officially sanctioned by the Gladstone Committee of 1895, this view has as yet been only partially exposed as myth by subsequent studies of the habitual, adult offender, and thus continues to lend added preventive urgency to the investigation of juvenile delinquency (2).

But current discussions about juvenile criminality in this country almost invariably take cognisance of other ideas and techniques in addition to those deriving from our own sociological tradition. Indeed, our reliance upon theories developed in other countries and particularly in the United States is sometimes so pronounced in the teaching context that students gain the impression of an almost complete hiatus in British research. Erroneous as such an impression may be, the fact remains that the heavy traffic in ideas about delinquency has tended to flow almost exclusively in one direction. As a result, we have reached the point where a working knowledge of the American literature becomes a prerequisite to making sense of most British investigations.

The famous school of sociology which began to flourish at the University of Chicago during the years after the First World War provides us with our starting point. Here, in the city that more than any other epitomised the cultural changes and urban expansion going on in America, the city 'first in violence, deepest in dirt, loud, lawless, unlovely, ill-smelling, irreverent, new' (3), an ex-journalist called Robert E. Park gathered a number of young researchers around him and guided their interests in the direction of urban sociology (4). Within this general context, the perspective which these investigators adopted towards various aspects of city life, including delinquency, was specifically ecological. That is to say, they not only directed their energies towards measuring the incidence of various. behavioural phenomena within specified areas of the city but also towards discovering the connection which they believed to exist between the social organisation of such areas and their distinctive physical characteristics.

The existence of such a connection was implicit in Park's own concept of the 'natural area', a relatively small area of residence with physical boundaries and inhabited by natural groups characterised by distinctive social and cultural homogeneities. To this somewhat static conception, which more than anything else implied the need for depth investigation of the differences between areas, was added a more dynamic element with the so-called zonal hypothesis. The city, according to this view, was more than a collection of differing natural areas, it was divisible into zones extending concentrically from the centre to the periphery and reflecting the ongoing processes of industrialisation and urban growth; it was not just that areas were different but that they were becoming different:

'The ecologists viewed population movements and changes in land utilisation in terms of the sequence of "invasion", "dominance" and "succession", stages observable in the plant community when new species come in and oust existing ones. Originally, the population of the city lived around the central business district, but this area was the most obvious choice for the location of new commercial and industrial enterprise. As industry moved in, so the wealthier inhabitants moved out, and as the area's decline in terms of desirability of residence depressed rentals it became the obvious choice for newcomers to the city, usually poor immigrants in search of housing at lowest possible cost. The respectable artisans were as a result encouraged to move out, and they in turn began to displace the well-to-do who moved out further still.' (5)

It was this more dynamic modification of the ecological perspective with its emphasis upon the 'interstitial area' in the throes of transition from one phase to another, that captured the attention of those members of the school who like Frederick Thrasher, Clifford Shaw and Henry D. McKay were particularly interested in the problems of delinquency and crime (6). For these investigators, such social phenomena were not so much explicable in terms of the character of an area, as in terms of its changing character. Hence in one of his earlier works (7) Shaw noted that the relevant rates not only varied inversely with the distance from the city centre, but also that the highest of them were located in areas of declining population and physical deterioration. Similarly, Thrasher's classic study of the gang was unequivocal in seeing this form of delinquency as characteristic of the interstitial area abutting Chicago's central business district, the famous 'Loop':

'The central tripartite area of the gang occupies what is often called the "Poverty belt" — a region characterised by deteriorating neighbourhoods, shifting populations, and the mobility and disorganisation of the slum. Abandoned by those seeking homes in the better residential districts, encroached upon by industry, this zone is a distinctly interstitial phase of the city's growth. . . . Gangland is a phenomenon of human ecology. As better residential districts recede before encroachments of business and industry, the gang develops as one manifestation of the economic, moral, and cultural frontier which marks the interstice.' (8)

Although the Chicago ecologists placed great emphasis upon characteristics of the delinquent area such as physical deterioration, and even though Shaw and McKay stressed the constancy of rates in particular areas despite substantial alterations in the composition of their populations (9), they were adamant that this did not entail any belief 'that delinquency is caused by the external fact of location.' (10) Rather, they saw delinquency factors as being inherent in a community which presented children with 'a variety of contradictory standards and forms of behaviour' (11), a community in which there existed 'a powerful competing system of values' (12) and one in which there was little or no community effort to deal with the problem. The key, in other words, was the social disorganisation endemic in areas of rapidly shifting population and physical deterioration:

'The common element (among social factors highly correlated with juvenile delinquency) is social disorganisation or the lack of organised community effort to deal with these conditions. . . . Juvenile delinquency, as shown in this study, follows the pattern of the physical and social structure of the city, being concentrated in areas of physical deterioration and neighbourhood disorganisation.' (13)

The use to which these and other sociologists have put social disorganisation has been criticised on several grounds including its tendency towards tautological definition — the forms of behaviour explained by the condition being used at the same time to demonstrate its very existence — and its failure to appreciate that the absence of conventional organisation

50

need only imply *different* social organisation, not disorganisation (14). Indeed, the maintenance of this latter distinction was to become an important facet of other descriptions of delinquency such as W. F. Whyte's study of 'Cornerville' and other theoretical formulations such as those advanced by Sutherland, Kobrin, and by Cloward and Ohlin (15).

The very real defects in the formulation and subsequent use of ideas about social disorganisation should not, however, be allowed to obscure the importance of the contribution which was made by the Chicago School. Quite apart from the collection of data on a massive and unprecedented scale, these researchers had so many sensitive insights into the sociology of delinquency that scarcely any modern theory emerges without some debt to them being acknowledged. Shaw and McKay recognised for example, that however 'disorganised' an area, delinquency could nonetheless be culturally transmitted as a traditional and indeed a demanded response in the slum (16). This idea as we shall see, is a central plank in the current subcultural theories about delinquency. At the same time, in their 'Juvenile Delinquency and Urban Areas' which was published in 1942, the same authors were alive to the dangers of over-emphasising this tradition of delinquency to the point where the culture of the delinquent area might be portrayed as too radically divergent from that prevailing in its more law-abiding counterparts. Here again is a sensitivity for complexity which has only been rediscovered in recent years (17). Indeed, even the current trend towards recognition of the need to appreciate the delinquent's subjective experience and the impact of society's reaction upon how he perceives himself, is not totally without its antecedents in the Chicago School:

'Although so much of a gang boy's life is fanciful it often has the utmost reality for him, and many times he does not distinguish between what is real and what is not. He interprets his own social situations in his own terms and with the utmost seriousness. To understand the gang boy one must enter into his world with a comprehension, on the one hand, of this seriousness behind the mask of flippancy or bravado, and on the other, of the role of the romantic in his activities and in his interpretation of the larger world of reality.' (18)

In a now famous passage in 'Juvenile Delinquency and Urban Areas', Shaw and McKay speculated at some length about the possible association of unconventional conduct with a discrepancy, particularly economic, between idealised status and the practical prospects of its attainment. 'Those persons who occupy a disadvantageous position are involved' they maintained, 'in a conflict between the goals assumed to be attainable in a free society and those actually attainable for a large proportion of the population' (19). In concluding that this situation could be conducive to deviant behaviour, Shaw and McKay came very close to endorsing the

51

coherent explanatory model of 'anomie' which Robert K. Merton had advanced some four years earlier (20) and upon which he was subsequently to elaborate at considerable length (21).

Although it has been claimed that Merton's formulation of 'anomie' displays a marked indebtedness to Weber, the more common interpretation is that he derived the concept from Durkheim's use of the same term to describe the condition of normlessness arising when the potentially insatiable desires of men are no longer controlled by the external, regulating force of collective order (22). But whereas Durkheim placed his main emphasis upon the correlation between this condition of normlessness and social changes of a relatively abrupt kind, Merton saw the anomic condition as endemic, at least in contemporary American society (23). The United States, he argued, approaches a polar extreme in which culturally defined goals, enjoined as legitimate objectives for all, are exaggerated to the corresponding detriment of the emphasis which is placed upon the means institutionally prescribed for their attainment. This cultural disequilibrium engenders a situation in which regulatory norms are so undermined that people may withdraw their emotional support from the rules and come to be controlled largely by considerations of technical expediency (24).

To this modification of Durkeim's notion of untrammelled aspirations, Merton added another element which he perceived as crucial for an understanding of deviance and, no less important, of its distribution within the social structure. Given a disproportionate emphasis on goals, he argued, it becomes apposite to enquire whether individuals can actually achieve satisfaction through pursuit of the prescribed means. Have they access, in other words, to the channels through which their culturally engendered aspirations may be fulfilled? On this score, Merton was convinced that not only do a substantial number of contemporary Americans lack such access but also that this disjunction between ends and means impinges more strongly on the members of some social strata than of others, thereby enhancing their propensity towards deviance:

'It is only when a system of cultural values extols, virtually above all else, certain *common* success goals *for the population at large* while the social structure rigorously restricts or completely closes access to approved modes of reaching these goals *for a considerable part of the same population*, that deviant behaviour ensues on a large scale. ... Goals are held to transcend class lines, not to be bounded by them, yet the actual social organisation is such that there exist class differentials in accessibility of the goals. In this setting, a cardinal American virtue, "ambition", promotes a cardinal American vice "deviant behaviour".' (25)

It is almost superfluous to add that the 'considerable part of the same population' which Merton saw as having its access most heavily restricted is located in the 'lower reaches of the social structure'. This, he held to account for the over-representation of the lower social strata among the deviant and criminal populations even though he never quite made up his mind about the reliability of the statistics upon which the assumption of over-representation is based (26).

This theory and its associated paradigm of possible adaptations to the situation of anomie — conformity, innovation, ritualism, retreatism and rebellion — has been heavily criticised on a number of grounds which, however interesting and important, cannot concern us here (27). A criticism which does concern us, however, is the one which Albert K. Cohen advanced in 1955 as part of his famous study of gang-culture (28). Merton's theory, he argues, may well account for 'adult professional crime and for the property delinquency of some older and semi-professional thieves' (our long quotation from Merton was indeed taken from his discussion of innovation), but it does not explain the non-utilitarian, negativistic and malicious behaviour of the delinquent subculture (29). The idea of a resort to illicit means, claims Cohen, simply does not come to grips with the essential nature of this particular brand of delinquency (30).

Cohen's own explanation for this exception to the Mertonian scheme takes the dominance of 'middle-class' values in American society as its point of departure. Whereas some societies, he argues, may employ differing criteria for the evaluation of children in different parts of their relatively rigid systems of stratification, modern America applies the same 'middle-class measuring rod' to all, irrespective of their social origins. As a result, the working-class boy finds himself caught up in a competition for status and approval that is dominated and judged by middle-class standards, particularly as applied in the school. But the pattern of his socialisation is not such as to facilitate success in these terms and, as a result, he is likely to experience a severe problem of adjustment.

To this problem, primarily one of status, Cohen sees three ideal-type patterns of response, although he concedes that the determinants of the actual choice remain obscure. Some boys may opt for what, borrowing W. F. Whyte's terminology (31), he calls the 'college-boy' way of life — a continued striving after the educational and occupational achievements so highly valued in the dominant culture. Others, again in Whyte's terms, may struggle on with a 'corner-boy' mode of adaptation which permits an uneasy adherence to working-class values and even a certain amount of minor delinquency without completely rupturing good relations with the powerful carriers of middle-class values. But some, says Cohen, find neither of these alternatives acceptable or, indeed, available; these are the boys who have resort to the specifically delinquent solution in the subculture.

The problem of adjustment faced by these boys — and to a lesser extent by those who adopt the stable corner-boy solution — is rendered all the

53

more acute by the fact that it is not easily circumvented on the psychological level: the pervasiveness of middle-class values in important areas of the working-class boy's life is such that he has to some extent internalised them. They therefore linger on to threaten his satisfaction with any solution other than the college-boy response which brings different, if not necessarily smaller problems in its train. The boy has, in other words, a secondary problem of anxiety because of his continuing ambivalence over middle-class criteria. To solve this, Cohen claims, he may resort to 'reaction-formation', an exaggerated and hostile rejection of the standards under which he is deemed so unsuccessful. By this mode of adjustment he secures some reassurance 'against an inner threat to his defences'. At the same time, he may be able to secure some redress for his deprivation of status by joining together with others who, sharing his problems on the social and psychological planes, will engage in a mutual redistribution of status in accordance with perceived success in attacking the discriminatory value-system. Thus is born, asserts Cohen, the malicious, non-utilitarian and negativistic subculture within which certain forms of behaviour become 'right' precisely because they are 'wrong' in terms of middle-class values. In this context, even stealing — the most obvious candidate for classification as a resort to illicit means — can assume a distinctive 'contra-cultural' (33) meaning:

'Group stealing, institutionalised in the delinquent subculture is not just a way of getting something. It is a means that is the antithesis of sober and diligent "labour in a calling". It expresses contempt for a way of life by making its opposite a criterion of status.' (34)

The careful reader can scarcely have failed to notice certain superficial similarities between these ideas and those which were earlier attributed to Merton. We must be careful, however, to avoid the common mistake of concluding from this that Cohen merely offers an interesting extension of Merton's ideas. For one thing, Cohen's model sees middle-class values 'impinging' upon the working-class boy, particularly through the criteria which are applied to him in middle-class dominated institutions like the school. While he may indeed internalise some of these values over time, and while we may talk in this sense of the 'pervasiveness' of middle-class values, this is not quite the same thing as the diffuse cultural consensus about goals that Merton describes. More important, not only does Cohen's description of the emerging delinquent subculture deal much more explicitly with the psychological problems which Merton appears content to infer from structure, but it also hypothesises that the 'delinquent system of values and way of life does its job of problem-solving most effectively when it is adopted as a group solution' (35). Cohen, in other words, makes much more use of reference group theory than does Merton whose plausible explanation seems to deal with the individual in an unduly

54

'atomised' and isolated fashion (36).

Like Merton, Cohen has not lacked his critics. A well-known and, in view of Cohen's emphasis on ambivalence, a not altogether fair caricature of the theory has been presented by Matza who alleges that the theory portrays the subculture as an 'oppositional response to the pious legality of bourgeois existence' (37). No less important as part of the background to the British material in this section, is Walter B. Miller's contention that the delinquent subculture merely reflects conformity to the focal concerns of working-class culture rather than any reaction to perceived lack of status in terms of internalised middle-class criteria (38). On an empirical basis, Short and Strodbeck as well as Reiss and Rhodes have cast doubt upon the reaction-formation hypothesis itself (39), while Yablonsky has criticised the assumption which Cohen, in common with other subcultural theorists, makes about the gang as a defined sociological group (40).

But the most systematically worked out and the most constructively utilised critique of Cohen's theory is to be found in the work of Cloward and Ohlin who take issue with what they see as his assumption that the member of the delinquent subculture typically desires (and is denied) middle-class status (41). Such may well be true of subcultures comprising frustrated 'college boys' but it does not apply to many other working-class boys who may still aspire far beyond their realistic expectations of achievement without coveting status in terms of middle-class reference groups. For these boys the means-ends discrepancy is primarily an economic one involving their relative position as measured by 'lower-class rather than middle-class criteria' (42).

According to Cloward and Ohlin, the adoption of a delinquent solution to this different order of problem does not necessarily involve the psychological process of 'reaction-formation' so plausibly advanced by Cohen as the gang member's way of dealing with lingering moral ambivalence. In a plural society, individuals can and do attach legitimacy to norms on bases other than moral validity. That is to say, they can accept them as 'an authoritative set of directives for *action*' without necessarily regarding them as morally superior (43). Conversely, they can just as easily withdraw legitimacy without repudiating the moral validity of a norm and, equally important, without experiencing any continuing crisis of moral dissonance. This, claim Cloward and Ohlin, is precisely what may happen in the case of the delinquent subculture. Under the pressure of a disjunction between ends and means, the working-class boy may blame the system rather than himself and, having done so, may selectively abrogate the legitimacy of conventional norms as applied to himself. He may, in other words, become alienated without having to face problems of guilt, fear and anxiety resulting from continued definition of the norms in question as morally valid.

The other major contribution made by these theorists relates specifically to Merton rather than to Cohen. Following the Durkheimian concept of anomie as he did, and accepting too his emphasis on a means-ends scheme, they pointed to a basic and unwarranted assumption that he had made, namely, that *differential access to legitimate means* is offset *by equality of access to illegitimate ones*. This, Cloward and Ohlin convincingly argue, is simply not true, the world of crime and deviance is just as prone to structural inequalities as is the world of legitimate behaviour. On this basis, they go on to construct a typology of subcultures — criminal, conflict and retreatist — which they relate and trace to differentials in the availability of illegitimate opportunities for boys already substantially precluded from the conventional channels to success (44). It is for this elaboration of Merton's analysis that Cloward and Ohlin are probably best known; and rightly so, for in arriving at their classification they achieved an unprecedented degree of synthesis between traditions as divergent as anomie on the one hand and cultural transmission and differential social organisation on the other (45).

This review of American literature brings us finally to the work of David Matza who has probably done as much as anyone else in recent years to inject new vigour into sociological discussions of delinquency and of deviance in general. In collaboration with Gresham Sykes in 1957, Matza published a paper under the title of 'Techniques of Neutralisation', which has become part of the standard literature on delinquency (46). Like alienation, techniques of neutralisation are explicitly presented in this paper as mechanisms preceding and facilitating delinquency rather than as rationalisations which protect the individual 'from self-blame and the blame of others after the act' (47). Essentially, they derive from the fact that social norms tend to be qualified guides for action rather than categorical imperatives — even the law, as Sykes and Matza observe, is flexible to the extent of permitting defences such as insanity or self-defence. The delinquent, according to their theory, merely stretches a series of such defences far beyond acceptable limits, thereby providing himself with the justification for delinquent behaviour and, at the same time, neutralising both internal and external disapproval in advance. He is not, in other words, unequivocally committed to any set of antithetical values; he has simply learnt a series of 'definitions favourable to violation' (48) while remaining at least partially committed to the dominant social order.

Conceived by its authors as a refutation of Cohen's argument, neutralisation is scarcely as incompatible with his theory as Sykes and Matza appear to have thought. As we have already suggested, Cohen not only recognised the possibility of continuing attachment to dominant values, but indeed, incorporated ambivalence on this very point as the sine qua non of psychological progression towards the negativistic subcultural solution. It is by no means paradoxical that in a later reworking of his ideas with Henry Short, Cohen was able to accept the neutralisation hypothesis as an elaboration rather than a refutation of his own 'Delinquent Boys' (49).

56

For Matza himself, however, this early tilting at theoretical windmills was full of portent. In a second paper with Sykes he takes the idea of the delinquent's continuing commitment to convention still further by arguing that many 'delinquent' values are merely expressive analogues of 'subterranean' values 'embodied in the leisure activities of the dominant society' (50). Still later, in 'Delinquency and Drift' Matza elaborates both ideas as part of a more comprehensive model of delinquency which depicts the individual as typically 'drifting', albeit uneasily, between deviance and convention, with undetermined chances of washing up on either shore (51). The important thing about this formulation is that it asserts neither complete freedom nor complete constraint in the aetiology of delinquency. True, there may be 'underlying influences which imperceptibly guide the process', but at the end of the day there is still some room for the idea of will. The subculture permits delinquency but does not demand it. Thus from the original neutralisation hypothesis, Matza arrives at the point where he rejects the total, harsh determinism of previous sociological explanations with their emphasis upon irresistible, if largely unidentifiable 'causes', and at the same time, resists the final sociological nihilism of accepting the complete centrality of will in human affairs.

In his most recent book 'Becoming Deviant' (52), Matza pursues the methodological ramifications of these ideas even further. Deviants of all kinds must be regarded as subjects rather than objects, as acting and self-reflecting rather than merely reacting to the constraints of external stimuli. The primary obligation of what he calls 'naturalism' must be to portray them in this way, for this, despite all the unavoidable complexities, is precisely what they are in reality. Notions of structure and predisposition have not here completely disappeared, it is true – or at least not yet (53). What Matza calls 'affinity' still has its part to play even if only in liberating individuals to the extent that they become willing to deviate rather than necessarily deviant (54). But a change of emphasis in his thinking is nonetheless fairly evident. Having earlier urged a return to 'soft determinism' he now recognises that this must entail increased attention to the subjective aspect of becoming delinquent or deviant. With this shift in emphasis and with the equally important role that he attributes to societal reactions – 'signification' – Matza takes his place among the increasing number of sociologists of deviance who subscribe to what is commonly called the 'interactionist perspective'. The ideas of this important school have particular relevance for an understanding of the material in our final section and will receive some brief examination there.

The articles, extracts and original contributions which appear in the present section reflect the partial assimilation of some of the above ideas into British sociological writing about juvenile delinquency in the post-war period. This is not to say, of course, that this assimilation has been whole-

sale and uncritical. Indeed, the major significance of several of the contributions lies in their asserting the limited applicability to this country of
theories developed in the United States. In a wider context we might even
say that they underline the general danger of theories becoming 'culture-
bound' when too much reliance is placed upon the experience of one
society. Most of the items make their own connections with the American
literature fairly explicit, and, as a result, nothing more than a quick resumé
of the major inter-relationships is necessary in this introduction.

As in our earlier review, we begin with ecology and social disorganisation. These are the organising themes in Sainsbury's contribution which,
although primarily concerned with the distribution and causes of suicide,
nonetheless makes a very important point about London's ecology and
subsequently about the sociology of delinquency in the metropolis. Unlike
the pattern in Chicago, the capital's areas of greatest poverty do not
coincide with those which, in Sainsbury's view, may be described as
socially disorganised. More important, he finds that although suicide is
indeed positively correlated with social disorganisation, delinquency is not.
Instead, it tends to follow the ecological distribution of poverty.

A similar conclusion about the lack of any connection between social
disorganisation and delinquency is arrived at in our extract from 'The
Criminal Area' one of the most frequently cited books in post-war British
criminology. Terence Morris, its author, goes much further than Sainsbury,
however, in positing an alternative explanation. In interpreting the
ecological distribution of delinquency, he argues, variables such as poverty
or the physical deterioration so heavily emphasised by the Chicago school
are not enough. The picture must be viewed from the much wider perspective of its connections with social policy — the planned, rather than the
natural area — and most important of all, from the standpoint of its
inextricable links with social class. In this latter context, he takes issue
with both the social disorganisation theorists and with Cohen. The delinquent area is organised but it is working-class, and the behaviour of many
of its subcultural delinquents merely reflects the distinctive process of
socialisation prevailing in that segment of the social structure.

This raises, of course, the thorny question of whether working-class
children are in fact over-represented among the delinquent population, a
question which, as we shall suggest in the more general context of our final
section, might seem less problematic if approached from the viewpoint of
the sociology of law. For the present, however, we include a brief paper by
Douglas and others who suggest that, at least as far as the official picture is
concerned, the over-representation hypothesis can be substantiated.
Although at least one later study of officially recorded delinquency does
not confirm this finding (55), we should note that Lynn McDonald's use
of self-reporting techniques led to substantially similar conclusions (56).

In the impressionistic but nonetheless incisive extract which we reproduce from Willmott's 'Adolescent Boys of East London', the 'cultural

58

normality' of certain kinds of delinquency, particularly theft, in such working-class areas is emphasised once again. But, unlike Morris, Willmott also finds that the more aggressively anti-social behaviour of some boys — those who came closest to being a gang — cannot be dismissed as the normal outworkings of cultural patterns prevailing in this working-class area. Nor indeed, can it be easily interpreted as the result of a search for illicit means in the sense used by Cloward and Ohlin. Rather, this more serious and, Willmott suspects, more persistent delinquency seems to symbolise a frustrated response to consistent rejection, 'a desire to strike at society', and as such, approximates more closely to the contra-cultural model put forward by Cohen.

This conclusion must be viewed, however, against the background of more typical delinquency described by Willmott himself and by Downes in his account of adolescent, working-class groups in Stepney and Poplar. There, while he indeed encountered a considerable amount of delinquency, this tended to occur — at least for boys of this age — within the context of what Cohen could only have categorised as a 'corner-boy' rather than a specifically 'delinquent' adaptation. Status-frustration in the latter's sense of the term was singularly lacking, as indeed was evidence of the alienation so central to the argument of Cloward and Ohlin. Instead, Downes sees the typical response to lack of educational and occupational success among his adolescents as 'dissociation'. They opted out in the sense that they stopped caring, and deflected their aspirations into the world of non-work, where *sharing* 'subterranean' values of the dominant culture, but still dissociating from its middle-class dominated institutions, the corner-boys found their access to *leisure* goals heavily restricted. In this differential access, the culmination of a process involving educational failure and dissociation from work, Downes sees the genesis of much of their delinquency.

In reproducing even a lengthy extract from this important and influential book we are extremely conscious of the danger that we may do violence to the author's closely argued reasoning. To minimise this possibility we have therefore attempted, apart from a brief discussion under the heading of anomie, to encapsulate his major conclusions about Cohen's theory in a brief summary at the beginning of the extract, leaving his examination of the hypotheses advanced by Cloward and Ohlin and by Sykes and Matza relatively unabridged. Unfortunately, the premium which a collection of this kind places upon space must also preclude any restatement of the implications, particularly for education, which emerge from the Downes' study. These, the reader is counselled to follow up for himself, if only to appreciate how investigations conceived on a fairly theoretical basis can lead to very practical, if all too often unheeded suggestions for social planning at a very basic level.

We can, however, pursue the possibly crucial role of education in the emergence of the delinquent subculture a little further at this stage (57).

In David Hargreaves' contribution, based partly on his well-known book, 'Social Relations in the Secondary School' (58), it is argued that the school provides one of the most important contexts within which concepts such as status deprivation come to have immediate meaning for individual boys. In the school he is streamed according to his ability and his commitment to values regarded as legitimate by the teachers. More important, if placed in a low stream on this basis, he is likely to become the object of invidious comparison and of other sanctions, both formal and informal. Little wonder, Hargreaves argues, that he becomes increasingly negative in his attitudes towards the school and its teachers, and along with others similarly placed — others whom he does not even have to seek out for himself — participates in a negatively oriented and 'delinquescent' subculture.

Finally, in a section which so frequently alludes to 'subculture' as its organising construct, it is appropriate to include a theoretical discussion of this concept itself. In Witkin's paper, it is argued that sociologists frequently make an unwarranted assumption about the subculture when they portray its emergence in terms of a process of 'pattern introjection'. Part of a wider constellation of assumptions about the nature of sociological man, this model presents, according to the author, an unduly inflexible view of the individual's relationship to his socio-cultural environment. Instead, we should allow for a sampling process of interaction between personality, culture and social structure — a process 'whereby certain organisations of attitudes are rendered more adaptive than others'. With such a view, Witkin asserts, we might more easily account for some of the differences between delinquency here and in the United States, and, moreover, might restore some element of creativity to our conceptualisation of man in his social environment.

1. For a discussion of the sociological problems involved in the definition of social problems, see H. S. Becker (ed) Social Problems New York, John Wiley (1966). See also R. C. Fuller and R. R. Myers 'The Natural History of a Social Problem' American Sociological Review, 6 (June 1941) p. 320; R. K. Merton and Robert A. Nisbet (eds), Contemporary Social Problems New York, Harcourt Brace & World (1961) pp. 697-737
2. See, for example, D. J. West The Habitual Prisoner London, Macmillan (1963)
3. Lincoln Steffens The Shame of the Cities quoted in Anthony M. Platt The Child Savers Chicago, University of Chicago Press (1969) p. 37
4. For a useful review to which this introduction is heavily indebted see T. Morris The Criminal Area London, Routledge & Kegan Paul (1957)
5. Ibid. p. 8.
6. Frederick M. Thrasher The Gang Chicago, University of Chicago Press (1927); Clifford R. Shaw and Henry D. McKay Juvenile Delinquency and Urban Areas Chicago, University of Chicago Press (1942), revised edition (1969)
7. Clifford R. Shaw Delinquency Areas Chicago, University of Chicago Press (1929)
8. Frederick M. Thrasher Op. Cit. (abridged edition) Chicago, Phoenix Books (1963) pp. 20-21

9. They were however, severely taken to task over the ecological determinism allegedly implicit in this argument. See C. T. Jonassen 'A Revaluation and Critique of some of the Methods of Shaw and McKay' American Sociological Review, 14 (1949) pp. 608-615
10. Clifford R. Shaw Op. Cit. p. 21
11. Clifford R. Shaw and Henry D. McKay Op. Cit. p. 172. The authors comment here on the similarity with Sutherland's theory of Differential Association. See E. H. Sutherland and Donald R. Cressey Principles of Criminology (Sixth Edition) New York, J. P. Lippincott (1960)
12. Clifford R. Shaw and Henry D. McKay Op. Cit. p. 317
13. Ibid. p. xxvi. See also Frederick M. Thrasher Op. Cit., p. 33
14. For a useful discussion of this criticism see Don C. Gibbons Society, Crime and Criminal Careers Englewood Cliffs, Prentice-Hall (1968) pp. 185-186
15. W. F. Whyte Street Corner Society Chicago, University of Chicago Press (1943); E. H. Sutherland and Donald R. Cressey Op. Cit., (Seventh Edition) pp. 101-121; Solomon Kobrin, 'The Conflict of Values in Delinquency Areas' American Sociological Review (October 1951) pp. 653-61; R. A. Cloward and Lloyd E. Ohlin Delinquency and Opportunity New York, Free Press (1960); See also Sutherland's own account of how he came to employ the term 'differential social organisation' in A. Cohen, A. Lindesmith and K. Schuessler (eds) The Sutherland Papers Bloomington, Indiana University Press (1956) p. 21 and David Matza's stimulating discussion in Becoming Deviant Englewood Cliffs, Prentice-Hall (1969) p. 45
16. Clifford R. Shaw and Henry D. McKay, Op. Cit., p. 174
17. See D. Matza Delinquency and Drift New York, John Wiley (1964) and D. Matza Becoming Deviant Englewood Cliffs, Prentice-Hall (1969)
18. Frederick M. Thrasher Op. Cit. p. 96. See also Clifford R. Shaw The Natural History of a Delinquent Career Chicago, University of Chicago Press (1931)
19. Clifford R. Shaw and Henry D. McKay Op. Cit. p. XXXIX
20. Robert K. Merton 'Social Structure and Anomie', American Sociological Review (October 1938) pp. 672-82
21. Robert K. Merton Social Theory and Social Structure, New York, Free Press (1949)
22. Emile Durkheim Suicide New York, Free Press (1951); for the alternative view of Merton's sources see M. B. Scott and R. Turner 'Weber and the Anomie Theory of Deviance' Sociological Quarterly VI (1965) pp. 233-240
23. Durkheim did, however, come close to this position in acknowledging that anomie could become chronic and even necessary in societies 'where progress is and should be rapid', ibid. p. 364. The editors are grateful to R. S. Schenk for his helpful comments on this part of the introduction
24. Robert K. Merton Social Theory and Social Structure (Revised edition) New York, Free Press (1957) Chaps. 4 and 5
25. Ibid. p. 146
26. Ibid. p.144 ff. See also D. Matza Becoming Deviant Englewood Cliffs Prentice-Hall (1969) pp. 96-97
27. See in particular: Marshall B. Clinard Anomie and Deviant Behaviour New York, Free Press (1964); Edwin M. Lemert Human Deviance, Social Problems and Social Control Englewood-Cliffs, Prentice-Hall (1967); R. Dubin 'Deviant Behaviour and Social Structure' American Sociological Review 24 (1959) pp. 147-164; R. A. Cloward 'Illegitimate Means, Anomie and Deviant Behaviour' American Sociological Review 24 (1959) pp. 164-176; A. K. Cohen 'The Sociology of the Deviant Act: Anomie Theory and Beyond' American Sociological Review 30 (1965) pp. 9-14
28. Albert K. Cohen Delinquent Boys New York, Free Press (1955)
29. Ibid. pp. 35-36. He is careful, however, to make clear that such behaviour is not characteristic of all juvenile delinquency. Ibid. p. 25

30. To these assertions Merton has replied that Cohen is probably right in claiming that the theory does not account for *all* deviant behaviour. But he also argues that it does *not* maintain that the resulting deviant behaviour is rationally calculated and utilitarian. Rather, the theory focusses on the acute pressures which may lead to a number of different responses. Robert K. Merton Social Theory and Social Structure (Revised edition) New York, Free Press (1957) p. 178
31. W. F. Whyte Op. Cit (Revised edition) (1955)
32. A. K. Cohen Op. Cit. p. 133
33. On the useful, conceptual framework of 'contraculture' into which Cohen's theory can easily be fitted, see J. Milton Yinger 'Contraculture and Subculture' American Sociological Review 25 (1960) pp. 625-635
34. A. K. Cohen Op. Cit. p. 134
35. Ibid. pp. 134-135
36. See Cohen's later discussion 'The Sociology of the Deviant Act: Anomie Theory and Beyond' American Sociological Review 30 (1965) pp. 9-14
37. D. Matza Delinquency and Drift New York, John Wiley (1964) p. 34
38. Walter B. Miller 'Lower Class Culture as a Generating Milieu of Gang Delinquency' Journal of Social Issues 14 (1958) pp. 5-19
39. J. Short and F. L. Strodbeck Group Process and Gang Delinquency Chicago, University of Chicago Press (1965); Albert J. Reiss and Albert L. Rhodes 'Delinquency and Social Class Structure' American Sociological Review 26 (1961) pp. 720-732
40. Lewis Yablonsky 'The Delinquent Gang as a Near-Group' Social Problems 7 (1959) pp. 108-17. See also Lewis Yablonsky The Violent Gang London, Pelican Books (1967)
41. Richard A. Cloward and Lloyd E. Ohlin Op. Cit. For an extremely useful point by point comparison of the two theories see D. Downes The Delinquent Solution London, Routledge & Kegan Paul (1966) pp. 22-61
42. Ibid. p. 92
43. Ibid. p. 16
44. Ibid. p. 150 ff. See also E. Spergel Slumtown Racketville and Haulburg Chicago, University of Chicago Press (1964), and A. K. Cohen and J. F. Short 'Research in Delinquent Subcultures' Journal of Social Issues 14 (1958) pp. 20-37
45. See Clifford R. Shaw and Henry D. McKay Op. Cit. (Revised edition) (1969) p. XXXV ff
46. G. M. Sykes and D. Matza 'Techniques of Neutralisation: A Theory of Delinquency' American Sociological Review 22 (1957) pp. 664-70
47. Ibid. p. 666
48. Ibid. Sykes and Matza point explicitly to the similarity between their hypothesis and that advanced in Sutherland's notion of 'differential association' quod vide, (E. H. Sutherland and Donald R. Cressey Op. Cit.)
49. A. K. Cohen and J. F. Short Op. Cit. p. 21
50. D. Matza and G. M. Sykes 'Delinquency and Subterranean Values' American Sociological Review 26 (1961) pp. 712-19
51. D. Matza Delinquency and Drift New York, John Wiley (1964)
52. D. Matza Becoming Deviant Englewood Cliffs, Prentice-Hall (1969)
53. Matza does concede that he is moving further away from determinism in this book Ibid. p. 7 f.n. 10
54. Ibid. p. 112
55. G. Palmai, P. B. Storey and O Briscoe 'Social Class and The Young Offender' British Journal of Psychiatry 113 (1967) pp. 1073-1082
56. Lynn McDonald Social Class and Delinquency London, Faber & Faber (1969)
57. See also the paper by C. M. Phillipson in the final section
58. D. Hargreaves Social Relations in a Secondary School London, Routledge & Kegan Paul (1967)

Suicide, Delinquency and the Ecology of London
by Peter Sainsbury
Reprinted from <u>*Suicide in London*</u> *London,*
Institute of Psychiatry (1955) Chap. 3

It has been shown, not only that the suicide rates of the London boroughs differ from one another but that these differences correlate with certain social characteristics of the boroughs — their social isolation, mobility and disorganization. The effect of these social factors, and of economic class, age, sex, marital status and illness on the suicide rates of neighbourhoods, will be discussed in the following pages. But first must be briefly examined the social processes which have determined the evolution in London of districts with special social attributes.

The Growth and Ecology of London

The diversity of districts within London is the unplanned product, of geographical, historical, economic and social causes. Since the Middle Ages there has been the major division of London into a commercial centre, the City, developing around the port in the east, and a political centre in the west at Westminster. In the former a zealous community of ambitious merchants pursued their trades, defying any interference from the court; and around this commercial hub were gathered the industries and the homes of the labourers. With increasing trade and industrialization, the working-class district expanded into the gargantuan slums of the present day. Though bleak and grim, this district is comparatively settled socially, for it is a community which has arisen and is maintained in response to local industrial demands. The high proportion of London-born among the inhabitants of the East End boroughs is evidence of social stability.

In the environs of Westminster the more erratic world of the court and government developed. Here were provided the diversion of the momentarily privileged and the entertainment of the wealthy and leisured. This division of London has persisted: the restless, meretricious West End, and the settled East End where the Cockney, the hereditary Londoner, lives by the commerce of his port and City.

London's growth was greatly hastened by the industrial and technical developments of the nineteenth century, and the consequent construction of a system of rapid local transport. Out of this arose a second differentiation: highly mobile districts for business, commerce and shopping at the centre, and at the periphery 'vast dormitories, an anonymous wilderness, neighbourhoods without neighbours' (Summerson 1945). The early parochial character of London was obliterated, and the shifting impersonality of the modern city emerged, this being especially marked in West and Central London.

Finally, There has been the delimitation of a mosaic of smaller districts, each with characteristic populations and activities. These were manifest in the eighteenth century. To-day there are the one-room flat, boarding-house and hotel areas of Kensington, Bayswater and Bloomsbury which cater for the immigrant; social isolation is pronounced here. There are districts, notably Hampstead, to which aspire the commercially successful, where occupational mobility might be expected to be a special social feature. Similarly, trades and professions gravitate to circumscribed districts; the doctors mecca to the north of Wigmore Street has a quality as unmistakable as that of the artists' or greengrocers' headquarters in Chelsea and Covent Garden.

So London has developed "natural areas", such as have been described in Chicago; they do not seem, however, to conform to the simple concentric pattern found in Chicago, although some characteristics, such as population density, are so arranged.

A most important respect in which the social structure of London differs from that of Chicago or Minneapolis is that London's most mobile and apparently most socially disorganized districts do not coincide with those of greatest poverty. The prosperous north-western boroughs have the highest rates for mobility, isolation and social disorganization; the poor eastern boroughs the lowest. Moreover, in London the zones of transition are not the most mobile, nor do they appear to be the centres in which immigrants are absorbed; the statistics clearly show that immigrants settle first in the north-west, and next in the peripheral southern boroughs (Smith 1934).

In the following sections the relationship of the natural areas of London to the incidence of suicide will be discussed.

Distinction between Poverty and Social Disorganization

The separation in London of the districts of greatest poverty from those of social disorganization provides an opportunity to examine the importance of these separately in relation to suicide. For in the American studies the coincidence of poverty and social disorganization at the city centre left in doubt the role of each in producing the high central suicide rates. The findings in London unequivocally support the view that social disorganization, not poverty, is the paramount factor.

As the boroughs are administrative areas of recent origin it is preferable to consider borough divisions or groups, if these more nearly correspond to the social, cultural or physical unit.

A comparison of the suicide-rank order of the boroughs during 1919-23, 1929-33 and 1940-44 showed that each borough, especially those with high rates, preserved a fairly consistent position. This finding strongly supports the hypothesis that some social characteristic of the borough controls its suicide rate. It is fair to suppose that during the war the borough populations changed considerably because of evacuation, conscription, and so on, but nevertheless the boroughs preserved their social peculiarities and retained their usual relative rates of suicide. A striking example of the tenacity with which a borough maintains a high suicide rate is provided by Westminster. From the figures for suicide in Westminster given by Winslow a hundred years ago it appears that the suicide rate during 1832-36 was 15.7 per 100,000, which is five times the rate for London as a whole in 1831 (Winslow 1840, population of London from Trevelyan 1944).

The alliance of a high incidence of suicide with social mobility, isolation and disorganization in the north-western boroughs has been sufficiently stressed; but the social characteristic primarily responsible for a high rate varies from borough to borough. In Mayfair, for example, the impersonal, fleeting nature of reationships and the lack of a consistent and generally accepted set of values seem to be especially important. In the rented single rooms of South Kensington, Bayswater and Bloomsbury the untoward consequences of loneliness and anonymity seem to prevail; and a high suicide rate was actually found in the Bloomsbury district of St. Pancras. In Hampstead the human problems to be expected are those of the parvenu adopting unaccustomed values and a new way of life, those of the immigrant adjusting to an unfamiliar culture, and those of the lonely boarding-house dweller. High suicide rates were observed in the two latter groups, and even the more prosperous tended to be over-represented among the suicides. The high mobility around the railway stations in the City and Paddington might well conduce to a high rate of suicide, such as was found in the districts adjoining the termini of St. Pancras.

The remaining boroughs north of the river and adjoining the high-suicide-rate group, Hammersmith, Fulham and Islington, have intermediate suicide rates, just as in social characteristics they share many features of both the high- and low-rate boroughs.

Two working-class districts may be distinguished: the first, the East Central group, comprising Shoreditch, Finsbury, Bethnal Green and Southwark, has the higher suicide rate. Shoreditch, in fact, is among the ten boroughs with highest rates, although it shows few of the social features so evident in the other nine. Its high suicide rate seems less anomalous when one considers its central position adjoining the high-rate district, its high-mobility rating and the abundance of "black" streets on the survey maps. The second working-class group, Poplar, Deptford, Stepney and Bermondsey, is more to the east; its suicide rate is well below the average for London. Reasons have been adduced for supposing that these working-class districts form a stable, well-knit community of perennial Londoners. Furthermore, these four boroughs have the four highest birth-rates of London (Smith 1932, 1934).

Wandsworth, Lewisham and Woolwich form the southern and outer ring of the county. They also have a low suicide rate. They comprise a socially homogeneous group of middle-class and skilled working-class residential boroughs. They show few signs of social disorganization; on the contrary, the impression is one of settled family life and owned homes, all three boroughs have an increasing population.

In London, suicide rates seem therefore to vary with the social character of a district. This was so in Chicago (Mowrer 1942, Cavan 1928), in Minneapolis (Schmid 1933) and in Hamburg (Gruhle 1940). In London, the suicide rate was highest in the more mobile central district and in lodging-house areas; it was lower in the more stable boroughs and the peripheral suburbs. What are the possible explanations for the distribution of suicide in the London boroughs?

The view must be sustained that the nature of community life, its cohesion and stability, and the opportunities it provides for satisfactory relationships, alone afford a comprehensive explanation of the variations in suicide rate of communities and other social groups.

Poverty in Relation to Suicide

In the published literature there is little precise information about the relationship of social status to suicide, so the findings in London merit further consideration.

In distribution, poverty and suicide are mutually exclusive for it has been shown that the boroughs with highest suicide rates are also those with the highest proportion of middle-class, moderately well-to-do inhabitants, and the poorest boroughs, Shoreditch apart, have an average, or more commonly, a less-than-average suicide rate. From the exceptions it is evident, however, that the relationship is not a simple inverse one. For example, St. Pancras with a suicide rate of 28.3 has considerable poverty and a smaller middle-class component than the other high-rate boroughs. In Lewisham and Woolwich, with suicide rates of 14.3 and 15.5, 31% and 17% of the population respectively belong to the middle class; both are boroughs which combine a relatively high social status with low indices of mobility and isolation. A lack of consistency between social status and suicide is also evident in the findings for the borough subdivisions.

If the neighbourhood status is narrowed down to the more immediate milieu of the street of the suicide's home, the over-representation of suicides in the streets of a higher social grade and their under-representation in the lower grades is striking.

Similarly, suicide was proportionately greater in the upper occupational classes than in the lower. This finding is in keeping with the findings of the Registrar-General and of allied studies undertaken in America (Dublin et al. 1933). The Registrar-General's Tables and the official statistics of other countries show a higher rate of suicide among those engaged in the professions and among owners of businesses (Miner 1922), careers in which individuality, independence and personal responsibility for one's actions, are important — conditions for Durkheim's egoistic suicide. Among the case studies on suicide, only Stearns gives figures for social status. He found that 65% of suicides were well-to-do (Stearns 1921).

But when the suicide's actual economic status at the time of his death is considered, a discrepancy becomes evident. It is then found that the proportion of suicides in poverty is much increased. This implies that among the suicides were many who had lost status, either through unemployment, illness, business failure or the poverty of old age. Unexpected poverty would seem to dispose to suicide to a greater extent than does habitual poverty.

The relationship between poverty and suicide is complex. The conclusions which may reasonably be deduced from this study are that indigenous poverty does not foster suicide. On the contrary, the suicide rate tends to increase with social status. On the other hand, poverty befalling those used to a better standard of living is a burden badly tolerated, and a factor predisposing to suicide; secondary poverty of this kind would account for the rise in the suicide rate in the upper occupational classes during the economic depression and the discrepant finding that the incidence of suicides living in poverty is greater when the suicide's actual economic level at the time of death is the criterion, rather than the economic status that might be inferred from occupation and neighbourhood.

Poverty and contentment are by no means incompatible, as both Booth and Smith stressed in their Surveys (Booth 1889, Smith 1932). There is a shared tradition and a neighbourly and cordial atmosphere in many of London's poor districts, which is in contrast to the cool formality of South Kensington and other more prosperous areas. A further important focus of community activity and feeling in London's working-class districts is the trade-union movement. The respective suicide rates reflect this difference.

The findings support the hypothesis that increased social mobility or isolation, whether of class, occupation or neighbourhood, conduces to suicide; for suicide prevails among the social classes and occupations which demand individuality, are less subject to group control, and have a high mobility of status (i.e. opportunity for changing status). The boroughs with the highest suicide rate have a high proportion of middle-class residents engaged in commercial occupations. They also have a high spatial mobility, with a consequent decrease in neighbourliness; and it is with these features that a high incidence of suicide seems to be associated.

It is interesting to compare the class status of the mentally disordered with that of suicides. Neustatter studied the effect of poor social conditions in producing neurosis among children. He concluded that low economic status did not directly determine neurosis among the poor children of South-East London, as the incidence was higher among the well-to-do children of the north-west boroughs (Neustatter 1938). American observations on mental disorder and neighbourhood have established that rates are higher in the slum districts (Faris et al. 1939), and decrease with rising social and economic status (Hyde et al. 1944). In both these studies, however, the poorest parts of the city were found to be the most mobile, which makes comparisons with London difficult.

The occupational rates for mental disorder show that persons of higher status have a lower incidence of mental illness (Clark 1939). The economic status of patients has been shown to vary with the type of psychosis. Manic-depressives are over-represented in the well-off, and the organic psychotics in the "dependent"; the number of the former is increased in periods of economic stress, but the number of the latter is little affected by economic conditions (Dayton 1940, Faris et al. 1939, Malzberg 1940). It may be concluded that those mental disorders in which environmental stresses play an important part in provoking illness most resemble suicide in their relation to social status.

Unemployment

From the low negative correlation found between unemployment and suicide in the London boroughs it seems probable that there are social factors more important than unemployment in determining suicide rates. Nevertheless, suicide and unemployment are regularly found to increase together during economic depressions. Stearns found that the two were closely correlated in Massachusetts (Stearns 1921).

In London the unemployed had a much greater suicide rate than the corresponding employed population: in about a third unemployment was a principal cause of suicide. Other findings give similar results. Lendrum gave the following figures: the proportion of attempted suicides who were unemployed was 22.6%, but the proportion of unemployment in the population of which they were a sample was 6.4% (Lendrum 1933). 26% of Hopkins's cases of attempted suicide were unemployed; but in only 6% was this considered the cause of suicide (Hopkins 1937). Lastly, Stearns found that 50% of suicides were unemployed, but this was never found to be the cause of suicide (Stearns 1921). Is this increased rate of suicide among the unemployed attributable to poverty or to another concomitant of unemployment?

It was calculated in the New Survey that unemployment persisting over six weeks would reduce the average family below the poverty line (Smith 1932). The majority of the unemployed in this study, therefore, would have been in poverty. But two observations suggest that poverty may be a secondary consideration: (1) the negligible increase in suicide found in the lowest social class during the 1931 depression, (2) the case studies indicate that aimlessness and hopelessness are the cause, not poverty (Smith 1932).

So it would appear that the unemployed experience in an exaggerated form the disturbance found in all classes at times of economic upheaval. The latter is the common factor causing both suicide and unemployment and so, in some measure, accounting for the association between them.

Overcrowding

No consistent relationship between overcrowding and suicide was observed. It is probable that the overcrowding indices are measuring two opposing effects: (1) that of socio-economic status, in which case overcrowding might be expected to go with a low suicide rate, (2) that of propinquity, an effect possibly allied to social disorganization, in which case overcrowding might be expected to raise the suicide rate. Only in St. Pancras was overcrowding associated with a high suicide rate, and this was in the socially disorganized district adjoining the railway stations. Of the remaining four boroughs in which the degree of overcrowding in the suicide's home was examined, the suicides were under-represented in the overcrowded districts.

It is sometimes alleged that suicide is in some way dependent upon density of population (Gruhle 1940) or city size, per se. What in fact this means is that city life, where overcrowding is admittedly a feature, is more inclined to foster suicide than is country life.

Social Isolation

'Hell is a city much like London': the impassive indifference of the metropolis and its capacity to engender feelings of insignificance and loneliness among its residents is a product of two major social processes: first, the differentiation of districts given over exclusively to lodging-houses, hotels and flatlets; and secondly, the isolation produced by a high mobility which debases human relationships to a formal level and compromises all values by offering so many alternatives.

In this investigation precise indices of solitary living have been correlated with suicide rates in different districts, to test the hypothesis that social isolation is a powerful cause of suicide.

The suicide rate was highest in those boroughs that provided ample opportunity for solitary living. Not only did these include by far the greater proportion of boarding-houses, but they showed a greater incidence of people living alone or as boarders than did the rest of London.

The purely statistical finding of a high correlation between suicide rates and rates of isolated living acquired more meaning when the results of the inquiry into the mode of living of 409 suicides were examined. In five London boroughs it was shown that: (a) the proportion of the suicides living alone was significantly greater than was the proportion of persons living alone in the corresponding borough populations, (b) the rank of the boroughs with respect to numbers living alone was similar to their suicide rates, and (c) the Bloomsbury lodging-house district of St. Pancras had a higher incidence of suicide than had the rest of the borough.

The relationship between suicide and solitary mode of life is probably one of cause and effect, for the individual records indicated that in 10% of cases loneliness had been regarded as a factor contributing to suicide. Allowing for the nature of the records, this is a substantial fraction. Loneliness was especially evident among the aged.

Many sociological studies have emphasized the close association between social isolation and suicide. Nevertheless, there is seldom, in case-studies reported by physicians, any reference to the suicides' mode of living. Stearns, however, found that nearly a third of suicides admitted to Massachusetts General Hospital lived in boarding-houses (Stearns 1921).

Social isolation is a wider concept than living alone. It includes: the social and cultural isolation of the immigrant; the solitude of old age arising from lack of contemporaries to share values and outlook; the unemployed's sense of social rejection; the ostracism resulting from infringement of a social taboo by divorce or a criminal act, or any similar activity that might diminish relatedness to the community. A high suicide rate is found in all these categories: only the concept of social isolation embraces and accounts for such a diversity of phenomena.

Social Mobility and Suicide

I have frequently mentioned the social effects of mobility, both spatial, i.e. movement of populations between districts, and vertical, i.e. movement between classes or occupational groups. For the study of suicide, the most important consequence is that mobility promotes social and cultural isolation. The immigrant into one of the more mobile districts of a city has to contend with alien and contradictory values which tend to undermine his accepted beliefs (and traditions); this may conduce to an attitude in which life loses purpose and significance.

The percentage of the residents of a borough entering and leaving it daily, and the proportion born outside London, when used as measures of mobility, correlated significantly with the borough's suicide rates. A further index, such as rate of change of address in a neighbourhood, would, of course, have been preferable but was impracticable.

Among the five boroughs studied in detail, Hampstead and St. Pancras had a high mobility, and both had high suicide rates. Their mobilities differ in type. In Hampstead a high proportion of the residents were born outside London, including an important foreign-born element; secondly, there is a raised class mobility, for this is a district into which the economically successful migrate: it contains more business men than any other part of London. In St. Pancras there is a high transiency in the neighbourhood of the railway stations, and a big daily turn-over of population. Suicides among transients caused a substantial rise in the suicide rates in the southern divisions of the borough, though the characteristically high rate of these divisions persists if the suicide rate is based on resident population only. About 12% of *all* suicides in the five boroughs were transients: by contrast, 14% of residents committed suicide away from their homes.

The studies of the distribution of suicides in Minneapolis, and of juvenile delinquency and mental disorder in Chicago, clearly indicate a close association with mobility. The present findings suggest a similar relationship between suicide and mobility in London.

London's immigrants differ from Chicago's in that they move into the better-class neighbourhoods, which suggests that the unsettled nature of a district where immigrants congregate is more important than its economic status.

The foreign-born immigrants in Hampstead had a disproportionately high suicide rate. High suicide rates among the foreign-born have also been recorded in New York (Miner 1922) and in Chicago. In the latter town the foreign populations were not found to account for the differences in suicide rates between communities (Cavan 1928).

Schmid found that in a group of American cities there was a positive correlation of 0.6 between the percentage of residents of the city who were born in some other state, and the cities' suicide rates (Schmid 1933). But there seem to have been no studies relating suicide to mobility comparable to those obtained for mental disorder (Faris et al. 1939, Queen 1940, Schroeder 1942). Tietze, studying the effect of mobility on the incidence of mental disorder, found that inter-city mobility was a better indicator of the disruptive effects of mobility than was intra-city mobility (Tietze et al. 1942). This is consistent with our finding that Deptford, Poplar, Bethnal Green and Hackney combine low suicide rates with a low percentage of immigrants from both outside London and other boroughs, and a high percentage of residents born in the boroughs (Smith 1934).

Social Disorganization and Suicide

It might be expected that if social control and integration in a neighbourhood are diminished, the conduct of its residents would lack restraint and moderation, and the incidence not only of suicide but also of illegitimacy, divorce and crime would be increased.

As regards the distribution of divorce and illegitimacy in London this expectation was realized; they are both more prevalent in the socially mobile boroughs, and show significant correlations with suicide. These findings are similar to those described in Chicago (Mowrer 1942, Cavan 1928). Mowrer records a correlation of 0.89 between the community rates for suicide and divorce during 1929-35.

The fact that the divorced have a high suicide rate does not explain the association, as the number of divorced in any borough is too small to alter the rates appreciably. On the other hand, a careful inspection of many case studies in which the cause of suicide was given revealed that an illegitimate pregnancy was seldom mentioned as a reason for suicide. The present study included only two such instances. Divorce and illegitimacy cannot, then, be said to cause high suicide rates in a district; all that is apparent is that suicide, divorce and illegitimacy tend to increase together in areas with certain social characteristics. Thus the rates for all three are high in the West End, where, for instance, night-life, intemperance, and what may be called meretricious values exist. The findings are different in the working-class and the middle-class boroughs of South-East London where the informal social control and surveillance commonly found in a well-knit community may reduce the incidence of suicide, divorce and illegitimacy. I calculated from the Registrar-General's occupational tables a significant correlation ($\tau=0.44$) between borough suicide rates and proportion of population professionally engaged in amusements — an occupational class closely associated with those aspects of city life which may connote social instability.

The lack of correlation between juvenile delinquency and suicide was unexpected; Shaw's work in Chicago made it seem probable that juvenile delinquency and social disorganization might also be found together in London. Burt in London and Shaw in Chicago had shown that poverty areas and delinquency areas were closely associated; but it has already been mentioned, when contrasting the social structures of London and Chicago, that the areas of poverty and social disorganization are separated in the former, but coincide in the latter. Therefore, in Chicago, areas with high rates for suicide, delinquency, poverty and social disorganization are found together; in London, juvenile delinquency and poverty are associated, but not suicide which is the highest in the disorganized areas.

The conclusion which it seems reasonable to draw from these facts is that economic factors may be of relatively greater importance in determining juvenile delinquency than is social disorganization; for if the two factors are separately correlated with juvenile delinquency, only the former shows a significant association.

The position as regards adult crime may well be different, because in this study it was found that streets described in the New Survey as criminal and degraded contributed four times their expected number of suicides. Mowrer found that in Chicago the community rates for suicide and juvenile delinquency correlated to the extent of 0.14, but that suicide and arrests had a correlation of 0.71. This suggests that crime may be more closely allied to social disorganization (Mowrer 1942).

Sex, Age, Marital Status and Suicide

In every culture an individual's sex, age or marital status implies a definite social role, and the suicide rates of these categories in London must now be discussed in relation to the cultural and social roles they entail.

The suicide rates in these groups were much the same as those found elsewhere. The classification of the population by sex, age and marital status did not account for the differences in rates between boroughs: if the suicide rate of a borough was raised, the rates for all groups were increased. The origin, therefore, of the variation in borough suicide rates does not lie in the composition of their populations.

Sex

The male suicide rate in London was twice that of the female, which is less than that often found in Western countries; but an excess of male over female suicides is not an invariable phenomenon: in certain cultures the female rate is greater (Miner 1922). Before these differences can be interpreted, two further comparisons of the sexes ought to be made: the rates for attempted suicide, and the relative importance of factors which affect the rates.

Figures for attempted suicide in London were rather less than those for successful suicide; the sexes were equally represented. American and German statistics, however, show that twice as many females as males attempt suicide (Mowrer 1942, Donalies 1928). If the sexes are broken down into age groups, it is found that in both successful and attempted suicides male rates are higher in later life; female rates are higher than male for attempted suicides only in the second and third decades.

An explanation frequently offered for the difference between the sexes in the number of successful attempts is that the methods employed by men are more certainly lethal. This is little more than a restatement of the problem; moreover, the analysis of methods employed in the present series of cases shows asphyxiation and poison to be by far the commonest method for both sexes. Availability is more likely to be an important factor in determining method. In urban areas, for example, gas is commonly used, in rural areas firearms (Dublin et al. 1933).

A possible interpretation of the differences between the sexes in rate of successful suicide is suggested by two observations: (1) when one compares groups of suicides showing large differences in rate, such as urban and rural, or wartime and peacetime figures, the fall or increase in suicide is proportionally greater among the males than among the females (Mowrer 1942, Metropolitan Life Insurance 1946, Miner 1922): (2) economic factors are more important precipitants of male suicides, but domestic difficulties often preponderate with females (Hopkins 1937, Moore 1937, Lendrum 1933). Male suicide rates also correlate more highly with business conditions than do female rates (Dublin et al. 1933).

When the biological and social roles of the two sexes are compared, the female role appears more precisely defined, and her biological and social functions more harmonized. That of the urban male, on the other hand, is less restricted by social conformity; in fact, an aggressive individualism is encouraged in him. The responsibility for the support and welfare of his family devolves on him; he is more subject to the stresses of mobility and change. The male's more independent and arduous social role, as indicated by the marked lability of the male suicide rate in social and economic stresses, and the frequency among males of causes of suicide related to problems of social readjustment, affords a likely explanation of the excess of male over female suicides.

Age

The differences in suicide rate of the various age groups are also in keeping with the hypothesis that participation in, and control by, the social group diminishes suicide, whereas isolation favours it. Suicide in the first fifteen years of life is rare (1 in London during 1929-33). It is when the support and authority of the family group is first discarded that suicides become numerous. After the fourth decade the male suicide rate is very high.

Studies undertaken among the aged in London clearly indicate both their distressing loneliness and the suicidal thoughts which accompany the feeling that their lives are valueless. Loneliness and lack of occupation appear to be a more urgent problem among the aged than is poverty (Rowntree 1947, Smith 1932). These two difficulties were also evident among the aged suicides in this study.

The lability of suicide rate in the aged suggests that social factors are as important as biological ones in accounting for their high rate of suicide. During the war, for example, when elderly men were able to obtain useful employment, the suicide rate among them fell more than that of younger men. The proper provision of hostels and occupation for the elderly might well be included in a social programme designed to diminish suicide.

Marital Status

The married persons in this series had a higher suicide rate than the single; but their average age is above that of the single, so that the usual tendency

74

for married persons to have a lower suicide rate would not be evident unless they were compared with the single by age groups.

The widowed and divorced had the customary high rates. Others have shown that the high rate among the widowed is partly due to their high average age. With age held constant the suicide rate of the widowed is still greater than that of the married, but less than that of the single (Dublin et al. 1933). 5% of the present suicides were described as separated or divorced: the incidence of divorce in the whole of London is 0.24% of the population.

The bonds of family life and the social pressure to live up to family responsibilities are deterrents of suicide. The single have not adopted this socially approved family role, the widowed have been separated from it, and the divorced have incurred social disapproval by rejecting it: their suicide rates may be said to measure the extent to which they participate in the social and cultural pattern.

Physical Illness and Suicide

Physical illness was a factor determining 29% of the suicides. This is higher than is usually reported. The incidences found by other investigators were 23% (Cavan 1928), 14% (Stearns 1921), 12% (Metropolitan Life Insurance 1927). For attempted suicide the incidence was: 24% (Andics 1947), 13% (Hopkins 1937), and 10% (Lendrum 1933); Siewers and Davidoff found 30% among patients admitted to mental hospitals, but only 10% among those admitted to a general hospital (Siewers et al. 1943).

Suicidal attempts prompted by physical illness are more often successful than those made from any other cause (Metropolitan Life Insurance, 1945). Hendin similarly observed that the seriousness of the intention to die was especially high in this group (Hendin 1950).

Many of those who formed the subject of this group complained not only of the physical illness but of its social consequences, e.g. loss of employment or of money. Andics, who made a detailed examination of her cases of attempted suicide, also remarked that the physically ill complained that loss of work and separation from the community made their illnesses intolerable (Andics 1947). This isolating effect of illness suggests a possible explanation of the 10 cases in which a physical deformity was the implicated cause of suicide.

Mental Disorders in Relation to Suicide

Unfortunately, rates for first admissions to mental hospitals from the London boroughs were not obtainable. The Public Health Department of the London County Council, however, very kindly provided figures for the

75

number of admissions from each of the boroughs to the observation wards of London during two months in 1949. The admission rates for mental disorder from the boroughs correlated significantly with their mean 1946-48 suicide rates (τ=0.39).

The six boroughs with the highest rates for admission of mental patients were, in order, the City, Stoke Newington, St. Marylebone, Westminster, Southwark, Chelsea. The six with the lowest rates were Shoreditch, Bermondsey, Deptford, Woolwich, Poplar, Bethnal Green. This finding is also supported by the figures for all the certified patients chargeable to the boroughs — grouped into nine areas (London statistics 1931-2) — which showed that area 4, composed of Hampstead, Holborn, St. Marylebone and St. Pancras, had the highest rate of certified patients.

As far as they go, these figures suggest that mental disorder in London has a higher incidence in the more mobile and socially disorganized districts, where suicide is also found. They are interesting because of their obvious similarity to the valuable and painstaking studies undertaken in American cities. One explanation of this association is that as the mentally ill are prone to suicide, mental illness and suicide will be found together; but a comparison of other statistics of suicide and mental disorder, such as their rates by economic class, shows no correspondence; moreover, this explanation merely alters the problem to one of explaining why mental disorder is more prevalent in one locality than another. The more likely explanation is that the difference in community rates of both mental disorder and suicide is the effect of a common cause — the social organization of the neighbourhood. This view is supported by the ecological studies of Cavan, Schmid and Faris on suicide, and those of Faris and Dunham, Schroeder, Tietze on mental disorder, in which both conditions were closely associated with social mobility, isolation and disorganization.

The complexity of the relationship of suicide to mental disorder is due to the fact that both are ultimately determined by the same order of social, psychological and biological causes, compounded in one individual to dispose to suicide, in another to mental illness, and in a third to both.

In Conclusion

The variations in suicide rate in the London boroughs can be explained by the hypothesis that the social character of city districts is determined by the extent of social mobility, isolation, or cohesion, and that these factors also predispose to or diminish the tendency to suicide. The hypothesis brings order to a number of apparently contradictory observations.

Thus, socially mobile, isolated and disorganized districts had most suicides; social isolation explains the correlations found between suicide and living alone or in boarding-houses, suicide and districts with a large immigrant population, suicide and the incidence of divorce and illegiti-

76

macy. The higher suicide rates in the more mobile and individualistic occupations and classes, and among the unemployed, and the rates for sex, age and marital groups may all, likewise, be interpreted in terms of the degree of social isolation or participation to which these groups are subject.

The sociological approach to the study of suicide by an analysis of the incidence of suicide in differing social groups and contexts provides a body of fact that may help to prevent suicide or alleviate the distress of many who, though not suicidal, suffer in unhappiness or some other way the effects of the social disorder of which suicide is the visible distress signal.

Andics, M. von (1947). Suicide and the Meaning of Life, London, 1st ed

Booth C. (1889). Labour and Life of the People, London, 2nd ed., vol. 1

Burt, C. (1944a). The Young Delinquent, London 4th ed

Cavan, R. S. (1928). Suicide, Chicago, 1st ed

Clark, R. E. (1939). Bulletin of the Society for Social Research, Dec., p. 8, quoted by Mowrer, E. R. (1942), Disorganisation Personal and Social, Philadelphia, 1st ed

Dayton, N. A. (1940). New Facts on Mental Disorder, Springfield, Ill., 1st ed

Donalies. G. (1928). Mschr. Psychiat. Neurol., 69

Dublin, L. I., and Bunzel, B. C. (1933). To Be or Not To Be, a Study of Suicide, New York, 1st ed

Faris, R. E. L., and Dunham, H. W. (1939). Mental Disorders in Urban Areas, Chicago, 1st ed

Gruhle, H. W. (1940). Nervenarzt, 13

Hendin, H. (1950). Psychiat. Quart., 24

Hopkins, F. (1937). J. ment. Sci., 83

Hyde, R. W., and Kingsley, L. V. (1944). New Engl. J. Med., 231

Lendrum. F. C. (1933). Amer. J. Psychiat., 90

Malzberg. B. (1940). Social and Biological Aspects of Mental Disease, New York

Metropolitan Life Insurance Co. (1927). Statistical Bulletin, vol. 8, No. 4; vol. 26, No. 2, and (1946), vol. 27, No. 4

Miner, J. R. (1922). Amer. J. Hyg., Monograph No. 2

Moore, M. (1937). New Engl. J. Med., 217

Mowrer, E. R. (1942). Disorganisation Personal and Social, Philadelphia

Myerson, A. (1940). Amer. J. Psychiat., 96, p. 995

Neustatter, W. L. (1938). Lancet, 234, part I

Queen, S. A. (1940). Amer. Social. Rev., 5

Rowntree, B. S. (1947). Old People, Report of a Survey Committee on the Problems of Ageing and the Care of Old People, London, 1st ed

Schmid, C. F. (1933). Amer. J. Sociol., 39

Shroeder, C. W. (1942). Amer. J. Sociol., 48

Siewers. A. B., and Davidoff, E. (1943). Psychiat. Quart., 17

Smith, H. L. (1930). The New Survey London Life and Labour I, London, 1st ed

Smith, H. L. (1932). The New Survey London Life and Labour II, London, 1st ed

Smith, H. L. (1934). The New Survey London Life and Labour III, London, 1st ed

Stearns, A. W. (1921). Ment. Hyg. Concord, 5

Summerson, J. (1945). Georgian London, London, 1st ed

Tietze, C., Lemkau, P., and Cooper, M. (1942), Amer. J. Sociol., 48

Trevelyan, G. M. (1944). English Social History, London, 1st ed

Winslow, F. (1840). The Anatomy of Suicide, London, 1st ed

Delinquency and the Culture of the Criminal Area
by Terence Morris
Reprinted from The Criminal Area London, Routledge
& Kegan Paul (1957) Chap. 10

As a people, we often foster the notion that social class differences are superficial, perpetuated largely by those who have a vested interest in social and economic inequality. It is over half a century since Kipling wrote

'The Colonel's lady and Judy O'Grady
Are sisters under the skin.'

Indeed, such are the sentiments of almost every radical or egalitarian philosophy which sees equality of opportunity at the basis of an efficient society. The evidence of a great deal of social research, however, indicates that even in a welfare state the facts of social class continue to determine in an extraordinary degree the course of an individual's life from the cradle to the grave. The differences in health and infant mortality, for example, still persist, notwithstanding the rise in the standard of living of the lowest classes and the benefits of socialised medicine. In a society where educational opportunity is the primary avenue to upward social mobility through the acquisition of jobs with higher status and pay, we know that the unskilled worker's children are likely to stay unskilled workers and the professional man's children professional men because of the entrenchment of inequality in our class system.

Although for our purpose we talk of "social class" on the basis of data about occupation, it is clear that the notion of social class extends further. Occupation is a useful criterion of definition in that jobs carry not only status but also definitions of income which go far to establish a pattern of consumption and a way of life. However intangible arbitrary definitions of class may be, it is a fact that in the real world individuals are aware of class and class differences to a degree of unusual subtlety. Such awareness comes about very largely as a result of differences in the way of life between individuals with differential amounts of status and income, not merely in the pattern of consumption but in the organisation of attitudes and behaviour. Even in the United States where a hereditary class system such as our own is scarcely known and there is an almost standarised consumption pattern, class differences in status and achievement are still clearly discernible. For our purpose, however, the importance of social class is that it determines through the mechanism of a subculture the social norms, attitudes, and responses of the individual. Individuals grow up in families and families exist in a socio-economic matrix which we call the class system, and it is possible therefore to examine the behaviour of individuals in terms of their class membership. It may well be that for

78

some purposes it represents the most meaningful frame of reference. We know for example, that fox-hunting is behaviour which relates to membership of a rural upper and upper middle class, and not specifically religious or political groupings. It is part of a way of life; it is sub-culturally determined behaviour. Our problem is whether crime and delinquency may be understood in similar terms.

The problem is posed quite simply because, however reluctant we may be to feel that the poor are less honest or the rich more law-abiding, the facts of the matter are that crime and delinquency are almost exclusively a proletarian phenomenon. Such is the experience of every Probation Officer, Approved School Teacher and Prison Governor. In the Croydon material, amongst the series of persons charged (Series II) "Labourer", "dealer" and "no gainful occupation" occurred with monotonous regularity. Amongst the Probation and Approved School cases (Series III) not one child came from Classes I or II although in the population of the town these two classes were larger than Classes IV and V. 35 boys came from the families of unskilled workers and the like, compared with 18 from those of the semi-skilled and 11 from those of skilled artisans and minor "white collar" workers. Taking both boys and girls together, and the Census estimate of the social classes (expressed in terms of the occupational distribution of employed and retired males), the distribution appears as follows: Class III, 1 case per 3,003, Class IV, 1 case per 380 and Class V, 1 case per 187.

The assumption that there is a valid class differential suggests that delinquency may be studied within a class frame of reference. This is not saying that morality varies inversely with social status, but merely that *legally defined* delinquency is a social characteristic of the working classes in general and the family of the unskilled worker in particular. The behaviour of individuals in other social classes is so organised that departure from established norms is far less likely to bring the non-conformist into collision with the criminal law.

From this material it appears that the *proportional* distribution of those factors which characterise families with serious problems of social inadequacy or mental ill health are relatively similar for each of the three classes in question, with Class V taking a rather larger share of some of them. Parental separation, for example, occurs in about 1/3 of all the cases in each class, maladjustment or emotional disturbance in about half the cases. Other factors which have social or cultural rather than purely psychiatric connotations seem less evenly distributed. Traumatic experiences such as being left alone in an air raid or the sudden desertion of the mother occur in about 1/4 of the Class V cases but only in 1/8th of those in Class III.

In general terms the data from Series III suggest four things:

1 That serious delinquency occurs more frequently among the families of

unskilled workers than amongst semi-skilled workers, white-collar workers or skilled artisans.

2 That in each occupational group there is a hard core of "psychiatric delinquency" related to serious emotional disturbance in the family, or mental ill health, which accounts for between 1/5th and 1/4 of all the cases.

3 That the residue may be regarded as "social delinquency" related to the cultural milieu of the delinquent.

4 That the uneven distribution of delinquency between the social classes is indicative of the uneven distribution of the factors making for both "psychiatric delinquency" and "social delinquency".

TABLE 1 Family Relations and Mental Health by Social Class
Source: Data from Series III
Nos. of cases

	Class III	Class IV	Class V	Factor No.
Parental disharmony	3	7	7	13
Parental rejection	2	6	9	8
Parental separation	5	3	13	11
Maternal deprivation	3	1	4	6
Low standard of hygiene	2	2	13	14
Both parents at work	3	6	6	12
Maladjustment/emotional disturbance	8	10	17	5
Behaviour problems in family	–	1	4	9
Mental disorder or epilepsy in family	3	3	12	10
Traumatic experience	2	6	10	7
Discipline { inconsistent	4	9	6 ⎫	
severe	3	–	8 ⎬	23
lax	4	2	18 ⎭	
Total Nos. in each Class	16	19	44	

The efficiency of the family as an effective agency of social control must inevitably be impared when relationships within it are subjected to stress. These stresses may arise from personality problems, from the failure of parents to live in equanimity together, or from factors which are predominantly economic. Undoubtedly among the most important of these is housing. By and large, inadequate housing is a concomitant of low social class, for those with a strong position in the market are able to secure adequate housing for themselves even in a time of housing shortage. Those whose position is weakest must be content with what they can get. Legislation concerning housing (in Britain) is primarily concerned with the problem of public health. It defines minimum standards of accommodation and sanitation which are designed to minimise the unhealthful effects

80

of over-crowding and inadequate sanitation. But the demands of public health legislation seldom extend to the social consequences of inadequate housing, and it is precisely these factors which contribute to the stress placed upon families in unsuitable accommodation. The relationship between overcrowding, social class and delinquency is demonstrated from correlations between rates of delinquent residence and social class and over-crowding.

TABLE 2 Overcrowding and Social Class Correlated
with Rates of Delinquent Residence

	With Overcrowding	With % middle class households
Under 17	+ 0.71	−0.69
17-39	+0.69	−0.65
40 and over	+0.71	−0.65
All ages	+0.74	−0.76

For the purpose of this calculation an overcrowding index was based upon the percentage of households in each ward living at a density of 2 persons per room or more, the average density in the whole Borough being 0.69 persons per room. The percentage of middle class households was based upon the Juror's Index.

In each case the correlation was significant at the 1% level, meaning that the element of chance in the association of the variables was small. Correlations, however, do not provide *proof*, through this may not be the crucial issue. Rather, it is important to demonstrate that factors which relate to an objective class situation provide the *possibility* of certain stressful experiences occurring which, by complex interaction with other more specific and unique factors may result in delinquency.

Why are some classes more delinquent than others?

This is a question which must inevitably be posed. There are some people who would reject its validity altogether, on the grounds that "delinquent" means not only "legally delinquent" but "legally delinquent *and apprehended*". Such is the view of distinguished criminologists like Barnes and Teeters and the late Edwin Sutherland. There are naughty boys in Public Schools and naughty boys in Secondary Modern Schools, but in the main Public schoolboys do not commit actions which are likely to result in their transfer to an Approved School. Sutherland suggested that the allegedly conforming middle classes contain in reality a large number of criminals, but of the "white collar" variety. On this basis one might argue that the

81

problem of the class differential was largely one of academic definition, but it remains nevertheless that the vast majority of crimes consist of the straightforward stealing of property and their numbers are by no means balanced by elaborately contrived frauds and deceit on the part of business men and large corporations. It seems much more reasonable to say that the class differential in legal delinquency results from the cultural differences between the social classes, in that anti-social behaviour may be expressed in a variety of ways depending upon the forms of expression made available to an individual by his class membership.

The most fundamental differences relate to the socialisation of the child. It is in childhood that the foundations of a way of life are laid, for the child constantly inquiring and experimenting with behaviour is quick and eager to learn the most satisfactory means of exploiting his environment and satisfying his own needs and desires. There have been in the United States a number of important studies of the problem of child rearing in different class situations, (1) and although the American material indicates what may ultimately happen in Western Europe, it is complicated by special American factors such as ethnic and national cultural differences. Undoubtedly the best study in Britain to date has been Betty Spinley's *The Deprived and the Privileged*, (2) and although her middle class group of controls is undoubtedly upper middle class and rather atypical for the mass of the population, her analysis of socialisation in a London slum area is extremely valuable. The picture it presents confirms that drawn by Jephcott and Carter in their study of Radby, of life overshadowed by economic insecurity and dominated by the demands of the moment.

The middle class child is brought up in an atmosphere of controlled care. As a baby his feeds are regulated, his periods of sleep and play carefully ordered. An early bedtime becomes an institutional ritual. Toilet training and table manners are enforced by patient and persistent exhortation; sanctions against bad behaviour consist of the threat to withdraw mother love rather than physical violence. The child may grow up without siblings, or in a family in which births are deliberately planned at convenient intervals. Play is confined to the house or garden; the street play group scarcely exists because other children are "brought home" to play. The family itself tends to act as a corporate unit, and although father and mother may have their own individual interests, the joint family holiday or outing is as important as the joint entertainment of friends at home.

In contrast, the working class child grows up in an atmosphere in which restraint is often conspicuous for its absence. The baby is quietened by the dummy or crust dipped into mother's tea. He may be carried hither and thither, to the cinema or the fish and chip shop in the evening regardless of the hour. His diet soon becomes that of the adult members of the family; he is seldom dry. Punishment and indulgence may follow in swift succession; other babies will arrive inconveniently and displace him as the family

82

pet. His play will be largely in the street in which he will form an autonomous social group with boys of his own age. As a social unit his family will only be united on relatively rare ritual occasions such as weddings and funerals, the rest of the time father and mother will spend their leisure separately.

Cohen has summed up the differences in the sentence ". . . middle class socialisation, in comparison with working class socialisation is conscious, rational, deliberate and demanding". (3) The middle class child is conditioned to control and restraint from his earliest years; the immediate gratification of desires is discouraged and the virtues of thrift and abstinence emphasised. In almost every sphere of life he is made aware of the desirability of restraint and order. He does not urinate in the gutter or take food out into the street; mealtimes and bedtime are as fixed as the amount of his weekly pocket money. The working class child in contrast is allowed to develop in relative freedom. Because he is cast at an early age, maybe three or four, into street play-group society, the process of his social maturation is accelerated in some aspects and retarded in others. It is accelerated in that he is exposed to the influences of the outside world much earlier than the middle class child; at five or six, for example, he goes shopping regularly and travels alone or with his pals on public transport. At the same time, the fact of being so much in the company of his peers and left free to do as he pleases with his leisure time, means that the opportunity of learning about a wider system of adult values — which may indeed conflict with those of his own parents — will be severely limited to contacts with the school and perhaps the social worker or Probation Officer.

Emotional sophistication does not necessarily proceed at an equal rate with social and sexual sophistication. From the age of eleven or twelve the sexes begin to interact. On winter evenings the girls will sit on a low wall or seat by the park entrance and hold court for a group of boys on bicycles which are never ridden further than a few blocks. It is essentially group interaction one suspects because the group is able to provide the emotional security which is not possessed individually. At fifteen they cease to be children and become wage-earners. This dramatic precipitation into the adult world tends to accentuate the difficulties which arise out of what might be termed "uneven maturation". Sexuality assumes an enormous importance, and with it sexual experimentation. By sixteen or seventeen a girl considers herself lacking if she does not have a steady boyfriend, by eighteen or nineteen she is contemplating marriage and motherhood. By such thinking she tends to become emotionally mature more rapidly than her boy friend, for whom at seventeen or eighteen boyish pursuits are still current.

Cohen has written of the activities of the delinquent gang as characterised by "short run hedonism" (4) but in fact this description may be regarded as a fundamental attribute of working class culture. The child

83

seeks immediate gratification and is seldom denied; in the autonomous play group activities are organised only on a short run basis to secure an immediate end without thought of the consequences. Sexual behaviour ultimately follows the same pattern, and the resistances of working class adults to middle class birth control propaganda become more meaningful when considered in this light. The norms of behaviour which the child acquires for himself tend to be of the most rudimentary kind and their observance related as much to the effectiveness of external social pressures as to the degree of self-control which has become internalised. By contrast with the middle class child, the working class child is more likely to react to stressful situations in flagrantly anti-social terms because he has not been conditioned to restraint from his earliest years. Whereas the middle class way of life tends to inhibit spontaneity, working class culture tends to encourage it. In particular, aggression is seldom the subject of social disapproval.

The working class child is not only less able to cope with stressful situations but more likely to encounter them. The task of bringing up a family on a limited budget, particularly when the husband keeps her "short" seldom fails to leave its mark on the working class mother. Because husbands allot their wives a fixed rather than proportional amount of their wages, the mother must frequently work as well as run a home. The tensions and discords which result from disagreements over money are augmented by sexual difficulties. The woman's interest in sex rapidly becomes a pre-occupation with avoiding unwanted pregnancies; "good" husbands are those that make no sexual demands. Parental discord is undoubtedly one of the most disturbing experiences any child has to face because it strikes at the very foundations of his emotional security. But because no premium is put on restraint, husbands and wives may fight like tigers or simply desert the home. It is not intended to suggest that marital discord and "broken homes" are to be found only amongst working class families, but that in contrast with the middle class situation there are fewer mechanisms of control.

The working class child cannot escape from the bad or unhappy home except into the street and until he goes to work his activities out of school are likely to be severely limited by the amount of money he can get hold of. Stealing therefore pays dividends, whether it be cash from mother's purse or junk which can be sold for cash. Not for him is the boarding school where he can seek out parent substitutes more satisfactory than his own, except if he should commit an offence and be sent to one by order of the Juvenile Court. The middle class child by reason of his superior economic position has more outlets for his feelings. He does not need to roam the streets when he can create a world of fantasy with his toys or lose himself in a world of books.

Why are not all working class children delinquent?

The reader may feel that the picture of working class life which has been drawn is unduly pessimistic, but the picture of life in the delinquency areas of Croydon's older housing estates is very much of this order. Lest it be suggested that this in an argument from the particular to the general, the evidence of Jephcott and Carter and Spinley seems to indicate that the pattern is "normative" at least in a statistical sense. If all working class children grow up in a culture which exerts few social controls on the one hand and produces stressful situations on the other, how is it that not all of them succumb and appear in the Juvenile Court?

Mays' answer would probably be that most of them *do* in fact succumb but only a few are unlucky enough to get caught (5). There can of course, be no absolute refutation of this view, but it seems likely nevertheless that if the majority of delinquent acts are impulsive and seldom efficiently planned, then the chances of detection and prosecution are fairly high. On the other hand, amongst working class adults at least, larceny must run at a fantastic level. "Whipping" or "knocking off" are universally legitimate activities. Electric light bulbs, scrap metal or wood, towels, paper, food, almost any commodity which can be utilised is stolen from the employer without a qualm. It is an attitude of mind encouraged by army experience where the theft of kit penalises the victim and not the thief, resulting in an almost Hobbesian situation of a war of all against all.

The question can be answered by analogy. In the 19th century conditions of housing and sanitation in urban areas were such that mortality rates especially from contagious diseases such as cholera were extremely high. But even in a time of epidemic not everyone was stricken down, nor indeed did all those who were necessarily die. In other words, although everyone was exposed to virtually the same risks of contagion, some managed to escape the worst effects of the disease and some to escape infection altogether. The reason for this was simply the differential resistance offered by different individuals. A similar situation may be observed with regard to the stressful experiences which may engender delinquency. While socio-economic factors such as housing and income may make life difficult for the unskilled labourer and his family, the degree of stress which they create within the family depends very much upon the adaptability of the individuals concerned in the situation. Cultural norms are frequently "tailored" to fit the needs and capacities of individual personality, and if husband and wife are relatively well adjusted to each other they are less likely to come into violent conflict over money, the control of children or their sexual life. What we have earlier termed "psychiatric" delinquency is unlikely to be a feature of the behaviour of children who grow up in families which are well adjusted, even though they may nevertheless grow up in the cultural milieu of the street play group and its hedonistic philosophy. Their delinquency is more likely to be if anything "social", that is to say anti-social behaviour which is well integrated within the confines of the play group.

Those who come into marked conflict with the criminal law, who progress from Probation to Approved School, from Approved School to Borstal, from Borstal to Prison and ultimately to Preventive Detention (6), are those who have as it were, succumbed "mortally" in that their lives are firmly fixed on the path of crime. They are "outside" society almost as the dead are beyond life in their complete and utter rejection of societal norms. For them the sanctions of punishment have but little effect and then only in the short run. Ultimately they become a-social as well as anti-social. Such individuals are few in number and are drawn almost exclusively from the hard core of "psychiatric" delinquents. The "social delinquents" in contrast are those who get into trouble, sometimes seriously, but who nevertheless pass through the delinquent phase. They are like the individuals who sicken but do not die, and who recover with varying degrees of success. Some will, as it were, carry the marks of delinquency all their lives; they will "whip" and "knock off" when the opportunity presents itself. Others when they grow up will put dishonesty behind them forever.

The stressful situations which result in "psychiatric" delinquency cannot be classified as wholly economic or wholly cultural in origin but as an admixture of both aggravated by personality factors in the individual family. "Psychiatric" delinquency as a consequence occurs in all social classes, and in the Croydon material with only slight differences in its proportional frequency among the cases in each class. "Social" delinquency on the other hand flourishes in working class neighbourhoods because of the support it finds in working class culture. The older teen-agers and adults are still like "carriers" of disease, because although they do not actively come into conflict with the law their attitudes and behaviour represent a logical continuity with the delinquent phase of their earlier years. Attitudes to property remain egoistic and unaltered, irresponsible lateness and absenteeism replaces truancy; the boss takes the place of the schoolmaster as the unreasonable over-demanding figure of alien authority whom to deceive or defy is a mark of cleverness and success.

The reasons for not all working class children becoming delinquent may be listed then as follows:

1 The degree of stress resulting in "psychiatric" delinquency tends to vary with the circumstances of individual families and personalities.
2 Not all delinquents whether "psychiatric" or "social" will necessarily commit delinquent acts which are specifically *illegal*.
3 By no means all those who commit illegal acts will be detected and prosecuted and identified as delinquents within the definition of law.

Social control in the working class neighbourhood

Park described the process of social control in the ecological community as characterised by restraints which are internal and moral, and based on some kind of consensus. The stability of the social order is seen as dependent upon the stability of relationships which have a spatial base. The absence of such a stable order has been equated by Clifford Shaw and others with "social disorganisation".

On the surface it would seem indeed that the working class neighbourhood which was also a delinquency area was "socially disorganised" in this sense. But anyone who has worked or lived in such a neighbourhood soon realises that this is by no means so. On the contrary, one is confronted with a sub-culture unambiguously defined and in some aspects blatantly at variance with widely accepted middle class norms. Because the working class way of life rejects so many of the norms of middle class society it has been erroneously equated on occasion with social disorganisation. The problem of consensus and normative system of behaviour was examined by Durkheim in *Suicide* and his statement of it is usefully paraphrased by Parsons in *The Structure of Social Action*:

> '. . . not merely contractual relations but social relations in general, and even the personal equilibrium of members of a social group are seen to be dependent on the existence of a normative structure in relation to conduct, generally accepted as having moral authority by members of the community, and upon their effective subordination to these norms. They do not merely regulate the individual's choice of means to his ends, but his very needs and desires are determined in part by them. When this controlling normative structure is upset and disorganised, individual conduct is equally disorganised and chaotic — the individual loses himself in a void of meaningless activities.' (7)

Such disorganisation is infrequent in human society, and as Sainsbury has shown, is characteristic of areas of high suicide rates and not of delinquency areas, neither of which incidentally coincide (8). The normative structure of conduct may appear to be an inversion of that of the world at large but it is by no means disorganised. Nor indeed is a neighbourhood "disorganised" if there is no perceptible structure at all which is dependent upon a local consensus. If it were, then many middle class suburban neighbourhoods where social contracts over the garden fence may take years to establish, would be areas of social disorganisation. The maintenance of normative structures of action in an urban population with a high degree of physical mobility depends as much upon the existence of reference groups as upon local groups for their legitimation. These may be work groups, religious denominations, professional organisations or even the concept of membership of a social class. The effectiveness of social

87

pressures within the neighbourhood as a means of achieving social control must depend in considerable degree upon the amount of time the individual actually spends within its confines and the extent to which he interacts with his neighbours.

The differences which exist between systems of social control in middle class and working class neighbourhoods relate largely to the content of the cultural norms themselves. Middle class culture stresses the importance of the family as a social unit and the family therefore tends to accept collective responsibility for the behaviour of its members. If little Charles falls foul of the law, the whole family suffers in the disgrace; if father goes to prison, although he may actually have spent little of his time in the neighbourhood every family member must expect to face ostracism and social disgrace. In the working class neighbourhood because the family is much less of an identifiable social unit it is the actions of individuals which are judged rather than whole families.

The family as a whole has, therefore, less interest in controlling the activities of its members, and because of this tends to be much less effective than its middle class counterpart as an agency of social control. The experience of every Juvenile Court must endorse this fact when, for example, fathers are not only unaware of the doings of their children but usually express extreme reluctance to appear in Court when they are in trouble. When out of sight they are also out of mind. To walk down a street in any typical delinquency area, one might wonder how it was that other people did not exert some control over the children swarming everywhere, but any such interference by outsiders tends to evoke the most primitive feelings of familial solidarity. In one instance noted by the writer, a group of boys were beseiging another group in a house where both mother and father were out at work. The doors and windows were barred and so the attackers seized a pickaxe and began to belabour the front door. The woman next door seeing this, took action and dispersed the group, that evening going round to see the father of the boy who had wielded the pickaxe, only to be met with a stream of angry resentment for her pains. The next night her own front door was bombarded with cabbage stalks and garbage.

The virtual impossibility of any single community member being able to exert authority on behalf of the neighbourhood in enforcement of conduct norms, would suggest that no such norms exist. Paradoxically this is not so, for neighbours are continually evaluating behaviour, but always the behaviour of third parties not present. A woman who is pregnant by her lover or who has had her children taken into care, is a "no-good" or a "lazy bitch". The women castigating her immorality may nevertheless have all been pregnant out of wedlock or have sons who have been fined or put on probation. In contrast to a middle class situation where families keep up a front of conformity for fear of social ostracism, social controls have not been internalised in the process of socialisation. Ostracism and hostility on the part of neighbours are less effective because there is scarcely any guilt upon which they may operate. Judgements of behaviour by neighbours are seen not so much as evaluations of behaviour on the basis of normative criteria but as an expression of hostility to be met characteristically with hostility. The mother of the Approved School boy does not therefore hang her head in shame but ensures that any detractors feel the sharp end of her tongue.

Against this background of acrimonious moral judgement must be seen the street play group. The group is in effect one of a series of groups recruited on the basis of age and territory which grows up together in the neighbourhood. So much has already been written on the subject of the juvenile gang that it would be superfluous to summarise it here. Among the most important points which have emerged, however, is that the street play group is essentially autonomous in that it establishes and enforces its own norms independently of adult or other external interference. It has in addition to satisfy the emotional needs of its members for security, feelings of competence, or being wanted, when they cannot be supplied in a socially inadequate or grossly unhappy home. When the activities of the group become seriously anti-social and illegal it can only be restrained by the formal agencies of law enforcement which belong to society at large, the Police and the Courts. Because of the social gulf which exists between the group and most of the personnel of such agencies, their function is seen as hostile, aggressive and negative rather than positive and helpful in safeguarding the rights of individuals and the community.

Effective social controls then, are largely external and formal and stem from outside the local community. As a result the only kinds of anti-social behaviour which can be successfully limited are almost always illegal. Those delinquencies which are not illegal, and which would be kept in check by the informal pressure of public opinion in a middle class neighbourhood are integrated within a normative cultural pattern, the only control being exerted by an adaptation of the *lex talionis*. Feuds and reprisals, however, are essentially group activities and are confined therefore to those sections of the population which are organised on a group basis the children and adolescents. For the rest, the principle of "giving as good as you take" operates, so that abuse over the garden fence must be met by further abuse, slanders by counter-slanders and so on. Such a way of life is essentially unsatisfying and frequently mentally unhealthy. It is not surprising that almost all those individuals who can, seek to abandon it and adopt the norms of the middle class. The fulfilment of middle class norms necessitates far reaching changes in style of life and expenditure, but those who have benefitted by full employment and the redistribution of income are able, generally for the first time in their lives, to realise their social aspirations. They therefore send their children to Secretarial Schools if they fail at 11+, and place a premium on "respectability". But sooner or later they come up against the fact that to make their new status position secure they must move away, and herein lies a major difficulty. The situation in the housing market is such that there is little accommodation at medium rentals, and because their resources will not stretch always to the highest rentals or home ownership, they are compelled to stay in Council housing or other comparatively low cost accommodation.

In discussing the ecological concept of the natural area the point may be made that "cultural differentiation" between urban neighbourhoods for the most part results from the fact that the social classes tend to be residentially segregated through the operations of the housing market and through individual choices made with reference to class determined systems of cultural values. I have suggested that anti-social behaviour in general and delinquency in particular may be meaningfully studied in terms of the subcultural differences between the social classes. It would seem at first sight then, that the study of the delinquency *area* was not only a procedure whose usefulness might be called into question but whose validity might also be doubted. Now while it is true that instances of "psychiatric" delinquency may crop up anywhere in the city, "social" delinquency tends to be much more highly localised. The Croydon evidence confirms that whilst the former is more evenly distributed over the middle and working class areas of the town "social" delinquency predominates in old working class areas and on the inter-war housing estates.

Croydon has not developed radially as so many American cities appear to have done and there are as a result no well defined zones to which variations in the rates can be meaningfully related, nevertheless, the three highest ward rates occur in those wards which make up and immediately surround the central business district. It is unlikely, however, that this is either relevant or indeed exactly true. Considering the precise areas of delinquent residence one finds them to be spatially separate from the central area and highly varied in their ecological characteristics. The suggestion implicit in so much of the work of Clifford Shaw and his collaborators is that the physical deterioration of a neighbourhood is somehow vitally related to the problem of delinquency and crime. The evidence, at least from Croydon, suggest that the physical characteristics of the area are of little relevance save as an indirect determinant of the social status of an area. Low status and low rentals are normally found together in urban areas and physical deterioration, where it helps to depress both status and rentals, can be said to be a feature likely to attract those individuals who may be loosely described as the core of the "social problem group". But where the provision of housing is not solely within the province of the market, and the local authority has stepped in to provide housing as a social amenity for a not inconsiderable proportion of the population, then the natural ecological processes of selection manifesting themselves in the cycle of "invasion-dominance-succession" are likely to be severely modified by social policy with strikingly different results. The ecological process may be modified yet there is still crime and delinquency, though this is not to suggest that the concept of a criminal or delinquent sub-culture resulting from the interplay of ecological influences is necessarily invalidated; far from it. It does suggest, however, that there must be a shift of interest from the natural area which has grown up of its own accord to the "planned" area which has resulted from conscious social and political deliberation. In particular, emphasis must be laid upon the individual cultural unit, the family, which remains essentially unaltered as a social institution for the transmission of cultural values and as an agency of social control.

1. See, for example, Allison Davis, 'Socialisation and Adolescent Personality' in Readings in Social Psychology, ed. Newcomb and Hartley, New York, 1952. Davis and Havnighurst, 'Social Class and Color Differences in Child Rearing', American Sociological Review, Vol. 53, 1946
2. London, 1954
3. Cohen, A. K., Delinquent Boys, The Culture of the Gang, London, 1956
4. Cohen, op. cit., p. 30
5. Mays, J. B., Growing up in the City
6. Preventive Detention abolished by the Criminal Justice Act, 1967. (eds)
7. Parsons, T., The Structure of Social Action, p. 377
8. Sainsbury, P., Suicide in London, London, 1955. See also the preceding paper in this book.

Delinquency and Social Class by J. W. B. Douglas, J. M. Ross, W. A. Hammond and D. G. Mulligan
Reprinted from The British Journal of Criminology *(1966)*
Vol. 6 pp. 294-302

An opportunity to study delinquent behaviour in a relatively large sample of young people from all parts of Great Britain and from all social classes is provided by the National Survey of Health and Development. This paper describes certain social characteristics of the boys in the sample who, between the ages of eight and seventeen years, have been before the courts.

The National Survey sample is selected from the 12,468 legitimate single births occurring throughout England, Wales and Scotland during the week March 3 to 9, 1946: it includes all births to agricultural workers' wives and to the wives of non-manual workers and one-quarter of the births to all others. This selection from the larger total number gives a sample of 5,362 children approximately half of whom come from the middle (or non-manual working) class. The high weighting of middle class families in the Survey is an advantage when studying problems of, for example, higher education, but is a disadvantage when studying problems of delinquency and crime. The original social structure of the complete week's sample can be regained by giving the middle class and agricultural workers' children a weight of unity and the rest a weight of four. When this is done the rates obtained for infant mortality, grammar school selection, etc., are close to the national figures, and this also holds for the incidence of delinquency. In the following discussion the term "population estimate" means that this adjustment has been made to restore the original population balance. In general, however, the figures given are based on the actual number of young people who have been followed up.

This paper is concerned with only the 2,402 boys in the sample who were living in Great Britain in 1963, of whom 288 had appeared before the courts or been cautioned for an offence. The girls are excluded (except for the rates given in Table I) because only thirty-five of them were delinquent.

A delinquent in this discussion is a boy who, before the age of seventeen years, has been cautioned or who has appeared before the courts and been sentenced for an offence. Four groups of delinquents are described — first, all those cautioned or sentenced on one or more occasion, regardless of the type or severity of the offence — in other words, the total delinquent population of the 288 boys. Second, those who have been cautioned or have committed trivial offences only. Third, those who have committed one or more indictable offence, *i.e.*, the more trivial offenders are excluded. Last, those who have committed more than one indictable offence before the age of seventeen years — these are referred to as the "repeaters." These four groups are not in all instances mutually exclusive: the first includes indictable as well as non-indictable offences and those convicted on more than one occasion as well as those cautioned only. The third group — the "serious offenders" — also includes the "repeaters."

The proportion of delinquents falling into each of the four categories is shown in Table I. The first line gives the proportion of the 2,402 boys actually followed up, of whom 12.0 per cent. are delinquent. The second line shows the proportions of the estimated population of 5,642 boys *i.e.*, the number obtained after the weighting adjustment has been made; of these an estimated 825, or 14.6 per cent., are delinquent. It will be noted that the delinquency rates are higher for the estimated population (14.6 per cent. as opposed to 12.0 per cent.) but this is to be expected because delinquents tend to come more from the manual working class, of whom only one in four was included in the selected sample that was followed up. (If allowances were made for the exclusion of the illegitimate children from the National Survey sample the delinquency figures would be slightly higher.)

Two social descriptions of the families are used in this paper. The first, or occupational classification, based on a home visit in 1961, divides them into eight groups according to the occupations of the fathers at the time when the boys were fifteen years old (these groups are shown on the left in Table II). Not all the families could be grouped by the father's occupa-

TABLE I Per Cent. Delinquency Rates for the Boys in the National Survey, based on: (a) Actual Numbers (b) Population Estimates

	All types of Offenders		Cautions and Non-indict		Indictable Offenders		Repeaters		Total No. of Children (100%)
	No.	%	No.	%	No.	%	No.	%	
Boys, Survey Sample (Actual nos.)	288	12.0	96	4.0	192	8.0	67	2.8	2,402
Population Estimates	825	14.6	237	4.2	588	*10.4	229	4.1	5,642
Girls Survey Sample (actual nos.)	35	1.6	14	0.6	21	1.0	7	0.03	2,190
Population Estimates	**		**		**		**		5,226

* This number is slightly below that expected from the official Home Office Supplementary Statistics (unpublished analysis). This is no doubt due, in part at any rate, to the exclusion of the illegitimate children from the follow-up study.
** Population estimates are not given because of small numbers.

tion in 1961, however, since 6 per cent. were without a male wage earner and a further 14 per cent. were unclassified because the fathers were unemployed or because the family had withdrawn from the Survey or was untraced. This 20 per cent. of families which lack the 1961 occupation were classified by the nearest known occupation of the father, *i.e.*, in 1957, or failing that in 1946. In this way only four families remain unclassified.

The second classification is based on the education and social origins of *both* father and mother, after making an initial crude division of the fathers by their occupation in 1957 into non-manual and manual workers. The definitions of the four social classes arrived at are given in the Appendix. In this way all but 70 of the families were allocated to one of the four social classes. This classification has the merit that, by the very nature of its derivation, it does not change from year to year. Education and social origins are fixed and the only point where change can occur is between manual and non-manual workers — a boundary that is not often crossed. Such change between manual and non-manual workers as there was took place mainly in the early years of this study, and for this reason the social classification was tied to the 1957 occupation of the father. In contrast the first classification — by father's occupation alone — was highly unstable as shown by the fact that during the first fifteen years of the Survey more than half the families changed their occupational group

93

on one or more occasion.

The distribution of the Survey families in both the occupational and social class classification is given in Table II. First is shown the actual number of families falling into each occupational group or social class, and second the estimated number, *i.e.*, after correcting for the original sampling procedure.

Table III shows the proportion of delinquents in each occupational group. On the average the children of non-manual workers are only half as likely to be cautioned or come before the courts as the children of manual workers, and within the non-manual working class, the children of black-coated workers are twice as likely to be in trouble as the children of salaried or professional workers, indeed the rate of this group tends to fall between that of the salaried group and the manual workers. Between the four groups of manual workers' families the proportions of delinquent children show comparatively small variation — there is no sharp increase in delinquency in passing from the semi-skilled to the unskilled, as might have been expected.

There are different patterns of offence within the occupational groups; a higher proportion of the middle class delinquents have committed non-indictable offences or were cautioned only, whereas a higher proportion of

Table II Actual and Estimated Numbers of Boys Grouped by:
(a) Father's Occupation in 1961
(b) The Social Origins and Education of both Parents

Father's Occupation 1961	Numbers: Actual	Popul. Estim.	Social Class		Numbers: Actual	Popul. Estim.
Professional	241	298	Middle	Upper	260	287
Salaried	401	518	Class	Lower	738	1,116
Black-coated	331	517				
Foremen and skilled	716	2,420	Manual Working	Upper	392	1,202
Semi-skilled	194	662	Class	Lower	942	2,883†
Agricultural	151	172*				
Unskilled	165	534	Not classified		70	154
Self-employed	199	505				
Not classified	4	16				
Total	2,402	5,642			2,402	5,642

* Population estimates for agricultural workers are higher than actual numbers owing to movement of other manual workers into agricultural work between 1946-1961.
† The excess of lower manual workers in the population estimates is accounted for by the inclusion of the self-employed, only one-quarter of whom was taken for the Survey sample.

94

TABLE III The Percentage Delinquency Rates of the Boys, Grouped
by Father's Occupation Based on Actual Numbers

Father's Occupation 1961	Percentage Delinquent:				
	All types of Offenders	Cautions and Non-indict.	Indictable Offenders	Repeaters	Number of Children
Professional	5.0	3.3	1.7	0.4	241
Salaried	4.5	2.5	2.0	0.2	401
Black-coated	10.3	5.2	5.1	0.9	331
Foremen and skilled	15.1	4.3	10.8	3.8	716
Semi-skilled	20.1	4.6	15.5	8.2	194
Agricultural	14.6	6.0	8.6	3.3	151
Unskilled	20.6	4.2	16.4	6.7	165
Self-employed	9.0	2.5	6.5	1.0	199
Not classified	(3)*	nil	(3)*	(1)*	4
Total	12.0	4.0	8.0	2.8	2,402

* Number of boys

manual working class children were repeaters or serious offenders. The
agricultural workers' children, however, are an exception to this pattern.
These differences suggested that offences may be dealt with in different
ways depending on the social background of the family and on whether
they occur in town or country. In actual numbers (as opposed to
population estimates) only 7 per cent. of all children who are repeatedly
delinquent come from non-manual workers' families as against an expected
41 per cent. if the same rate were to apply to both groups. With these
small numbers no comparisons between the risks of the children of
professional, salaried and clerical workers are possible as they all contain
less than 1 per cent. of repeaters. Repeated offences are much more
common among the manual workers' children and most common of all
among the semi-skilled workers, with the unskilled workers' children being
slightly, but not significantly, less likely to repeat. The risk of repeating
for the agricultural workers' children is less than half that recorded for the
semi-skilled and unskilled, and approximately equal to that of the children
of foremen and skilled manual workers.

The same families are re-grouped in Table IV into the four social classes
based on the education and social origins of both parents. The lowest
incidence of delinquency is found in the upper middle class. The lower
middle class and the upper manual working class have approximately the
same incidence, which is roughly three times that in the upper middle
class. The lower manual working class stands out as having the highest

95

incidence of all, approximately seven times that of the upper middle class. When indictable offences only are considered, the relative differences between the social classes are increased and the upper and lower manual working classes move away from each other. With the "repeaters" social class differences are still further exaggerated: there are no upper middle class children who appear before the courts on more than one occasion, whereas 0.7 per cent. of the lower middle class, 1.8 per cent. of the upper manual working class and 5.6 per cent. of the lower manual working class boys do so.

TABLE IV The Percentage Delinquency rares of the Boys, Grouped by Social Class Based on Actual Numbers

Social Class	Percentage Delinquent:				Number of Children
	All types of Offenders	Cautions and Non-indict.	Indictable Offenders	Repeaters	
Middle Class Upper	2.7	1.9	0.8	nil	260
Middle Class Lower	8.3	4.1	4.2	0.7	738
Manual Working Class Upper	9.7	3.6	6.1	1.8	392
Manual Working Class Lower	18.7	4.9	13.8	5.6	942
Not classified	8.6	1.5	7.1	2.6	70
Total	12.0	4.0	8.0	2.8	2,402

The following diagram compaies the risk of delinquency in the same families grouped by the two different methods. The area of each cell in this diagram is proportional to the number of families to which it refers (the self-employed and the unclassified have been omitted).

The implication from this diagram and Tables III and IV is that the education and origins of the parents are as important, in relation to the delinquent behaviour of their children, as the achieved occupational position of the fathers.

Prof 298 5.0%	Salaried 518 4.5%	Black-coated 517 10.3%	Foremen and Skilled 2,420 15.1%		Semi-skilled 662 20.1%	Ag. 172 14.6%	Unskilled 534 20.6%

Upper Mid. 287 2.7%	Lower Middle 1,116 8.3%	Upper Manual Working 1,202 9.7%	Lower Manual Working 2,883 18.7%

The families shown in Tables III and IV include those broken by death, divorce or separation. We do not intend to discuss here the contribution of broken homes to the pool of delinquency but the crude figures for delinquency in these families, as well as those in which the mother has remarried, are needed for comparison with the figures given above. There were 296 boys (1) in all types of broken family, whether there had been a remarriage or not, fifty-one of whom were delinquent. This amounts to a total delinquency rate of 17 per cent., roughly the proportion reported for the lower manual working class. As these broken families are distributed over all social classes this is 'a rather higher rate than might be expected and further examination shows that it is the families broken by divorce or separation that produce the high incidence of delinquency — 23 per cent. of children in these families were delinquent as compared with 12 per cent. of those in families broken by death, and this difference cannot be explained in terms of the social classes from which these families came. (2)

Social Class Classification in the National Survey.

The classification is based, for the most part, on the 1957 occupation of the father of the survey child; where this is not known, on the 1946 occupation.

Upper Middle Class
    The father is a non-manual worker, and
(a) both parents went to secondary school and were brought up in middle class families, or
(b) both parents went to secondary school and one parent was brought up in a middle class family, or
(c) both parents were brought up in middle class families and one parent went to secondary school.

Lower Middle Class
    The rest of the non-manual workers' families.

Upper Manual-Working Class
    The father is a manual worker, and
        either the father or mother or both of them had a secondary school education, and/or one or both of them were brought up in a middle class family.

Lower Manual-Working Class
    The father is a manual worker, and
        both the father and the mother had elementary schooling only, and both the father and the mother were brought up in manual-working class families.

1. The 296 refers to known breaks at the time at which this analysis was begun — March 1965.
2. Dr. Annette Lawson, of this M.R.C Unit, has kindly supplied us with these figures from her work on the broken families within the National Survey.

Delinquent Subcultures in East London *by Peter Willmott*
Reprinted from <u>Adolescent Boys of East London</u> London, Routledge & Kegan Paul (1966) Chap. 8

The most publicized problem that adolescents, particularly working-class boys, present to adult society is their tendency to misbehave. If court convictions for law-breaking are taken as an indication of anti-social behaviour, it is predominantly the province of adolescents rather than adults, of boys than girls, and of the working rather than the middle class. It is true that the social class difference may be less marked than it seems from the crime figures: delinquency may, for instance, be just as much a feature of middle and upper-class adolescence, but unrecorded because more often dealt with unofficially, by headmasters and university proctors, and treated more leniently by public, police and courts. (1) Even so, there is obviously some delinquency among the subjects of our study.

Our main sample survey does not itself provide any direct information about delinquency. When we tried, in the earliest series of standardized interviews, to ask systematically about the boys' criminal experiences, we could not tell how far they were suppressing the facts, how often they exaggerated or dramatized them. Because we did not feel we could put much reliance upon what they said, we decided to exclude these questions from doorstep interviews. We did, however, discuss delinquency with the boys fairly fully in longer interviews and group discussions; here they talked more freely and, as far as we could judge, frankly. This illustrative material can fortunately be supplemented from two statistical studies of juvenile offenders in East London. The first, by Power and his colleagues at the Social Medicine Research Unit of the Medical Research Council (London Hospital), covered the boys and girls under 17 who appeared before the Courts from January 1958 onwards and who lived in what is now Tower Hamlets — Bethnal Green, Stepney and Poplar. (2) The research workers kindly made available some separate figures for Bethnal Green boys, as well as allowing access to their other data. The second study, by Downes, was an analysis of all the people aged 8 to 25 who lived in Stepney and Poplar and who were convicted by the Courts in 1960 for offences committed during the same year. (3) Downes also carried out some 'informal observation' of boys in Stepney and Poplar. (4) My hope is, by drawing upon these various sources of information, to build up a reasonably accurate picture of the place of delinquency in the lives of the Bethnal Green adolescents.

98

How much delinquency

As Power points out, 'In London the police do not in general caution juveniles; in almost all instances juveniles found breaking the law are brought before the Courts'; (5) this means that his figures, based upon Court appearances, are, in his own words, 'as full as the present system permits' for boys up to 17 (the age at which adult Courts take over from juvenile). When the present book was in preparation, he was able to give us detailed information for Bethnal Green covering the five years 1958 to 1962; the information included the ages of offenders, their offences, number of previous Court appearances, and present or former school.

These figures show that, of the boys living in Bethnal Green who were aged 14, 15 or 16 during those years, about 7 per cent each year came before the juvenile Courts and were found guilty. Just over half appeared only once, a quarter twice, and the rest more often. The annual 'juvenile delinquency rate', measured by the proportion of boys under 17 coming before the Courts for the first time during one year, was about 4 per cent.

These Bethnal Green rates are close to Power's figures for the East End as a whole. They do not in themselves suggest a very worrying juvenile crime problem. But the figures look more serious if a 'cumulative rate' is calculated − in other words, if we ask how many local boys are likely to come before the Courts at least once at some time during the span of their adolescence. The Tower Hamlets study has been able to follow boys through the years up to 17; its calculations suggest that, by this age, more than one local boy in four − from Bethnal Green, as from Stepney and Poplar − is likely to appear in Court. This still leaves out of account the years from 17 to 20, for which detailed figures are not to hand. If one draws upon national figures for an indication of what happens during these years, (6) it seems probable that something like one Bethnal Green boy in three may appear in Court before his 21st birthday. Measured in this way, delinquency is obviously fairly common.

What crimes do the boys commit? The 14, 15 and 16-year-old Bethnal Greeners who came before the Courts over the five years from 1958 were more often charged with theft than anything else. Altogether 40 per cent of the offences were some kind of theft. The stealing was mainly of a petty kind, but more than a quarter of it was 'breaking and entering'. Stealing was, however, more common among the 14 year olds than the 15 and 16 year olds: 65 per cent of the offences committed by the former were stealing, compared with 29 per cent of those committed by the latter. This age difference fits the pattern of juvenile crime in Tower Hamlets as a whole between the ages of 8 and 17. Power reports that stealing and similar offences rise to a peak at 14 and then fall off. (7)

Among 14, 15 and 16-year-old Bethnal Green offenders, 19 per cent of the offences were 'taking and driving away' (in other words, 'borrowing' a motor cycle, scooter or car), 16 per cent traffic offences, mainly driving a motor cycle or scooter without a licence, and 12 per cent one of the misdemeanours associated with hooliganism and violence — 'insulting behaviour', carrying an 'offensive weapon' and so on. These various offences — 'take and drive away', traffic offences, hooliganism or violence — accounted for 19 per cent of all the offences among boys aged 14, 51 per cent at 15 and 66 per cent at 16. Although there are no figures for Bethnal Green boys aged 17 and over, the evidence from Downes' research near by is that crime in general falls off sharply after about 20, as it does in the country as a whole, and that these offences other than stealing start to become important at about 15 and reach their peak at about 17. (8)

Stealing is General

How does all this match up with what the boys had to say? Their own account suggested that certain sorts of law-breaking — particularly stealing were even more widespread than the official figures indicate. Stealing, it seems, is part of the 'normal' behaviour of boys in Bethnal Green, as it apparently is in other working-class areas. (9) An 18 year old said of himself and his friends a few years earlier:

'We used to thieve now and again, same as anyone else, but I don't think we was bad — it was just a normal thing we used to do.'

And a 16 year old was probably exaggerating only slightly when he said:

'There's not a boy I know who hasn't in fact knocked something off at some time or another.'

A friend who was present commented:

'They're not thieves or anything like that, they're just normal.'

There were many examples of the kind of petty crime that, as the figures suggest, was common at about 13 or 14.

'We used to pinch ordinary little things, particularly when we were in the last couple of years at school. I remember when we went out on a school party once — there was about sixty of us and we went to this place in the country where there was a little village store that sold souvenirs. I reckon that out of that sixty, about fifty of the kids thieved something out of the store. We laughed about it when we were going away after- wards, saying that the store was almost cleaned out by the time we'd finished.' (17 year old.)

Some of course went on stealing.

'The first time I was pinched was when I was about 11. It was when my sister was getting married and I wanted to buy her a wedding present. We used to play in the bombed houses and there was this bloke in there — I'll always remember, he was a little bit older than us. He was stripping the lead out of this house and he said to us, "Do you want to earn something?" and we said, "Yes", so he said, "See this lead? I'll just go and stand on the corner and you walk up with it." He had an old wireless set he put it all in. And when me and my mate were walking up to him there were two blokes standing there. They looked just like ordinary blokes, but they turned out to be detectives and they pinched us, and when we looked round this bloke was gone. We told the detectives that some bloke had given it to us, but they never believed us and they found out what house it had come from and it was down to us. We got into trouble over that — up the Juvenile Court and both bound over. After that we pinched all sorts of things out of shops and off stalls. Then when I was about 16 or 17 a mate and I started breaking in. We started with a bicycle shop — we went round the back and climbed over a wall and got in. It looked so easy — just a little wall — and we broke in there and stole quite a few things. After we'd done the bicycle shop, it gave us encouragement and we did some more after that. We used to go round at night and break into shops and cafés. Mind you, all that stopped a couple of years ago. I must sound like a real thief to you, but I don't thieve now.' (20 year old.)

It seems from the figures that most other boys who continue stealing from shops, warehouses and the like after about 14 stop by about 19 or 20. What goes on, up to and beyond this age, is stealing from or defrauding one's employer — often dignified by being described as 'knocking-off' or 'fiddling'. 'I stole a table-top from my firm,' said an 18 year old, 'but I don't call that stealing.' Another said:

'I've knocked off things from work — spare parts, light switches, mirrors and given them to people or sometimes sold them.'

An 18 year old, working for a local trouser manufacturer, explained:

'I work a fiddle if I ever get the chance. Say a load of material comes in, and it's marked on the ticket 45 yards. After a few days that ticket may come away and the governor may say, "What's the yardage?" You tell him you don't know, so you measure it on the machine and you find that it's 50 yards. You look in the book and you find that it's supposed

101

to be 45 yards. You've got five yards over, haven't you? If you tell the governor about it, he'll keep it for himself. He's not going to send it back to the mills and tell them they've made a mistake. So what I do, I take it myself. I don't see any reason why I shouldn't. To take off your governor is the usual practice, I should say. Governors fiddle, don't they? And they cheat each other. So why shouldn't you do the same?'

The same justification was used by others.

'They're out to rook you first, I mean the employers, ain't they? Docking this and that off your money? No, I don't reckon there's much wrong with pinching at work.' (18, store-keeper.)

Thus theft from employers is not by any means an entirely adolescent phenomenon, though it may be more common amongst them. I have heard similar views expressed by their fathers and men like their fathers interviewed in Bethnal Green. Similar attitudes are reported among adults as well as young people in other working-class districts. (10)

Along with this tolerance towards those who take things from employers, there is a widespread view that theft from a friend or relative is morally wrong, as stealing from rich people or large firms is not. (11)

'If you steal off someone who's a friend of yours, someone you know, that's bad. I don't see as there's anything wrong with stealing from a big shop or from a bank or somewhere like that. Ordinary people don't have to find the money out of their own pockets — it's all covered by insurance anyway.' (17 year old.)

'If someone pinches something from a big shop or from the back of a Rolls-Royce, or something like that, and they get away with it, I say good luck to them. What does it matter? It's only a crime against society, so who cares? It's not at all the same thing as knocking down some poor little old lady who's walking along leaning on a stick and with a big purse in her hand. I don't like to think that people around here would knock an old lady like that down for her purse.' (19 year old.)

A few boys did not make this distinction: to them stealing from large shops or wealthy people was also wrong. But it seemed as if the two just quoted were expressing the views of the majority.

Attitudes to the offences connected with motor vehicles were more mixed.

'I started with scooters. You know, you come home from school and you see a scooter parked there. You've found out how to get it started from your mates and you think "I'd just like to ride one of those things around the block". If it's dark and there's no one about you get on and ride away on it. If nothing goes wrong, you're tempted to do the same thing the next day and the day after that.' (18 year old.)

Most, however, said they would not do it themselves. As one put it, 'It's mad. You might get away with it a couple of times and you might think you're all right, but it's very easy to get caught. I reckon it's a mug's game. I've had two mates who've been nabbed for pinching motor bikes or scooters.' It will be noted that the suggestion here is not that it was wrong to 'borrow' someone else's scooter, only reckless. But, as with the distinction between stealing from friends compared with 'impersonal' organizations, there was widespread disapproval of car or scooter thefts which caused harm or suffering. Several boys, for instance, condemned an incident in 1960, in which a woman of 64 had been knocked down and gravely injured by a 'borrowed' car driven by a 17 year old boy. Another example came from a 17 year old.

'I've done my share of "borrowing" cars and scooters in the past. I don't think it's right, particularly sometimes. Two blokes from round here came out of the Lyceum ballroom one night and pinched a Mini to get home because they reckoned there weren't any more buses running. Well, this car belonged to a young out-of-work actor, who's got polio. It puts him in a right fix. The police find this car abandoned down Bethnal Green and someone grasses about these two blokes and they get pinched. Then the story comes out. Of course the two chaps say they're sorry about the polio bloke and all that, but the beak says they're only sorry because they got caught. Still they only got fined. The point is it just shows how you can hurt people who haven't done anything to you. It's daft really, thoughtless.'

The Cult of Toughness

Views about violence are also mixed. Some boys were members of groups that sometimes fought others. Jimmy Grove said:

'We like a punch-up now and then. We fight for a reason, we don't just go out to sort somebody out. If one of our people gets hit by a mob, well we go after that group. We go over Victoria Park, there's a mob over there and they grabbed one of our boys, so we went back after them. If they hadn't started on a couple of our mates, we wouldn't have done anything. If I was going along the road tonight and a couple of blokes jumped me and I've got quite a few mates near by, well, what do I do? I jump on *them*. That's how we look at it.'

His friend Alan added:

'We don't go looking for trouble in places outside our area, we don't go up towards Brick Lane because they'd come down and jump on *us*. We don't start on them. Anyone who wants to come in our area, they can as long as they don't start on us. We don't even go over to Stepney, because if we went over there, one night they would come over here, and they've got so many more than we have got that we wouldn't have a chance.'

Another described how conflicts suddenly developed:

'It generally starts through looks. Somebody looks at somebody else and the other bloke says, "Who do you think you're looking at?" Or someone says, "Looking for trouble, mate?" And you say, "Yeah, got any?" And one thing leads to another, he gets a kick somewhere and then it starts.' (16 year old.)

Generally, the boys seemed to feel that Bethnal Green was a 'tough' district — in the praiseworthy sense of a 'manly' one. A boy, aged 15, who had moved to Bethnal Green from Suffolk when he was eight, remarked:

'When I first got here I thought all the kids were harder — you know, tougher — than in the village where I used to live. I've got used to it now, and I'm the same myself. I think that East End boys are definitely harder than in other districts.'

The conventions, among age peers, about loyalty and pride sometimes impose an obligation on a boy to fight, whether he really wants to or not. 'Us two go together,' said one 15 year old. 'If he gets in a fight I help him and it's the same with me.'
Another 15 year old said that he was always expected to support his friends.

'If you don't join in a fight you get called all the names under the sun. "What did you stand there for?" "Why didn't you join in?" Even if two of your mates are on to two others, they still expect you to join in. You must stick by your mates. They call you chicken otherwise.'

Yet another, aged 16, explained how he had been led by pressure from his friends into a fight he had not particularly wanted:

'I heard this fellow was calling me names — it was over a girl I took off him. He was going round saying I was a cunt and he'd murder me and all that. My mates said, "You going to get him?" sort of thing. So of course I said, "Yes, if I see him." Four days ago I was with eight of my mates and he was with two of his. I called him round the alley and had a fight with him. I only hit him twice and he was on the ground. I was scared beforehand; I always am before a fight. But I had to fight him, because all my mates were backing me up. They were all there. I would have looked small if I hadn't fought him then.'

These examples illustrate an important point about the influence of peers. There is, locally and particularly among the adolescent boys, a general 'cult of toughness', a respect for physical prowess and for 'spirit', which sometimes pushes into aggression even boys who have no special taste for it. But in practice the 'toughness' is much more a matter of convention of folklore than of day-to-day behaviour. There was plenty of evidence that most boys seldom fought and disliked violence. Some, for example, said that they had left one or other of the local youth clubs because 'it was too rough there' or 'there seemed to be a lot of fighting'. Some who belonged to another club remarked that its appeal was that 'the manager up there is good — he comes down on anyone who tries to start any rough stuff'. And the answers of the members of the sample, when asked what they thought of the recently reported clashes between rival groups of teenagers at seaside resorts, were revealing. While about one in ten seemed to accept or approve of the fighting, as many as two-thirds of the sample firmly condemned the participants.

'It's terrible, It's only a few get together and spoil it for everybody else.' (15, secondary modern schoolboy.)

'I think the way they carry on is ridiculous. It shows teenagers up.' (17, plumber's mate.)

'It's stupid. I don't see how they can go at each other. When it comes to fighting, I don't see that. Anyway, how can you fight someone you don't know?' (18, shop assistant.)

In fact, systematic fighting and mob battles are a rare occurrence in the East End. A 16 year old said, 'There are some who say they fight with bottles and knives and go out for big punch-ups and all that, but it's mostly talk.' (12)

The Threat to Adult Order

Just the same, there are other forms of aggressive and destructive behaviour that threaten the orderliness of the adult world and are seen as distinctively 'adolescent'. If there is sympathy amongst the local adults for some of the fighting — on the ground that it is 'manly' to settle a quarrel 'with your fists' — there is hardly any for the apparently senseless rowdyism and damage to property in which some boys indulge.

A 15 year old thought that the habit of destructiveness started at an early age.

'When you're a little kid, you smash up the things people chuck on the bomb sites, like old baths, old prams, old boxes and that. And motor-cars — there's always old motor vans on the bomb sites that the kids smash up. At first they think the bits they pull off are going to be useful for something, but when they get them off there's always something wrong with them, say some bracket won't come off, so then they do some more smashing up. It goes in crazes. After that we used to smash up builder's boards and "House to Let" notices. We didn't do it very much, but I know for a time we was pulling up those "House to Let" boards, and we used to dump them in the canal or in the Victoria Park Lake, I don't know why we did it; it was for a giggle.'

We were also given current examples of characteristic boisterousness. One boy, aged 17, described what happened one Sunday afternoon with three friends:

'We decided to go down to Southend in this little van — me and Charlie and Alan and Tom. Charlie was driving. We got down to Southend about 5.30, we jumped out and went in a telephone box to comb our hair in the mirror. We went to the Kursaal and started bilking the dodgem cars, you just jump over the fence, you see, and get in the queue; you say you've lost your ticket and get away with it. Then we went in the bar and had a few drinks. Then we went in the ghost train and Alan got off the train in the dark, I thought he would; we were all waiting for him to jump on us and somebody jumps on the top of us, it's Alan. Then we went on the scenic railway and they wouldn't strap us in (i.e. they were not allowed to ride): they could see what we was like. Then we went on the beach and Charlie shouted out there was a lot of bottles down there. We filled them with water and started throwing them about; they smashed against the stones; I stood there and thought if someone's going to come down in the morning they'll cut their feet to pieces. Then Alan stood on the end of this pier and started swinging round a big tin can on a string, he was going to throw it out to sea, he misjudged it, instead of throwing it upwards he let go too late and it went straight over his shoulder, just missed this old lady. So we ran and jumped in the van and drove away.'

There are, in some of these examples, a number of common themes. First, much of what the boys are doing, is, in strictly rational terms,

106

pointless and senseless — much of the behaviour is an expression of bubbling exuberance, of animal high spirits. As a 17 year old said, 'When you're young you want to let off a bit of steam. It's an attitude everybody experiences — it's a way of expressing yourself.' Secondly, this is almost never done by boys on their own or in pairs; the members of the peer group support each other.

'When they're together there's a sort of devil-may-care attitude. They're all in one bunch and they feel the others don't seem to care — well, they're pretending not to care, anyway — so why should I care. I won't care either. They sort of get carried away with each other. One tries to outdo the other. They say to themselves, if he's not afraid to shout out at that old lady over the road, I'm not afraid to put a stone through that window over there.' (18 year old.)

Finally, much of this behaviour is literally 'anti-social'; property is damaged, other people may be injured, frightened or disturbed. This is why adults, including those in Bethnal Green, disapprove. The boys themselves are either unconcerned or actually want to strike at adult society. Certainly some of them thought this last was true of themselves or their fellows. A 16-year-old grammar school boy said, 'A lot of us feel like it. It's the result of boredom. There's a natural instinct to rebel against somebody'. And a 19 year old, looking back, 'A lot of young people enjoy annoying adults. It may be because other people treat them badly, I suppose — in their work or at home or something like that. They think to themselves we'll do it just for spite. They want to take it out on someone else.'

One boy of 18 suggested that the hostility was often generated by adults.

'Adults tend to hold teenagers down a lot. If a crowd of you go into a pub and you're having a drink, you're with a crowd so you have a laugh. The older people look across at you and stare and say to each other "Mad hooligans" or something like that. They're sort of against us, they're upset by the noise we're making, they're frightened that we're drinking too much. We can take as much as they can, in fact more in some cases. As a matter of fact, one rule we always have in our crowd is that if anybody's driving, they don't have a single drink. If one boy is driving, he sits and drinks lemonade while the rest of us drink beer or spirits. But the older people look across at you and think you're getting drunk and making too much noise and all that sort of thing. It's no wonder that youngsters go a bit wild occasionally, open up now and again.'

The sense that adults are sometimes intent upon 'holding them down' seems to be held by a sizeable minority. Their feeling that adult society is against them is expressed in their attitudes to the police. 'I don't like the bloody coppers; I don't think any young boy likes a policeman,' said a 16 year old sweepingly. An 18-year-old carpenter, echoing a suggestion raised at the beginning of this chapter, argued that the treatment of working-class boys was different from that accorded to university students and the like, and that this discrimination was practised by the police and by people in general.

'We don't learn to speak properly. We've been brought up pretty rough. The things these students do are not all that different from what we do. But people don't look at it the same way. They say, "They are studying and they need to let off steam" — you know, exuberance and all that. But when any of us do it, I mean even the general public — it's not only the law — people turn round and say, "Look, they're mad gits, sit on them".'

Examples were given of police discrimination locally against boys, as they themselves saw it, just because they were adolescent.

'They always push you off the pavement, even though next door there's a load of older people they don't touch. If you're a teenager they'll have you for anything; you just stand on the corner and they have you for loitering. If you're riding your bike, they stop you and say, 'Where are you going, where have you been, whose bike have you got?" It happened to me once. Say you have a fight and they come along, they don't *have* to clip you round the earhole.' (17 year old.)

Given this resentment against the police, it is perhaps not surprising that some boys occasionally, as they put it, 'take the mickey' out of policemen.

Michael: There was a fight between a couple of people round in our block, someone went round the phone box to call the coppers. This copper came up and we started taking the mickey out of him. Everybody knew the police would be coming round. We were sort of standing in his way, and he came up and said, "Is this Norfolk House?" So I said to him, "You got eyes, mate?" It's up in big letters in front of him. He says to me, "Don't be funny." I says, "They're probably expecting you." He says, "Why?" I said, "How should I know?" He said, "You just told me they might be expecting me." I says, "I never said nothing."

Peter: I said, "No, he never said nothing, copper." The copper said, "Don't you start playing around with me." I said to Michael, "Have you got four coppers. I want them for the telephone box?" The copper went absolutely mad.

Michael: Anyway, he went up to the flat, and when he was coming out he said to us, "Watch it", like that. As he was walking away, I shouted out after him. I bawled out at the top of my voice, "You dirty great cunt." As soon as I said it, we turned round and belted off in the opposite direction.

Not that most are seriously antagonistic to the police. But many of them, at least some of the time, do have the sense that adult society is suspicious and hostile, and the police likewise. They in their turn are sometimes anti-adult and anti-police, and this is probably part of the explanation for the occasional defiance and hooliganism.

Family Influences

The adults with whom the boys clash may of course include their own parents. But parental attitudes to juvenile crime, and their influence upon their sons, are more complex matters deserving special attention. In a few families fathers in particular themselves openly break the law and are hostile to the police.

'When this copper started shoving my friend around,' said a 17 year old, 'I hit him with a bottle. I was put on probation for two years for that. My old man said, "Jolly good luck — sod the coppers." He don't like coppers because he's a lorry driver; and before he drove lorries he was pinched lots of times for being a street trader.'

Clearly there are some 'criminal families' in Bethnal Green. Power found that, in Tower Hamlets generally, boys were more likely to come before the Courts if one of their siblings had been there already. (13) And we came across families where serious crime was commonplace.

'Look at my family — everyone goes inside from time to time. One of my uncles has just come out after doing six years. Another uncle goes in now and then for three months. Another one is selling stolen goods — he's been doing that for two years and he ain't been caught. He's making loads of money. It runs like that in the family.' (16 year old.)

Such families are rare. Even among the rest, however, minor 'fiddling' or 'knocking off' from employers is commonly tolerated, even approved — probably almost as much, as I suggested earlier, among the adults as the adolescents. The extent of pilfering from the near-by docks is one indication. (14) Many adults in Bethnal Green, too, though they would not themselves steal from large stores or 'impersonal' concerns, are like their sons in regarding such thefts with relative tolerance. It would be wrong to think that this shows manual workers to be particularly immoral. Sutherland has convincingly shown that 'white-collar' crime is widespread; (15) and tax evasion, expense account 'fiddling' and sharp business practice are by no means unknown to many of those who would be quick to condemn pilfering by a dock or railway employee. As Wootton remarks, 'The truth is that the anti-social behaviour of one social circle takes one form, while the members of other circles both behave and misbehave differently.' (16)

In practice the Bethnal Green father who 'lifts' at work comes to terms with his minor thefts in just the same way as his more illustrious fellows with their own forms of misdemeanour — by refusing to regard them as crimes at all. They have not really done anything wrong: they are therefore in their own eyes not 'criminals' and certainly not against the police or the law in general. Similarly fathers who have themselves been 'in trouble' as adolescents are likely to be relatively tolerant of minor transgressions — 'It's just high spirits. Boys will be boys' — but do not, because of this, condone 'serious' law-breaking. All in all, to judge not only from what the boys told us about their parents but also from our earlier studies and our continuing contacts with the district, most adults in Bethnal Green think that the law is in general on their side and are ready to uphold it. Even among those who do not wholeheartedly share this opinion, most certainly think that law-breaking should be discouraged because of the risk.

The Place of Delinquency

The theme is by now familiar. What the boys themselves told us corroborates the figures given at the beginning. To recapitulate, there are two distinct cycles in juvenile law-breaking. The first is in theft, mainly petty; after the peak at about 14, some boys go on stealing, though most even of these stop by about 19 or 20. 'Fiddling' and 'lifting' from work does persist, and is regarded as fairly trivial by most people locally.

The second cycle is in the offences mainly 'associated with hooliganism and disorder'. (17) This cycle starts later and reaches its peak at about 17. In Downes' words, 'The first stage (of juvenile crime) begins about the age of 9 or 10 and persists to 14-15, i.e. from pre- to mid-adolescence. It involves almost exclusively break-ins and petty larcenies. . . . The second stage begins around 15-16 and persists until 18-19, i.e. from mid- to late-adolescence. It involves take-and-drive-away, rowdyism, some violence. . .' (18) It is striking that this second stage, in which the law-breaking is predominantly of the disorderly, 'defiant' or violent kind, coincides with the period of adolescence which earlier chapters have suggested is that of greatest strain and conflict. It seems, however, from what the boys say,

110

that this second sort of delinquency is less common than the stealing in which so many indulge when they are younger.

Altogether something like a third of the local boys may come before the Courts during their adolescence. Many others break the law, mainly by shoplifting and other petty theft and mainly in early adolescence or before. Among the older boys, particularly those of about 17, some occasionally do something wild or dangerous. But most of the offences are relatively trivial and for most boys the incident is relatively transitory. Of the boys who come before the Courts about half do so once and another quarter twice, and for virtually all boys the whole thing is over by the age of about 20. The conclusion is that delinquency is neither one of the main activities nor a continuing activity of most boys or most adolescent groups.

Explanations for Delinquency

Is it possible to identify the boys most likely to be delinquent? One finding is that the type of school is related to delinquency. A comparison of the past or present schools of the 14, 15 and 16-year-old Bethnal Green offenders with those of boys of the same age in our sample shows this. The boys before the Courts contained proportionately more boys at secondary modern schools; 89 per cent of them went to such schools compared with 58 per cent of the boys in the sample.

Downes found the same thing in Poplar and Stepney. He also had information on the occupations of offenders, and he adds:

> 'Where he is not still at school, the delinquent is most likely to be an unskilled, semi-skilled or unemployed worker. Occupationally, as educationally, the delinquent is "bottom of the heap". . . .' (19)

The 'open' interviews and group discussions in Bethnal Green pointed to the same conclusion about the 'seriously' delinquent. They suggested too that there was, among some boys, a consistent pattern of behaviour and attitudes, into which violence and law-breaking fitted. The 'deviants' among the Bethnal Green boys — those who disliked school, who could not settle in their job, who either did not go to youth clubs or, when they went, caused so much trouble that they were expelled are not all the same boys. One who dislikes school does not necessarily find it difficult to settle into a job, nor does the job-changer necessarily stay away from youth clubs. But there is some overlapping. Discontent at school and at work, for instance, often go together. Correlation analysis provides evidence of further links also. In particular, boys critical of school or work more often said their parents did not 'understand' them. (20) Andry found, in his comparison of samples of 'delinquents' and 'non-delinquents', that the

111

delinquent boys tended to get on less well than the others with their parents, particularly their fathers. (21) Delinquency, in other words, as some of our interviews seemed to indicate, fits in with other kinds of discontent inside and outside the home.

I can illustrate this by drawing on the experience of Jimmy Grove and his friends – the boys who come closest to being a 'gang' out of those we talked to in our research. First, school. Jimmy and his friends all went to secondary modern schools, and most of them disliked school. They described their schools as 'crap schools' and complained about the injustices of the 'eleven-plus'. In the main, they were not successful at school; they resented its discipline; they saw it as something to be accepted rather than enjoyed, a nuisance rather than of any value. In a word, they were in greater or lesser degree the failures and the rebels of secondary education. None of them had gone on to any kind of further education since they had left.

As for work, they were in the main in unskilled jobs, and most of them changed jobs often. Jimmy said:

'None of us worry what jobs we do. We are all the same, right, boys? We'll do any job as long as the money is high. We don't care what work we do, we don't care what the foreman's like, as long as the money's there at the end of the week.'

About apprenticeships, they said that they could not afford to take them on and that, in any case, they wanted to 'enjoy life, not sit at night school every night'. They were also among those who told stories about misbehaviour in youth clubs and being expelled for it.

They were certainly not content with their lot. For instance, Jimmy said:

'I want to be *it*. I want to be higher than millions of people with my name mentioned every day in the papers – when that happens you are *it*.'

The same boys engaged in organized theft – or as they put it, 'did jobs'. They told stories of breaking into shops and warehouses, driving away cars and scooters, and so on. They were also more violent than most of the other boys we talked to – 'We go in for punch-ups more than most of the fellows round here.'

We have no firm evidence whether these few boys illustrate a pattern that applies more widely. But the elements seem to hang together. The argument is that such boys are consistently rejected; respond with frustration, expressed in aggression; try to kick against society through delinquency and violence. This corresponds closely with a prominent sociological theory on delinquency, that of 'delinquent sub-cultures', which is

112

drawn largely from the United States. (22) In the debate on 'delinquent subcultures' there are differences of emphasis in detail, but a broad measure of agreement that the origins of delinquency are to be found in the contrast between the values of a prosperous and democratic society and the lot of the working-class boy within it. These boys live, so the argument goes, in a society which values success, above all material success, and in which, too, advertising and the mass media generally are constantly at work to sharpen aspirations. But, in a democratic society which prizes achievement, those who do not get on are branded as failures — and this applies most to working-class youngsters. Their sense of failure, according to the theory, is especially sharp when, as now, education is the main ladder of success and when they have been openly rejected by the educational system.

The suggestion is that this sense of failure and frustration is the mainspring of unlawful behaviour, particularly theft, violence and hooliganism. Here the interpretations differ. Some see the law-breaking as an attempt to get, by illegitimate means, the material trappings that successful people get by legitimate. Some, on the other hand, argue that the motive is above all 'status-frustration' — that is, the boys behave as they do to hit back at the society that has rejected them and to show their contempt for its values.

There has, in fact, been virtually no research in the United States or in Britain to test this theory on a satisfactory scale. Our study cannot provide such a test, but it is none the less instructive to see how the theory stands up to the findings of this research. The attitudes and behaviour of the delinquent boys just described correspond closely to what the theory would predict, and above all to the suggestion that their main motive is a desire to strike at society rather than acquire wealth.

So in broad outline the theory seems to apply. But only to some boys, not to most. There is no widespread and continuing sense of resentment, revolt or frustration among the local boys. Many boys are 'delinquent', in the sense that they sometimes break the law, and particularly steal. But, since most boys do not feel rejected or frustrated, the theory does not explain their transgressions. It can help to explain only the delinquency of the minority. My interpretation, though again I cannot demonstrate it, is that such boys engage more often in persistent and 'serious' crime, and are probably more likely to turn into adult criminals. If this is true, it still does not tell us why certain boys respond to a poor school record and a low-status job with a sense of frustration and bitterness, while others whose experience is apparently similar do not. There is no obvious sociological explanation for the difference; we probably have to look instead to psychology.

How, finally, is the relatively trivial delinquency of the majority to be explained? It can, I think, best be interpreted as part of the process of working out adolescent tensions and adolescent resentments against adults. Delinquency is encouraged, too, by the peer group. The process which

113

makes boys withdraw into a peer group of their own sex also withdraws them, to some extent, from the influence of social disapproval. They care less than formerly what their parents think, but have not yet acquired a girl friend whose opinion of them matters. When they do acquire one, and move towards a family of their own, they become once again more subject to the social controls of the local community and the national society.

1. See two American discussions of this: Cohen, A. K., Delinquent Boys, pp. 37-38, and Warner, W. L. and Lunt, P. S., The Social Life of a Modern Community, p. 427
2. The papers so far published on this study are Power, M. J., 'Trends in Juvenile Delinquency', and Power, M. J., 'An Attempt to Identify at First Appearance Before the Courts Those at Risk of Becoming Persistent Juvenile Offenders'. From now on I refer to these as 'Trends' and 'First Appearance' respectively
3. Downes, D. M., The Delinquent Solution, Chapter 6. See also the next extract in this section
4. Ibid., Chapter 7
5. Power, M. J., 'Trends'
6. See Little, A., 'The "Prevalence" of Recorded Delinquency and Recidivism in England and Wales', Table I, p. 261
7. Power, M. J., 'Trends'
8. Downes, D. M., op. cit., pp. 158-64
9. See Mays, J. B., Growing Up in the City, p. 81; in this study of working-class youths in Liverpool, Mays found that over three-quarters admitted breaking the law, mostly by stealing. Andry, R. G., Delinquency and Parental Pathology found that two-thirds of a sample of 'non-delinquents' in London admitted stealing (p. 94)
10. For instance, Downes in Stepney and Poplar (op. cit., p. 204), Mays, J. B., in Liverpool (op. cit., p. 117) and Jephcott, P. and Carter, M. P., in 'Radby', a Midlands mining and industrial town (The Social Background of Delinquency, pp. 67-68)
11. This distinction, too, was noted in the research in Stepney and Poplar, Liverpool and 'Radby'
12. This is what Downes reported of Stepney and Poplar: 'In both Stepney and Poplar, no inter-gang, and barely any inter-group, fighting was reported or observed, though there was a generally disseminated proclivity towards limited forms of toughness and aggression.' (Downes, D. M., op. cit., p. 212)
13. Power, M. J., 'First Appearance'. A study in Glasgow found the same: 'To a remarkable extent the convictions of the boys and of other members of their family run parallel.' (Ferguson, T., The Young Delinquent in His Social Setting: a Glasgow Study, p. 151)
14. See Downes, D. M., op. cit., p. 193. The studies in Liverpool and 'Radby' cited earlier, also bear this out
15. Sutherland, E. H., 'White-Collar Criminality'; this is an American article but it seems likely that much of it applies to Britain as well
16. Wootton, B., Social Science and Social Pathology, p. 70
17. Power, M. J., 'Trends'
18. Downes, D. M., op. cit., p. 164
19. Downes, D. M., op. cit., p. 184
20. The correlation coefficients were as follows. Between fathers 'not understanding' and (a) criticizing school lessons, .263; (b) criticizing school rules, .260; (c) dissatisfaction with job generally, .154; (d) dissatisfaction with job prospects,

.225. Comparable coefficients with mothers 'not understanding' were: (a) .186; (b) .177; (c) no significant correlation; (d) .305

21. Andry, R. G., op. cit., pp. 26-27, p. 45, pp. 60-61 and p. 88. A similar connection was noted in a study of eighty-five 18 year olds in an outer London borough: 'There was some evidence that unhappy family relationships were reflected in the boy's choice of job. . . . A group who seemed to be reacting against a disturbed family situation were the "drifters" found working in the semi-skilled and unskilled jobs.' (Logan, R. F. L. and Goldberg, E. M., 'Rising Eighteen in a London Suburb', p. 328)

22. See e.g. Cohen, A. K., op. cit., Cloward, R. A. and Ohlin, L. E., Delinquency and Opportunity, Miller, W. B., 'Lower-Class Culture as a Generating Milieu of Gang Delinquency', Matza, D., Delinquency and Drift. The whole debate is reviewed and related to the English scene in Downes, D. M., op. cit.

British Delinquents and American Subcultural Theories
by David Downes
Reprinted from The Delinquent Solution London, Routledge & Kegan Paul (1966) Chap. 7

The main question from both the Cohen and the Cloward-Ohlin viewpoints is; what response(s) does the male, working class adolescent give to being accounted a failure — in middle class terms — in the middle class contexts of school and the job-market? A corollary question is: irrespective of response, is the working class adolescent at any time a victim of 'status frustration'?

With some exceptions, observations pointed to the absence of any 'problem of adjustment' of the kind envisaged by Cohen in the lives of both the Poplar boys and those adolescents encountered in Stepney. There was an almost monolithic conformity to the traditional working class value-system and little discontent with working class status, especially in the occupational sphere. This is not to say that there were no economic dissatisfactions, but these are not peculiar to working class adolescents: they permeate the working class at all skill and age levels.

Status-frustration, as portrayed by Cohen, appeared to be found in inverse, rather than direct, correlation with the 'subcultural' delinquency. Discontent with role allotment, and resentment at structural blockage to upward mobility, seemed to be associated with lower-stream grammar and technical school, and upper echelon 'A' stream secondary modern school boys, rather than the products of the typical 'black' secondary modern school. It must be emphasised that Cohen's theorisation stressed the occurrence of status-frustration at an earlier stage than late adolescence and only research at the pre-school leaving stage in secondary moderns would supply any valid data on this point. Also, where status-frustration *did* occur in a lower unskilled and semi-skilled working class context, it produced a degree of desperation

115

which found some outlet – 'but' no 'gang' status 'solution' – in delinquency.

No group is in stasis. In the period of time – relatively short – in which the Poplar group were contacted, their delinquent behaviour appeared to lack two further elements crucial to Cohen's construct of the delinquent subculture, i.e. malice and negativism. The absence of these elements signifies the 'corner boy' rather than the 'delinquent boy' adaptation, although their involvement in delinquency was far greater than Cohen postulated for the typical corner-group, whose delinquent activities implicitly stop at truancy and do not involve property or personal aggression. However, this is not to deny that the group had been subcultural delinquents at an earlier age while still at school, the forcing house for the delinquent subculture.

According to Cohen, the parent male subculture tapers off at about age 15-16. In this way, the Poplar group can be viewed as en route from subcultural delinquency to young adult 'corner boy' conformity. The question of interpretation must remain open.*

'Gang' or Group?

Delinquent groups in the East End lacked both the structured cohesion of the New York gangs described by Cloward and Ohlin, and the fissile impermanence of Yablonsky's 'near-group'. If the definition of delinquent gang is that of a group whose central tenet is the requirement to commit delinquent acts – i.e. 'delinquent subcultures' as defined by Cloward and Ohlin – then observation and information combined point to the absence of delinquent gangs in the East End, except as a thoroughly atypical collectivity. The possible exceptions that were heard of were – by repute – conflict-oriented and 'near-group' in structure, and neither criminal- nor retreatist-oriented gangs were mentioned by respondents even in the legendary sense. The groups responsible for the bulk of delinquency were simply small cliques whose members committed illegal acts sometimes collectively, sometimes in pairs, sometimes individually, in some cases regularly, in others only rarely. Delinquency was no more the central requirement for membership than the experience of sexual intercourse, though the group and the peer group gave collective support to the commission of delinquent acts, much as they would to sexual prowess. Average group size was 4-5, with a few individuals on the periphery. While these street-corner groups persisted over time, and invariably possessed a dominant personality, all the other features commonly attributed to the delinquent 'gang' were absent: i.e. leadership, role allocation, hierarchical

*To permit a relatively unabridged presentation of Downes' discussion of Cloward and Ohlin and Sykes and Matza, we have restricted his discussion of Cohen's theory to this brief summary. (Editors)

structure, consensus on membership, uniform, and name. Girls were attached to the groups only in so far as they were acquainted with individual members, but rarely took part in any delinquent activity. The norm, then, is the fluid, street-corner clique, averse to any form of structure and organisation, but with persistence over time.

The non-existence in Stepney and Poplar of both gangs and groups based on the pursuit of delinquent activity *per se* is not, however, necessarily a proof of the non-existence of delinquent subcultures. The bulk of delinquency is committed by groups: but the delinquency is one aspect of the group's way of life, not the controlling factor in its formation. The issue now at stake is not what gangs there are, but why none — or very few — exist. What relevance have the Cloward-Ohlin concepts to this type of delinquency situation?

Criminal

The three categories of the Cloward-Ohlin typology are discussed here not as delinquent subcultures, but as patterns of behaviour generalised throughout the social and geographical areas studied. The ultimate criterion for the existence of a criminal opportunity structure in an area must be that such a structure has a separable existence as an institution within the area. By this criterion, Stepney can hardly be considered a 'criminal' area, and Poplar even less so. While there are in the East End several well-known (to the police) criminal cliques, and families of a 'professional' nature, i.e. solely engaged in the utilitarian pursuit of break-ins, robbery, and drug-trafficking, these groups are largely independent of each other, and are not organised in such a way as to constitute a visible, coherently patterned criminal opportunity structure on a quasi-bureaucratic basis, as are the big American syndicates. The set-up of adult crime in the East End seems to be that of small autonomous groups, some with their own 'guv'nor', some recruited on a completely *ad hoc* basis. Allerton (1) — in one of the few 'life-histories' of an East End professional criminal available — describes his recruitment for a specific 'job' into just such an *ad hoc* clique. This adult set-up is naturally reflected in the structure and aims of adolescent delinquents, among whom there are very few groups dedicated to deliberate and positive criminality, and these are almost certainly composed of boys with much Approved School and Borstal history. Small pockets of organised crime undoubtedly exist in Stepney, and it has traditionally acted as a magnet for ex-cons and receivers, as well as for the social 'inadequates' who fill the hostels and whose last resort is the bomb-site. Traditional Stepney crime comprises 'screwing', the used-car racket, H.P. rackets, dog-doping, and — more recently — drug-trafficking, as well as prostitution and illegal gambling and small-time 'protection' exercised against cafes and betting-shops. In a continuum of

117

adult crime in west Stepney in particular, the most organised activities — 'screwing', robbery, doping, drug-traffic — would have least personnel involved; more numerous would be those engaged in prostitution, immoral earnings, illegal gambling, drug-use and proneness to violence; mid-way would be larger numbers purposefully engaged in crime as a supplement to their jobs; and finally even more would take the opportunities inherent in their jobs to 'fiddle' extras in a fairly systematic way. The last category, which includes such activities as dockers 'whipping' goods, cannot be considered a criminal 'career', but is rather what Sykes and Matza might term a 'subterranean' aspect of conventional job-routine. 'Fiddled' goods are generally consumed personally or by immediate family, or are sold cheaply on a kind of informal community network, in which those who will buy suspected stolen goods, and those who would disapprove, or who might even 'inform', are known in advance. Where goods whose origin is fairly anonymous are concerned, such as nylons or canned soup, the risk is sometimes taken of hawking them round local pubs. There is little interaction between this kind of amateur crime — where recourse is rarely had to established 'fences' — and the first two categories mentioned. This is not to say that the promising dock 'whipper' or car-borrower never progresses to more ambitious and better-organised crime: but in the cases where this happens, the process is largely one of self-recruitment to a way of life, rather than attraction into a stable hierarchy which provides an alternative route to upward mobility. The latter feasibly occurs more frequently in those activities which are essentially crime-promoting but technically legal, such as property-racketeering and certain forms of bookmaking, and gambling.

The absence of a conspicuously successful adult criminal élite is reflected in the lack of any perceptible aspiring towards professional crime among adolescent delinquents; it is also reflected in the areas of adolescent congregation — which are restricted to stable working-class or wholly teenage locales — and their avoidance of specifically 'criminal' milieux. The self-image of the Poplar boys, for example, was that of the 'hooligan', not the criminal. This is not to say that they had no contact with individual adult criminals — a relative of the café owner was 'inside' for dealing in stolen cars — or that none of them had ever envisaged a full-scale 'job':

I asked Pete what he'd be doing in ten years time. 'Swinging by the fucking neck', he said. I asked what for. 'Well, if I ever run out of money again, I'm going to go out and do a job for some.' He told me that last weekend a kid had offered to go in with him on a job they'd get £200 each from, 'but why should I?' said Pete. 'If I got caught I could get five or ten years for that. Five years for two hundred quid, it's not worth it. Anyway, the next job I do I'm going to do by myself. I've been to court four times but I've never been caught yet, have I? I've always been split on. Every single time one of my mates has given me away. . . . But there's one job I'm gonna do, as soon as I break up with my girl. I'll get a couple of thousand quid out of it' – The pub radio gave out a bulletin on a mail-van raid when the bandits got away with £4,000 – 'Good luck to 'em, mate', said Pete vehemently. 'Behind every robbery like that, there's a brain. They do the job and he pays them off. The bloke who gives the inside information gets £500. They don't have to worry about getting rid of the stuff. The brain does that. I read it in the papers.'

This story shows – for one boy at least – intense sympathy for, if not identification with, the adult professional criminal. It also testifies to the efficiency of the various media as vehicles for the dissemination of criminal techniques. This example of aspiration towards the 'big score' was atypical, and probably paranoid. But it serves as a reminder that the tendency for offences to be non-utilitarian declines with age and growth of the appreciation of risk.

A factor which feasibly serves to deflect adolescents from certain offences in the East End, such as prostitution, poncing, drug-use and illegal gambling, is the association of these offences with the 'blacks', although long-established working-class families in the area are traditionally anti-pathetic towards prostitution. Prostitution is the notorious 'Stepney problem', a term which was actually used in one survey to differentiate the Stepney prostitute from the West-End type: ' "Stepney problem" is a special connotation used to describe those girls who were mainly the failures of Approved Schools and Borstals, and went to live in the coloured quarter of Stepney; mentally, physically, and morally they were in a lower grade than the ordinary prostitute.' (2) It is no longer so true that the Stepney prostitute is a pathetic and feeble-minded amateur, absconded from an institution or newly arrived by lorry from the North, sharing a bed often for nothing as the only means of finding one. Since the early and mid-1950's, the girls have been more organised, and a pattern established. There seems to be a distinction between the Cable Street and Spitalfields areas *vis-à-vis* prostitution, the former being centred on the caffs, the latter being much less public and tightly controlled by ethnic cliques, centred in all-night caffs and drinking-clubs. The clubs in Spitalfields are near the City, and cater for businessmen during the day, locals and 'tourists' at night. Many caffs rely on respectable trade during the day, and open at night simply as rendezvous for the girls, ponces and clients. Clubs which are closed simply re-open under a different name and management, on the by now well-established pattern. The Maltese reportedly run the girls in Spitalfields, and have been held to sell them to other cliques, such as Pakistanis, for sums around £10. Few girls are from Stepney or Poplar, and no attempt is made to recruit locally: the influx from the Northern conurbations is consistent. The occasional caff is 'queer' or lesbian, but these circles shift within short periods of time.

119

Underlying the prostitution situation, and in partial explanation of community attitudes towards the 'slags' and the 'blacks' are two main factors. First, the shrinkage of the native resident Cockney and Jewish population of Stepney from about 200,000 in 1939 to just over 90,000 in 1961, due to massive re-housing schemes and migration to the suburbs, both during the war and after, so that while the influx of coloured immigrants is well under 10,000 in number, they stand out disproportionately in the young male population. Second, the housing situation has left west Stepney in particular with tracts of slum, condemned property, some of which is not scheduled to be pulled down until 2005. But the property crucial to prostitution and property racketeering is especially that in re-development areas, with only a decade at most to stand. Whole areas have been bought up cheaply by agents and let off at exorbitant rents, or leased at high rates of interest, to landlords – often coloured – who connive at maximum short-term profits either from the girls and their ponces or sub-letting at exorbitant rents. Since the mid-1950's, therefore, prostitution has spread from the coloured enclave of Cable Street to Cavell Street, Spitalfields and, more recently, to Mile End, a pattern pre-determined by the ownership of crumbling property. Illegal gambling and drug-use has spread correlatively. Local white residents are bitter, but are now resigned to the spread of prostitution and the lack of official action apart from the occasional police raid. Neighbourhood organisation to tackle the problem came to an end with the break-up by the police of the 'Vigilantes' in 1957-58, an attempt by the community to administer the 'rough and ready' justice of the streets to what – in some areas – was beginning to threaten families and children. The fear was that 'children would come to regard prostitution as a possible way of life' but the impetus was given added violence by the identification of prostitution with 'the blacks', whose reliance on the girls was – to a large extent – forced by the absence of their own women, and the stigma attached by the stable working-class community to a girl who went with a coloured man. The only resort for unmarried negroes were those white women the local community itself rejected. White adolescents come to share the blanket aversion of their parents for 'the blacks and their women. . . . I bet you five quid you can't walk with me down Cavell Street and point to three houses that aren't brothels. It's the blacks. Send the cunts back from where they came from. . . . They import girls, most of 'em Irish. There hasn't been a pross nicked in two years.'

Conflict

Both the 'conflict' subculture of Cloward and Ohlin, and the 'conflict-oriented' adaptation of Cohen and Short, are based on the institutionalisation of violence in the street warfare ('rumbles') of juvenile delinquent

120

fighting gangs in New York, Chicago and other metropolitan centres. In both Stepney and Poplar, no inter-gang, and barely any inter-group, fighting was reported or observed, though there was a generally disseminated proclivity towards limited forms of toughness and aggression. A 'punch-up' that was witnessed in the Aldgate Wimpy appeared typical of the form taken by most adolescent aggression in the East End, though 'punch-ups' are supposed to be pre-arranged. This particular scuffle took place on a Friday evening about 10.30, began with one male teenager insulting another, blows were exchanged and — as the place was tightly packed with male teenagers and their girls — the fight snowballed so that those who were in the fight and those who were trying to watch became indistinguishable. A young P.C. came into the Wimpy, forced his way through the struggle, had his helmet knocked off but separated the two central protagonists, and ordered them outside. They apparently got away without being charged. This type of scuffle was frequent in this café, there were fights in or around or at the back of the building, usually at weekends following Friday pay-day. But:

'They're nothing much. . . . Nothing gets broken, except perhaps somebody's nose. There's no knives or anything more than a bottle, but hardly even that.'

The general view was that 'old-style' battles, between marauding mobs (as distinct from structured gangs) from nearby areas such as Hoxton and local mobs, were very much a thing of the past, of the 40's and early 50's. The 'Teds' never really 'caught on' in Stepney and Poplar, snuffed out by an essentially conservative working-class community which frowned on any real violence as a threat to family life and children. But even at its height, 'old-style' delinquency lacked the gang-structure, the concept of 'turf' and the idealisation of 'heart' which are held to be characteristic of the American street-gang warfare situation.

The Poplar boys were never seen to display even that degree of aggression that took place ritually in Stepney. Lacking in these boys was another characteristic of the American situation, the willingness to 'talk delinquency'. Axiomatic, however, was the absence of any 'real' aggression:

. . . I asked him if a big bunch had ever tried to take this particular café over, since it was the only one of its kind nearby. . . . Lennie said no, there was none of that kind of thing. 'It's only common sense. If a bunch came in now, there's not many of us here at the moment, they could clear us out. But we'd find out where they came from and we'd get all the boys from here, and all the boys from Bow, and we'd go and beat them up tomorrow night. No, there's never been anything like that. Stands to reason. If a negro boy comes in, he's going to feel scared

121

because we're all whites, but we don't take any notice. The other night four negro boys came in but nobody took any notice. If seven or eight of 'em come in, then we might tell 'em to clear out, but they'd never do that. No, about once a month you'll get a real fight between two of the boys here, but nothing like gangs fighting.'

In other words, conflict for 'neighbourhood hegemony' just doesn't apply in Poplar, or Stepney, or — with few exceptions — throughout London. Fights occur, but for more straightforward reasons:

'Bill's birthday party.... That ended up in a fight. These two boys turned up in a van and started messing about with Bill's girl, so we threw 'em out. They came back and there's five more of 'em in the back of the van with fucking great hooks from the docks. We beat 'em of throwing bottles at 'em. One of 'em gets his hook in Ray's jersey. Ray just says, "here, get your hook out of my jersey". The bloke takes it out and Ray just hits him in the face with this bottle. . . . Nobody got hurt bad.'

In general, however, the attitude was one of avoiding violence. Pete refused to use a snooker room because 'the yobs' who hung around the place used violence on newcomers:

'. . . They come from round Barking. If you go in there, they just beat you up. . . . That's their enjoyment, like ours is hanging around here and stealing cars. . . . They'd never let me in that gang down there, and I wouldn't want to, anyway. *They're too tough*. They don't even let you get to know them. You speak to them and they just walk past you in the street, then two or three of them'll split off and get you. . . .'

But this kind of vicious hostility was the exception, and clearly regarded as such by the boys themselves. Their own aggression, mostly verbal, followed the lines indicated by Miller in his analysis of aggression in a boys' street-corner group, i.e. narrow in content, target and range of expression, and playing itself out within the confines of the group.

The nearest approximation to conflict-orientated adolescent delinquency was the occasional short-term mobilisation for street forays. The difference was well summarised by the director of a well-organised Stepney youth club who had been to New York:

'. . . I went out to several locations. We have gangs here, there's no denying that, but they're nothing like the ones in New York. They have names, there, like the Comanches. . . . Here, the boys use bike-chains or knives and — occasionally — a kid gets killed by accident. But there they use guns and plan murder in advance, they premeditate that such and such a boy should be liquidated. . . . I give the street-workers there all credit, but they came too late. Here a boy leaves school and is working hard straightaway. There they stay at school until 16 or 17, they're bored, uninterested and don't get into a job when they leave school the way a boy does over here. . . . You can read the statistics any way you like. A twenty per cent rise in juvenile crime could mean just that the kids don't get away with it. When I was a kid, I stole, but I could run faster than any copper. Now the police have cars. . . . It's important to get this in perspective. Thirty years ago, you honestly couldn't walk through Stepney without fear of being molested. . . . Well, I've been here ten to fifteen years and I've never been beaten up yet, even in the worst districts. There's a lot of exaggeration. There's less *real* delinquency than ever before.'

Retreatist

While no evidence at all was found to suggest the existence of an adolescent retreatist subculture, characterised in its ideal-typical form, according to the Cloward-Ohlin criteria, by the consumption of alcohol, drugs, jazz and sex, two subgroups in the populations studied possessed affinities with Merton's category of retreatism, which does not postulate specifically delinquent or criminal behaviour, and which does not entail contracultural self-images of the subgroup as an élite. These two subgroups were the young coloured males who lived or hung around Cable Street and its environs — some of whom were involved in prostitution, gambling, hemp- or marihuana-smoking, heavy drinking and violence — and the young adult white 'yobs' or layabouts who shared this milieu, but who are characteristic of any inner urban working-class area, and are not confined to any specific 'quarter'.

Alienation

The concept of 'alienation' plays as central a role in the subcultural theorisation of Cloward and Ohlin as 'status-frustration' does in that of Cohen, and the largely negative findings for the latter apply even more forcibly for the former. There was barely any evidence to suggest that delinquent adolescents achieved any degree of alienation in the Cloward-Ohlin sense, i.e. 'withdrawal of attributions of legitimacy for conventional norms'. If the findings on 'status-frustration' were substantially correct, this is hardly a surprising conclusion: 'status-frustration' or profound disenchantment with available legitimate opportunities, is the stage in the delinquent subcultural sequence prior to the possible emergence of the alienated response. Alienation in this

123

context means much more than a boy 'not liking' his job, or feeling at odds with the machine he operates. It means rejection of the normative system by which he was allotted the job, came to operate the machine, in the first place. Yet the jobs of the Poplar boys and — notoriously — of a disproportionate number of male delinquents, including the most recalcitrant, were of low status even by working-class standards. These boys were not impervious to the working-class image of 'the good job', the autonomy of the craftsman, the physical toughness of the stevedore, the offbeat glamour and on-shore independence of the Merchant seaman, the high wages and security awaiting the apprentice. Enough of their peers occupy these jobs for the contrast to be ever-present. To deny on their behalf any real degree of status-frustration and alienation is not to present a picture of boys who are happy to be laggers — 'the lowest of the low' — van-boys, labourers, etc. What has been achieved, rather, is an opting-out of the joint middle- and skilled working-class value-system whereby work is extolled as a central life-issue, and whereby the male adolescent of semi- and unskilled origin is enjoined to either 'better himself' or 'accept his station in life'. To insulate themselves against the harsh implications of this creed, the adolescent in a 'dead-end' job, in a 'dead' neighbourhood, extricates himself from the belief in work as of any importance beyond the simple provision of income, and deflects what aspirations he has left into areas of what has been termed 'non-work' (rather than leisure).

This process has been best described as one of 'dissociation', as distinct from 'status-frustration' or 'alienation':

Satisfaction from work and the significance attached to it will depend not only on the nature of the work, but also on the expectations which the individual brings to his job. These in turn will be the result of complex processes of selection and socialisation, which begin at 11 + with entry to the grammar or modern school, each of which carries its stream of children on to broad groups of occupations. . . . For the less able child in the lower forms of the modern school, the dominant picture that emerges is one of school as a source of boredom and frustration. (3) In many schools the imposition of dull, mechanical tasks, which lack any apparent significance or relevance to the life of the child, effectively train him to accept the routine demands of industry. The transition from school to work involves little more than a change of routine. (4) Many expect little from work and are satisfied with what they find, even though the work is repetitive and makes few demands. The secondary modern boy leaving school at 15 has received early training in dissociating himself from the demands which 'they' make upon him. *He simply doesn't care.* It is not surprising that psychologists have discovered that many are content to carry out routine tasks. Dissatisfaction is a measure of the gap between aspiration and achievement. *For many, no such gap exists — their expectations and aspirations are centered on the world outside the factory.* (5)

In school, the problem is not one of structured protest, defiance and rebellion against middle-class norms, but of pupil inertia, boredom and passivity, with periodic outbursts of what Webb termed 'spontaneity, irrepressibility and rule-breaking' as a reaction against the shackling of their individualism by the school as a legitimised agency of control. In this connection, the apology offered by the father of a Stepney boy who refused to be interviewed is of interest. The boy had previously reluctantly agreed to be interviewed, but on the date, had gone out to the pictures with his wife. The father simply offered 'They don't take to people with education' as a reason, a classic instance of dissociation, of evasion and withdrawal, as opposed to outright annoyance and anger at being pestered.

Cotgrove and Parker, in reviewing recent studies in industrial sociology, go a long way towards establishing a frame of reference for the analysis of the work situation as a main determinant of attitudes and values in areas of non-work. They complain that

the sociologist, if he has looked outside the factory, has searched mainly for clues which would throw light on industrial behaviour. . . . The great weakness of such studies is their failure to sort out the components of the working-class situation and relate them to working-class culture, leisure and family life. . . . Short term hedonism, belief in fate, and the distinction between 'them' who decide and 'us' who passively carry out instructions . . . may well stem from the typical factory work-situation, characterised by a lack of autonomy and involvement. (6)

For the 'boys' in Stepney and Poplar, dissociation at work seemed to be coupled with dissociation in leisure. Granted the abundance of youth work in Stepney, the cause for surprise is not that this pattern has been broken down slightly, but that it has resisted such a variety of middle-class oriented blandishments. But it cannot be asserted that dissociation extends to the 'world view' of these adolescents, and it is this 'world-view' that affords least evidence of alienation in the Cloward-Ohlin sense. For example, the Poplar group showed firm loyalty to the monarchy, the government, etc. They disagreed with the way white Americans treated Negroes. Hatred of 'coppers' — 'the boys' sworn enemy — was not a manifestation of 'withdrawal of attributions of legitimacy from conventional norms', but rather a particularistic aversion to the kind of control enforced by the police. This was combined with an attitude verging on what Sykes and Matza termed 'techniques of neutralisation' — e.g. 'Coppers are a lot of cunts. They closed everything down, all the caffs. They stop us doing anything, always moving us along', etc. — i.e. 'accusing the accusers', though there is undoubted truth in their charge of

125

differential victimisation. Police justification for this would be valid, however, as the groupings they break up and 'move on' are often ripe for trouble-making: removal of the causes which led the groups to form and 'hang about' in this way is not the police's concern. Yet hatred of the police is often suspended. The friendly cop is a rarity, but is enormously respected. Also, on one occasion, Ray listened in to a police car bulletin. He expressed no resentment, just excitement. The police, normally repressive, had for once *been* a source of excitement. 'Plain-clothes', however, are quite beyond the pale.

'Dissociation' for 'the boys' is generally from middle-class dominated institutions, rather than from the total non-working-class society. One of a group of 'ton-kids' who used the caff occasionally expressed this almost too articulately:

> 'We go fast, but we watch it. We wait for straight stretches of road most of the time. *There's none of this defiance of society.* That's all in the newspapers and the newspapers are all wrong. They're just sensation-alising to sell more newspapers. . . .'

Even about the Remand Home, the group showed clear preference for conniving dissociation from its aims rather than alienation from its norms:

> 'It's better "inside" than out here. Prison's alright. And places like Stamford House, that's just a holiday camp. You go there and behave yourself for a fortnight and they make you a prefect. Then you get more time to watch the telly, you don't have to do jobs, things like that.'

Interaction between middle-class 'helpers' and working-class 'delinquents' in youth-clubs provides many instances of confrontation producing friction, but antagonism resulted in dissociation rather than open conflict on the part of the adolescent. Overt hostility is rarely the consequence of such interaction, even where middle-class intrusion is resented. By analogy, the 'inverted snobbery' peculiar to the English working-class is the hall-mark of dissociation and its maintenance is an antidote to feelings of alienation.

Anomie

Analysis so far has concentrated on what might be termed the consistently delinquent 'corner boy' — Cohen's clear-cut distinction between the 'corner' and the 'delinquent' boy appearing to be inappropriate at this juncture — and not on the working-class 'college' boy, the aspirant highly skilled manual and technical workers, or the conforming 'corner boy'. Also excluded are delinquent boys bent on pursuing a nascent professional criminal career — often on the basis of almost unbroken institutional-isation — and 'lone' offenders who commit delinquencies with no traceable pattern, e.g. those for whom delinquency is symptomatic of mental illness. It is still thought that the group delinquent 'corner boy' pattern accounts for the bulk of the major adolescent offences, i.e. the diversified activities of break-ins, car-borrowing, simple larcenies and theft from machines, rowdyism, receiving, weapon-carrying and — more atypically — vandalism and violence against the person. Yet these adolescents did not appear to be subject — or to have been subjected in the past — to any critical degree of status frustration or alienation. Interaction within middle-class institutions, and the experience of 'failure' in the context of both middle-class and upper working-class contexts, appeared to have evoked the response of dissociation from the ethic that work, and occupational status, were of crucial importance as a focal area for 'ego-involvement'. As a result, their reference- and membership-groups were pretty well aligned. This is not to deny that they were subject to a mild form of economic anomie, but this is not peculiar to the male working-class adolescent sector. It is built into the consumer economy as incentive for all classes and all age-levels. (7) But the strain towards anomie is not generated solely by frustrations encountered in monetary and occupational spheres. As Merton has repeatedly stressed:

> ... the general theory of social structure and anomie is *not* confined to the specific goal of monetary success and of social restrictions upon access to it. ... In terms of the general conception, *any* cultural goals which receive extreme and only negligibly qualified emphasis in the culture of a group will serve to attenuate the emphasis on institutional-ised practices and make for anomie. (8)

Dissociation from the goal of occupational achievement — which feasibly occurs long before entry into the job-market — forestalls Cohen's issue of status-frustration: the 'problem of adjustment', consequent upon internalisation of middle-class values to at least some extent, never occurs. There is little merging: working-class and middle-class value-systems meet in head-on clash. As Merton, again, has stated:

> ... the theory (of anomie) ... sees the conflict between culturally defined goals and institutional norms as one *source* of anomie; it does not *equate* value-conflict and anomie. Quite the contrary: conflict between the norms held by distinct subgroups in a society of course often results *in an increased adherence to the norms prevailing in each subgroup*. It is the conflict between culturally accepted values and the socially structured difficulties of living up to these values which exerts pressure towards deviant behaviour and disruption of the normative system. (9)

By acceptance of low job aspirations, the 'corner boy' is released from the pressures of upward mobility, and his view of the legitimacy of 'lower class culture' is endorsed. But dissociation – as has already been stated – means withdrawal of interest in work except as a source of income, and this has concomitant implications for his behaviour, with others similarly circumstanced, in areas of 'non-work'. Feasibly, the more debasing his job-content and the more dissociated he feels from work, the more the lower working-class 'corner boy' tries to recoup in leisure something of the freedom, achievement, autonomy and excitement he is denied in work. In other words, Cohen's concept of 'status frustration' might possibly apply in this country if 'status' is defined in the Weberian sense of 'style of life' and consumer behaviour, rather than in the narrower sense of occupational prestige and aspirations to middle-class orientated achievement.

'Subterranean' Values and Leisure Goals

Sykes and Matza, by viewing 'adolescents in general and delinquents in particular as the last leisure class', (10) have attacked the conception that the values underlying the delinquent's behaviour constitute a deviant normative system. They assert that: 'A number of supposedly delinquent values are closely akin to those embodied in the leisure activities of the dominant society'. They hold that: (a) the values behind much juvenile delinquency are far less deviant than commonly portrayed, and (b) the faulty picture is due to gross over-simplification of the middle-class value-system. Three major themes have emerged from the variety of classic accounts of delinquent behaviour and values, although consensus is limited to substance, and not interpretation: (i) delinquents are typically immersed in a restless search for excitement, thrills or 'kicks'; (ii) delinquents commonly exhibit a disdain for 'getting on' in the realm of work; (iii) delinquents characteristically accept aggressive toughness as a proof of masculinity.

(i) is not accommodated by legitimate outlets such as organised recreation, for the very fact that an activity involves breaking the law is precisely the source of excitement. In courting danger, provoking authority, etc., 'the delinquent is not simply enduring hazards: *he is also creating hazards in a deliberate attempt to manufacture excitement'*. The excitement that stems from danger and law-violation, e.g. especially in 'chicken runs' and 'rumbles', is not a by-product, but a – possibly the – motivating force.

(ii) places the delinquent firmly in the category of the unemployed, the casual worker, or the boy in the 'dead-end' job. Even where 'occupational goals involving the steady job or cautious advancement' are available, 'it takes deep faith – and naïveté – to believe that hard work at the lower end of the occupational hierarchy is a sure path to worldly success'. (In the words of a later-day 'courtesan', Mandy Rice-Davies, who began with a low-status background: 'Nobody ever made a bomb by plodding along in a dull job.' (paraphrase)).

(iii) is commonly interpreted as an index of the delinquent's alienation from the larger society, his aggression — whether verbal or physical — seen as an outlet for basic hostility, hatred, and the urge to injure and destroy. This may be so for atypical big-city 'structured' gangs. More typically, it expresses the delinquent's familiarity with the ethic that manhood is reached via an ability to 'take it' and 'hand it out'.

Far from taking this configuration of values as indicative of the delinquent's deviation from the dominant society, Sykes and Matza note its affinities with the code of Veblen's 'gentleman of leisure'. The emphasis on daring; rejection of the prosaic discipline of work; the flair for conspicuous consumption; the respect accorded to manhood demonstrated by force; all find a prototype in Veblen's leisured elite. Only the *mode* of expression — delinquency — is unfamiliar. *'The values are obscured by their context.'* Bur the context alone is not sufficient to account for the attribution of deviance to the delinquent's values. 'In our haste to create a standard from which deviance can be measured, we have reduced the value-system of the whole society to that of the middle-class', and our portrayal of that value-system is grossly over-simplified. By an over-emphasis on the individualistic pursuit of work-goals, the Protestant Ethic and the deferred gratification pattern, and by a similar inflation of the ethic of reciprocity, belief in luck and short-run hedonism, we have polarised middle-class and working-class value-systems. Sykes and Matza compare these value-system portrayals to the now outmoded racial group portrayals, i.e. they amount to 'a distinct grouping of specific values unique to the social class in which they are found', instead of basing analysis on the 'distribution of frequencies', i.e.: 'Most values . . . appear in most social classes; the social classes differ, however, in the frequency with which the values appear'.

In any event, and whatever degree of distinctiveness is held to obtain between the value-systems of the social classes, Sykes and Matza argue that *all* classes accommodate certain 'subterranean values' — values which are in conflict or competition with other deeply held values, but which are still recognised and accepted by many. (11) These contradictions in values . . . may exist in a single individual and give rise to profound feelings of ambivalence in many areas of life.' They are akin to private as opposed to public morality, but they are not — *per se* — deviant.

Delinquent values, therefore, have their counterparts in the dominant society, most crucially in the upper and middle class sectors. But their expression is muted, confined to certain circumstances, such as holidays, sport, recreations, private conversation. Members of the middle class — and of all classes — seek excitement in gambling, parties, night-clubbing etc. 'Most societies provide room for . . . a sort of periodic anomie, in which

129

thrill-seeking is allowed to emerge.' Indeed, 'the search for adventure, excitement . . . is a subterranean value that now often exists side by side with the values of security, routinisation, etc. It is not a deviant value . . . but must be held in abeyance until the proper circumstances for it arrive. . . . In many cases, the delinquent suffers from bad timing.' Likewise, it can hardly be claimed that the dominant society is fully and unquestioningly committed to hard work. The notion of 'pull' and 'contacts', the idea of the 'soft' job — for the working-class in England, the 'good skive' — are widespread. Riesman's 'inside-dopester', Whyte's 'organisation man' and Mills' 'fixer' are all concepts 'under-mining the Weberian sociologists' affirmation of *the* work values of society'. In his disdain for the monotony of manual labour and his desire for 'easy' money, 'the delinquent is . . . in step with his time'. As for aggression, the dominant society exhibits a widespread taste for violence; books, magazines, films and TV jointly peddle fantasies of violence, from James Bond to 'Psycho', as well as acting as vehicles for the dissemination of criminal techniques. The actual use of aggression and violence in war and law enforcement provide further endorsement of the acceptance of aggression and violence on the part of the dominant social order. The equation between physical toughness and virility is also widely accepted, though the use of aggression is surrounded by many prohibitions.

In brief, Sykes and Matza argue that, far from standing as an alien in the body of society, the delinquent may represent instead a dangerous reflection or caricature. By picking up and emphasising the subterranean part of the dominant value system, the delinquent serves to reinforce the overtly law-abiding in their tenure of its more respectable and publicly proclaimed values. 'These values bind the delinquent to the society whose laws he violates', and this sharing facilitates his 'reformation' with the coming of adult status. 'To the objection that much juvenile behaviour other than simply delinquent behaviour would then be analysed as an extension of the adult world rather than as a product of a distinctly adolescent subculture', Matza and Sykes reply that this is 'precisely their thesis'.

In approaching the relationship between delinquency and social class, however, the argument of Sykes and Matza comes to verge on the perverse. Because they have answered the question: 'What makes delinquency attractive in the first place?' exclusively in terms of leisure values, i.e. the values of what they term a 'leisure class', and because they assert these values apply to adolescents at all class levels, they are led to assert that delinquency is more or less evenly distributed throughout the social class structure. This argument is not only based largely on absence of evidence: it runs counter to the massive amount of evidence that exists. It is not enought to insist that the non-delinquent is a rarity. This is by now a criminological truism. Most evidence supports the view that group delinquency is more frequent, persistent, diversified and less amenable to

130

control among male, working-class, urban adolescents than in any other sector. Moreover, this view is consistent with the theorisation of Matza and Sykes, provided that the concept of *differential access to leisure goals* is utilised, along with theorisation on the differential *distribution* and *functions* of leisure among adolescents.

Temporarily leaving out of consideration a small, moneyed, upper class élite, the distribution of leisure in adolescence by social class is clearly determined by educational allotment. At school, the non-secondary modern boy is subject to a rigorous academic time-table, home-work, and frequently school-sponsored commitments in sport and voluntary associations. Increasingly, this pattern of obligations — which eats into non-school activities — is unbroken till the age of 18, with the transition from school to higher education or training. The early leaver at 16 typically moves into a white-collar job, where he pursues an achievement-oriented career, frequently involving part-time or further education. Hence, the non-secondary modern school-boy is institutionally restrained from the most basic delinquency-producing situation of all: an abundance of 'free' time. The same applies on a lesser scale to a sizeable minority of upper stream secondary modern boys, who obtain apprenticeship, lower-grade white-collar jobs, or trainee skilled occupations, which involve either day release or evening classes. But for the substantial majority of secondary modern boys, both at and after school, few commitments encroach on leisure time.

Paradoxically, these adolescents — who have most leisure — also *need* it most, and ask more of it. Matza and Sykes have stated that all adolescents are alike in that 'they move in a limbo between earlier parental domination and future integration with the social structure through the bonds of work and marriage'. But for the grammar, technical and skilled working-class boy, it is not so much a limbo as a period of structured training for future role performance. Society has invested much more heavily in this type of adolescent than in the average secondary modern 'drop out' destined for the narrow ranges of numerous and interchangeable semi- and unskilled manual jobs. The strong likelihood of dissociation from this latter type of work has already been discussed, as have the consequences of dissociation for involvement in areas of non-work. Home-centredness is clearly unthinkable for most working-class male adolescents before their own marriage: numerous studies have pointed to the early age at which the working-class adolescent — quite distinctly from the middle-class boy — disentangles himself from parental domination. Similarly, the nature of his work appears to disincline him towards political and community activity. The only non-work area to which he is unequivocally attracted is straight-forward, uncluttered leisure. Yet dissociation from the work situation, and from middle-class dominated authority contexts, has its corollary in leisure: the rejection of the youth club, except for those few which exert little discipline, do not insist on regular attendance, and do not intrude on the group's or the individual's autonomy. Hence the emphasis on commercial milieux, the caff, the cinema, the dance-hall. For work-oriented adolescents, no such prohibitions apply. School- and job-satisfaction often leave them self-sufficient in leisure: mere idleness, sheer relaxation, is enough. But the youth club, with its 'activities' and 'constructive' frame of reference, accommodates them if they feel the need for direction in leisure. Also, academically-oriented education has equipped them for individualistic leisure pursuits, such as reading, hobbies, etc. It is the 'corner boy' — who has most leisure, and lays most stress on it as the area for self-realisation — who has least resources at his disposal to use it positively.

It is in this situation that the adolescent 'corner boy' encounters blockage of access to certain leisure goals common to all adolescents. The concept of this group as a discriminated-against 'leisure class' involves little tampering with the formula proposed by Matza and Sykes. Leisure goals as a term is meant to subsume both 'subterranean values' — the search for excitement, the pursuit of aggression — and certain leisure aspirations and expectations reflected in and perpetuated by 'teenage' culture — sophistication (clothes, wit), smartness, 'exploit', 'kicks'. Achievement in some or all of these areas might be said to constitute 'success' in leisure for adolescents. 'Teenage culture' stresses the possession of these attributes and the pursuit of these collective goals. It also lays special emphasis on certain artefacts and institutions: the fast car or motor-bike, the 'regular' girl, record-players, parties, etc. Rising expectations of leisure over the last decade have brought goals formerly within the reach of a minority into the purview of all: the holiday abroad, trips to the country, all-night 'raves', the kick of speed. The genuinely leisured, upper-class adolescent has full access to these goals, as have most students. By contrast, the 'corner boy' is relatively deprived in access to arenas for this kind of 'exploit'. Law-breaking is the only area of excitement to which he has absolutely untrammelled access. 'Anything you get enjoyment from round here, you're breaking the law' and 'We did it for a bit of a giggle' or 'Just for laughs': these disavowals of malice are more than techniques of neutralisation: they are euphemisms for the absence of legitimate opportunities to realise leisure goals.

Observation in Stepney and Poplar gave some support for this view. A focal issue for the Poplar boys was what they termed the 'deadness' of the area, 'nothing going on', their aversion to the one institution — the youth club — which might have contained their 'periodic outbursts of anomie' (Matza and Sykes). Those with bikes had a valid outlet:

'We go fast, but we watch it. . . . There's none of this defiance of society. . . *The bikes for us are mainly a chance.* We can get to places on the bikes we'd never get a sniff at without. We go to the Isle of Wight, Maidstone and so on. We can take the girls out on them. . . .

132

There's a few nuts but not many. We never drink beer and I hardly smoke. We take good care when we're driving, even if we do go fast.'

Some did express the conventional 'ton-kid' persona, 'We go on "burn ups", playing "chicken" with each other. . . . For the kick, the speed, *you* know', but the dominant attitude inclined to the former. The caff was virtually the only milieu for those without bikes (none had scooters, though Bill eventually bought a car for £20): apart from the cinema and dancing at the 'Civic', it was their only legitimate arena for excitement. Their behaviour in the caff was characterised by a milling restlessness, punctuated by long bouts on the pinball machine, the jukebox, etc. Strain was generated by the sheer absence of tension, the feeling that something ought to be 'going on'. Outside the area, they looked for the same framework: 'We go up the West End sometimes, go in those amusement arcades', and once came back tattooed, skull-and-crossbones, etc. on the forearm. Only work, sleep, the cinema and 'courting' took them outside the caff. They were interested in no music except pop, no sport, no reading except the *Mirror* every day and comics. They themselves viewed delinquency as a pretext 'for .laughs', a diversion from the long periods of boredom, constriction and inertia of the caff, whose ethos was in 'negative polarity' to the constructive, busy 'activities' of the model youth club.

It is not suggested that these boys constitute a 'leisure class', only that the analogy itself is suggestive. In the absence of work-orientation and job-satisfaction, and lacking the compensations accruing from alternative areas of non-work, such as home-centredness, political activity and community service, the 'corner boy' attaches unusual importance to 'leisure'. There is no reason to suppose that the delinquent 'corner boy' does not share the more general, technically classless 'teenage culture', a culture whose active pursuit depends on freedom from the restraints of adult responsibility, but which reflects the 'subterranean values' of the conventional adult world. There is some reason to suppose, however, that the working-class 'corner boy' both lays greater stess on its leisure goals, and has far less legitimate access to them, than male adolescents differently placed in the social structure. This discrepancy is thought to be enough to provide immediate impetus to a great deal of group delinquency, limited in ferocity but diversified in content. The underlying sources, however, remain culture-conflict along class lines, school failure and subsequent dissociation from work-goals, and consequent non-involvement in desirable areas of non-work. This sequence appears crucial for the short-lived but intense emphasis on a particular set of leisure goals.

Conclusion

Informal observation among delinquent boys in mid- to late-adolescence supported the theorisation of Cloward and Ohlin that severe deprivation of access to the legitimate opportunity structure is a necessary basis for the emergence of delinquent contracultures, another determinant being the presence or absence of access to the illegitimate opportunity structure. Crucial in Stepney and Poplar was the existence of an adequate, if limited, legitimate opportunity structure, coupled with that of a petty and disorganised illegitimate opportunity structure, associated with downward mobility and ethnic out-groups. Neither is it thought that reactions to 'failure' in the context of middle-class dominated institutions are responsible for generating a sufficient degree of 'status-frustration' to produce a contracultural response. However, no attempt was made to assess these reactions in the principal such context, the school. Inferences were based on expressions concerning job-satisfaction, and occupational expectations and aspirations, subsequent to school-leaving. While a generalised pattern of delinquency resembling an extension through adolescence of Cohen's 'parent male subculture' was prevalent, the absence of any real degree of malice and negativism seemed to preclude a contra-cultural interpretation, although — again — study within the context of those schools containing the most deprived children would probably have yielded different behaviour patterns. Certain forms of acquisitive delinquency indulged in by male adolescents, e.g. miscellaneous larcenies, 'fiddling', etc., have their counterparts in the adult world at most class and age-levels, and merely serve to emphasise the subjection of the population as a whole to a condition of 'mild economic anomie'. Likewise, certain forms of violence committed by working-class male adolescents are paralleled in the lower sectors of the adult working class. Those forms of delinquent behaviour peculiar to male adolescents, however, the 'pointless' break-ins, take-and-drive-away, group rowdyism, are thought to originate in the process of dissociation from school and work areas, and a consequent over-emphasis on, combined with relative lack of legitimate access to, certain leisure goals common to the dominant society. Hence the existence of a delinquent subculture, as distinct from a delinquent contra-culture, i.e. commonly situated delinquents hold to a set of norms and share a set of values and beliefs hardly markedly different from those characteristic of other sub-groups in the population, as distinct from holding to and embracing a 'contra' normative system hostile to, and formed by reaction against, that of the dominant, 'middle-class' society.

1. R. Allerton and T. Parker, The Courage of his Convictions (1962), pp. 78-80
2. C. H. Roph (Ed.), Women of the Street (1955), p. 245
3. See M. P. Carter, Home, School and Work (1962)
4. See also Webb, 'Sociology of a School,' Brit. J. Sociol., Vol. 13, No. 3, Sept. 1962
5. See S. Cotgrove and S. Parker, 'Work and Non-Work', New Society, Vol. 41, 11/7/1963, pp. 18-19

6. Cited here are: N. Dennis, F. Henriques and C. Slaughter, Coal is our Life (1956); C. Sigal, Weekend in Dinlock (1960); J. Tunstall, The Fishermen (1962)
7. Cf. the discussion by T. H. Marshall, Sociology at the Crossroads (1963) pp. 317-318
8. R. K. Merton, Social Theory and Social Structure (1957), p. 181
9. Merton, op. cit., pp. 190-191
10. G. Sykes and D. Matza, 'Delinquency and Subterranean Values: American Sociological Review 26 (1961) pp. 712-719
11. Sykes and Matza fail to note that Cohen advanced much the same point, but regarded it as less crucial for an understanding of the middle-class value-system: 'The delinquent is the rogue male. His conduct may be viewed not only negatively . . .; positively it may be viewed as the exploitation of modes of behaviour which are traditionally symbolic of untrammelled masculinity, which are renounced by middle-class culture because incompatible with its ends, but which are not without . . . glamour and romance. . . . They find their way into the respectable culture . . . only in disciplined and attenuated forms. . . . *They are not, however, allowed to interfere with the serious business of life.* The delinquent . . . is freer to divert these *subterranean currents* of our cultural tradition to his own use.' Cohen, op. cit., p. 140

The Delinquent Subculture and the School *
by David Hargreaves

At Lumley Secondary Modern School, the boys are not distributed throughout the streams in a random way; rather, from our knowledge of a particular boy's stream we can within limits predict some of the main values he will tend to hold. The higher the stream, the greater the tendency for a boy to be committed to the school's values. His attendance at school is more regular and his participation in school activities is deeper. He likes school and the teachers, to whose expectations he conforms, whose values he supports and whose approval he seeks. This trend is particularly true of 4A boys, and as we move from the highest stream to the lowest, this trend tends to reverse itself, and the values held by low stream pupils are the opposite of those held by their peers in 4A.

Our examination of the normative structure of each form reveals a clear variation in the criteria on which boys assess one another and derive status or prestige in the informal group in different streams. We find that in the A stream informal status correlates positively with academic achievement and behaviour rating scores, whereas in the low streams informal status is a function of a negative orientation to the school's values. The A stream boys approve of the teacher's conception of his own role and define the pupil role in terms of conformity to the teacher expectations. In the low streams, the boys do not approve of the teacher's definition of the pupil role.

This process of differentiation reveals itself in the friendship choices

* This paper is based upon chapter 8 of Social Relations in a Secondary School, London, Routledge and Kegan Paul, (1967) by the same author.

135

made among the fourth year pupils. In each form the majority of boys choose their friends from their own form. This is hardly surprising, since it is with his class-mates that each individual interacts most frequently during school hours, and often outside school as well. But we must also note that although between a quarter and a third of friends are chosen from other streams, these extra-form choices are not random. The process of selection of friends from other streams can be summarized in the generalization that the greater the distance between streams, the lower the proportion of friendship ties.

In short, we are suggesting that the fourth year can be divided into two 'subcultures'. The upper stream subculture is characterized by values which are positively orientated to the school and the teachers. The lower stream subculture, embodied in the leadership of Clint, is characterized by values which are negatively orientated to the school. The lower streams take the upper stream values and 'turn them upside down' and thus form an example of what Cohen terms a *negative polarity*. The differentiation of values, though a continuum, is focused in two opposite poles of attraction which produce a gap in the friendship choices between the B and C streams.

We shall term these two suggested subcultures 'academic' and 'delinquescent'. 'Academic' indicates that the values are orientated to those of the school and the teachers; 'delinquescent' indicates that the values are negatively orientated towards school, and in the direction of delinquent values, though not of course being synonymous with delinquency. To posit the existence of such subcultures is to propose a model or 'ideal' type of the school's cultural structure. To what extent such an analysis 'fits' Lumley Secondary Modern School, that is to what extent it can serve as a meaningful and useful interpretative summary of our findings, has still to be justified. The 'ideal type' is presented pictorially in Diagram I. The dominant values of the A and B streams are academic, though this is less true for the B stream; delinquescent values in these forms are deviant. In the C and D streams, the dominant values are delinquescent, though this is less true for the C stream, and academic values are deviant. Thus the A and D streams become the poles or extremes of the normative differentiation.

For many years it has been a well established fact that the school experience of delinquents differs from that of the non-delinquent. Typical of such findings are those reported by the Gluecks (1), who showed that delinquents are more likely than matched non-delinquents to be retarded, to have poorer grades and to indulge more frequently in serious or persistent misbehaviour at school. Attitudes to school are perhaps the most telling index of the delinquents' subjective experience of school. The Gluecks categorized 62 per cent of their delinquent sample as showing marked dislike of school as against 10 per cent of the controls. The correlation between acceptance of school and delinquency is $-.61$. Similar

136

Diagram I Representation of Two Subcultures

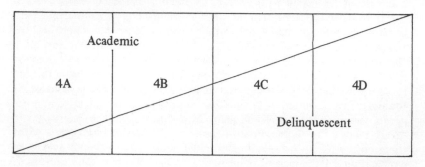

results are to be found in the data of Gold (2) where the correlation between delinquency and liking school is −.37.

During my stay at Lumley I managed to discuss problems of delinquency with every boy in the fourth year. Usually I was able to approach the subject during private conversation on the basis of more general discussions, such as the behaviour of the police in the area. When I had been in the school for nearly six months, the boys began to realize that in many respects I was not like a teacher, and that matters they mentioned to me would not be reported back to the staff. By the Spring Term, therefore, most of the boys felt able to trust me with their various confidences and, with two exceptions, seemed happy to discuss the extent of their own and others' delinquency. From what the boys reported I was able to take two measures. The first was the number of times every boy in the fourth year had appeared in the Juvenile Court, figures which could be confirmed from the official records. In this respect I found no example of a boy who denied an appearance in Court but was subsequently proved a liar by the records. The second measure was the unverifiable admission by each boy whether or not he was engaged in petty thieving and shoplifting.

The results of these two measures are given in Table I:

TABLE 1 Delinquency

Form	% Who Admit at Least One Appearance in Court	% Who Admit Current Petty Thieving	N
4A	3	7	30
4B	14	43	28
4C	37	73	22
4D	55	64	22
A11	24	43	102

137

These figures conform to the trends we have noted previously: negative behaviour is associated with lowness of stream. In the D stream over half the boys have appeared at least once in Court *and* admit current petty larceny. By contrast, in 4A only one boy has a Court conviction, and that was some years previously, and only two boys admit current thieving. In the Lumley study the correlations with positive attitudes to school are −.50 for delinquents and −.68 for those who admit current petty thieving.

From the figures it is clear that delinquency plays an important part in the normative structure of 4A in so far as its absence is indicative of norms *against* breaking the law. There seems little doubt from the discussion with these A boys that home environment was a force in establishing within these boys values which exclude criminal tendencies. Although part of the explanation for the lack of delinquency in the A stream derives from the home background, this is not in itself a sufficient explanation. Were it as simple as this, then we should not find any delinquent boy in the school with parents with anti-criminal values. In reality, as we shall see, some of the boys who were highly involved in petty theft knew only too well that apprehension would completely appal their parents. Many other factors, such as the personality of the individual, must be involved. The factor we wish to stress here is the pressure in the peer group. The norms in 4A would *necessarily* have to proscribe delinquent behaviour, since this would be inconsistent with the other predominating norms, which advocated behaviour in conformity with the teachers' expectations. To accept and internalize the teachers' values is to reject delinquent behaviour: 'Good lads do not steal'. Such support for these values as comes from the home will act in two ways. It will *predispose* boys to accepting the teachers' role expectations and to being integrated into the A stream, and it will *reinforce* the group's own norms. Likewise, where neither the group nor the home prohibit delinquent behaviour, the forces will draw the boy towards delinquency. In those cases where the home influence is not sharply defined in this respect, the peer group norms will become increasingly powerful in determining the attitude and values and behaviour of the boy.

The boys in 4B represent once again a compromise between the A and the C/D streams. Although only 14 per cent have appeared in Court, 43 per cent admit current petty larceny, which is a sharp increase on the 7 per cent in the A stream. Not surprisingly this figure disproportionately represents those boys of *high* informal status in the form: 9 of the 12 boys admitting petty larceny come from the upper half of the form and includes the first five positions of the informal status hierarchy.

The majority of the delinquent group had a Court record and were involved in current petty crime. Many of the accounts are very similar to those reported by members of 4B, such as the *collective* nature of the commission of the crimes. But there are important differences. In the B stream the main form of theft is incidental and petty. Cigarettes, sweets,

138

cakes, minerals and small trinkets from multiple stores are the most common of the articles stolen. Although this also occurred in the delinquent group, there are important differences. Firstly, criminality is more purposeful and organized. Rather than taking place, as was the case of 4B, 'on the way', on an incidental basis, it is planned before hand and often a special journey into the town is made. And when the boys get there, they arrange more carefully who will play which role.

We would expect to find an even greater cluster of delinquent boys occupying ranks of high informal status in 4C. Such is the case: only one of the eleven boys in the upper half of the informal status rank does not admit current thieving as against six in the lower half; six of the upper half have court records against two in the lower half. There are similar results in 4D. Nine of the eleven boys in the upper half of the informal status rank admit current thieving, against five in the lower half; and of the twelve boys with court records, only three fall in the lower half. In these two forms, therefore, we see that high status is associated with a court record and current petty thieving.

They learn by experience which shops are 'easier' than others. In addition, the quality of the stolen articles tends to increase in price. Clothes — significantly — become a major item of interest. Again whilst I could find little evidence of 'malicious damage' in 4B, such acts were fairly common among the delinquent group.

It will be evident that the delinquent group would frequently be involved in conflict with the teachers. On a number of occasions the incompatibility between teacher expectations and group norms was made quite explicit. We shall consider one example. This illustration is illuminating, in that it represents not one isolated event, but a continuous clash between the standards the teachers wish to impose and the norms of the delinquent group.

At the time of the study many of the 'pop' groups playing 'beat' music had long hair styles — the Beatles, the Rolling Stones, the Kinks and so on. Throughout the town many teenage boys imitated these styles. It is not surprising, therefore, that at the beginning of the Autumn Term 1964 a few boys in the fourth year arrived at school with long hair. The origin of this fashion, which by the middle of the fourth year had spread to many high status boys in the B stream, was in the delinquent group.

> Clint says, 'I'm going to get my hair flicking up', so I says, 'I'm going to let mine grow too', so he says, 'O.K.' So then we started letting it grow and then everyone did.   (Derek)

Many of the older boys had been wearing jeans in school for some time and the staff had made regular but not entirely successful attempts to ban jeans in school. Although the Headmaster was aware that the Local Education Authority would not support his refusal to accept a boy in school because of wearing jeans, he announced in Assembly that jeans were against the school rules. This rule was strongly resented by many boys for several reasons. Several other schools in the area did not enforce rules against jeans at school. Some felt that when the fashionable narrow trousers were worn at school they tended to become shapeless very quickly. Also some boys possessed only one pair of trousers and they wished to keep these as a 'best' pair.

A few days after the beginning of the Autumn Term, the Deputy-Headmaster called the top four informal status boys of 4D out of their classroom and told them that he would not tolerate this flouting of the school rules and that in future they must wear trousers to school. He explained to me afterwards that he hoped in this way to nip this incipient revolt in the bud. Yet the wearing of jeans continued intermittently, so a few weeks later one of the teachers asked for guidance on this matter at a Staff Meeting. The Headmaster pointed out that they could expect no support from the L.E.A. for their policy, and that the staff must therefore use informal sanctions against the wearing of jeans. All privileges would be withheld from offending pupils. One teacher pointed out that the offending pupils were the ones who in any case did not want privileges. The Head teacher retracted his remarks and stated that a boy must not be penalized simply because he wore jeans at school.

Many of the staff were not satisfied by this. Lengthy, informal discussions took place in the Staff Room and over lunch. The most vociferous members of staff were strongly opposed to jeans and long hair, and expressed their opinion in no uncertain terms. They argued that long hair was unhygenic and encouraged the spread of lice in the school; that it was dangerous, especially in the school workshops; that it was very unsightly and effeminate.

By November, when a second Staff Meeting was held, many tempers had been roused. As a result the Headmaster authorized the use of informal sanctions against the offenders. They were to be excluded from participation in the school concert, and from school visits. He also said, 'They'll get no help from me and I shan't give them a reference when they leave'. One of the teachers strongly objected to this policy, arguing that the academic development of the children was the school's real function, not the determination of styles of dress. No other teacher supported this objection, though one teacher expressed his agreement to me privately. The Deputy Headmaster countered the objection with a justification of the policy on the grounds that these boys were in any case disobeying their parents by having long hair and jeans and that the boys concerned were simply trying to be awkward in school. It was suggested that a long-haired member of 2A should be transferred to the E stream as 'an example' but this was not in fact carried out.

The more general policy was put into effect. Boys with long hair or jeans were excluded from school visits, though this affected very few boys

140

since only 4A and 4B were involved in these visits. The few offenders in these upper streams tended to capitulate and conform to teacher expectations as the year progressed. (One persistent deviant in 4A stayed at school for a fifth year, but since one master refused to teach him unless he had his hair cut, he left a few weeks after the beginning of his fifth year.) Teachers constantly made adverse and derogatory remarks about long hair and jeans. Such comments usually took the form of ridicule or an attempt to shame the pupils for their 'scruffy' appearance. Most of the teachers seemed almost completely unaware that such pressures would be unavailing since group norms were much more attractive and compelling than teacher expectations.

At the end of the Autumn Term the local Inspector of Schools attended the school's Carol Service and criticized the appearance of many boys. This caused the Headmaster to instigate a sort of 'purge' on jeans and long hair, and on lack of cleanliness, which he tended to see as synonymous. In an announcement to the whole school he said that boys who came to school in a dirty state in the Spring Term would be sent to the Chief Education Officer with a note to the effect that he, the Headmaster, would not accept these boys in school until they were more presentable. He also repeated that those boys with long hair could not expect a reference from him when they left school. He stated publicly that offenders would be excluded from extra-curricular activities. Finally he indicated that such boys would experience great difficulty in finding an employer when they left school.

At lunch that day a heated discussion ensued amongst the teachers. The majority agreed that long hair was a sign of anti-social behaviour and must be stamped out. Two teachers thought that long hair was a part of an adolescent phase and bore little relevance to the teacher's function.

The Spring Term marked the beginning of concerted opposition to jeans and long hair. On the first day of term boys with jeans were excluded from Assembly and lectured about the matter. One fourth year teacher openly admitted that he had caned six boys for having hair over their eyes and would continue to do so daily until they had it cut. The application of informal sanctions continued. The Headmaster wrote on one boy's report to the Youth Employment Officer, 'Has long hair.' The Headmaster refused to let boys with long hair have time off school to visit their future employers. He told the low stream boys:

Make yourself look normal. Make your appearance normal, instead of being like nothing on earth, or you'll not get a job. If an employer has two lads to choose from, he'll pick the normal one not you.

One teacher began cutting the hair of these pupils, an act which caused considerable dismay amongst the boys. The teacher did not, perhaps significantly, cut the hair of the leaders of the delinquent group, but of low status boys. However, one irate parent complained to the Education Offices about this, and the matter was hastily hushed up. The less drastic pressures continued. Bert of 4B was not allowed to sell flags in a local cinema for charity because the Headmaster considered that the boy's appearance would give an unfavourable impression of the school. It was on these grounds that several high status low stream boys were forbidden to attend the Leavers' Service at a local Church at the end of the Spring Term.

The teachers who disagreed with the Headmaster's policy formed a very small minority. One part-time teacher spontaneously told me that he disagreed with the policy for two reasons: firstly, the rule against jeans and long hair provided a means for the boys to express their antagonism to the system; secondly, the rule was arbitrary, since dirty trousers were considered more acceptable than clean jeans. Other teachers would not follow this argument.

As a researcher I tried to avoid becoming involved in the argument, but when my opinion was asked I felt it best to be honest and express my disagreement with the Headmaster's policy. I pointed out that when I had visited a local beat club with some of the boys I had felt very uncomfortable and out of place because of my short hair. On these grounds, we should appreciate that the club was more attractive to these boys than school, so we could not expect to win. Secondly, although I agreed that it was part of the teacher's duty to make the boys clean and tidy, I did not feel it was part of the school's function to dictate styles of dress. Thirdly, I stated that the Headmaster had informed me, after a visit from the school nurse, that with exceptions it was not the boys with long hair who tended to carry lice, since they washed their hair frequently. Finally, I suggested that long hair was perhaps a symbol of the boys' rejection of the school's values and that our opposition would only exacerbate this rejection. These arguments were hotly refuted by many teachers who were present.

Conflict between staff and boys continued. The Deputy Headmaster refused to consider Don for appointment as a prefect because of his long hair, despite support for his candidature from several teachers. As one teacher said:

I don't care a damn over his long hair, but if that's the school policy it's O.K. by me.

One boy in 4C who was an aspirant member of Clint's group was offered ten shillings by his mother and the same amount by his grandmother to have his hair cut short. His refusal in spite of these incentives is an interesting index of the symbolic importance of long hair in aligning him so visibly with the delinquent group.

Most of the delinquent group were leaving school at Easter. Few of them made any real attempt to secure employment. Part of this was their reluctance to have their hair cut. One boy in 4C did have his cut prior to an interview with a prospective employer a few days before the end of term. He was, of course excessively teased by both teachers and peers. Derek had his hair cut short on the evening after he left school. He was not willing, one might infer, to let teachers or pupils see that he was willing to abandon his long hair in order to get a job. He maintained his opposition to the last.

Central to Albert Cohen's theory of gang delinquency (3) is the failure of the working class boy to achieve status in the middle class system. Society's major institutions are run by persons who share the dominant middle class values and who use such values as a 'measuring rod' against which to evaluate others. Among the working class these values appear in an attenuated form, with the consequence that the working class boy is handicapped in achieving status (by which Cohen also seems to mean a sense of personal worth) at the hands of middle class agents, because his socialization has failed to provide him with the requisite personal qualifications. Cohen's thesis rests on the assumption that the working class boy does in fact seek such status in the eyes of middle class persons, and that he is frustrated in the attempt.

Cohen rightly sees the importance of life at school in the development of status concerns and problems. The teachers are often the principal middle class agents with whom the working class boy is likely to come into contact. Teachers are committed to the middle class value system and tend to evaluate their pupils on middle class criteria. Positive evaluation will thus be given to pupils who work hard and who behave well by middle class standards. Work and behaviour are the basic dimensions of the teacher's evaluation of the pupil, not only because they are central to the middle class value system, but also because work, in the form of scholastic achievement, and behaviour, in the form of conformity to school discipline, are the bases on which the teacher's competence is assessed by colleagues and superiors. Yet in rewarding the 'good' pupil who conforms to these expectations, the teacher must at the same time by implication condemn and punish the non-conformist, who will find it difficult to be insensitive to such negative evaluation.

To what extend did the pupils at Lumley internalize and conform to middle class values, even though the school catchment area is working class? Cohen lists the middle class values as:

(i) Ambition is regarded as a virtue.

In our study we have seen that, the higher the stream the greater the parental support for desiring a better job than father's and the higher the occupational aspirations of the boys.

(ii) Individual responsibility, resourcefulness and self-reliance.

No direct measures are available for these at Lumley, but we may note, for example, that high stream boys are more anxious than others to convince the teachers thay they are able to work unsupervised, both in the class-room and at home, and they show greater interest in activities such as rock climbing and cycle tours.

(iii) Cultivation and possession of skills.

In our study the higher the stream, the more the boys prefer to work hard at school, approve boys who do likewise, and like teachers who make the pupils work hard and punish boys who misbehave.

(iv) Worldly asceticism, postponing immediate satisfaction in the interest of long-term achievement.

This trend is most marked in the A stream at Lumley where boys value academic achievement more than 'having fun'. In the low streams the reverse is true. This difference reveals itself particularly in the norms which govern copying.

(v) Rationality and planning.

When the boys were asked to express their agreement or disagreement with the statement, 'Planning for the future is a waste of time', there was an association between disagreement and high stream (chi-square = 8.37, D.f. = 3, P< .05).

(vi) Cultivation of manners, courtesy and personability.

Members of the low stream approve cheekiness to the teachers significantly more often than high stream boys, and a direct measure of approval of good manners differentiated between the streams.

(vii) Control of physical aggression and violence.

In the high streams, fighting ability is irrelevant to status, and fighting activity is deviant. In the low streams, physical powers and fighting ability form a major criterion of informal status.

(viii) Wholesome recreation.

High stream boys tend to join youth clubs which organize activities for their members, whereas low stream boys tend to join clubs which do not organize specific activities and in which members may play very passive roles. Approval of boys with 'interesting hobbies' is associated with high streams.

(ix) Respect for property.

Low stream boys, especially members of the delinquent group, are frequently involved in acts of theft and malicious damage, but this is not true for high stream boys.

In short, there is evidence in this study that the higher the stream the greater the degree of conformity to middle class values. Moreover, there were indications that high stream boys tend to come from homes which were more orientated to middle class values than were the homes of low stream boys.

Inevitably it is the low stream pupils with their lower commitment to middle class values who most frequently fail to act in accordance with teacher expectations. In consequence they were to the teachers the constant target of invidious comparison with high stream pupils, whose achievements and behaviour they could not emulate. The sanctions and pressures exerted against the low stream non-conformists took a wide variety of forms, including ridicule and derogation as well as formal punishments. In addition they were excluded from the opportunity of joining the school's holiday ventures, of making afternoon visits to local places of interest, of becoming a prefect. It was to them that the teachers least qualified and least competent in matters of discipline were allocated. Many such pupils complained to me that they were denied these privileges and that they were treated by the teachers as inferior and worthless. In response to the sentence completion test item 'Teachers here think of me as. . . . . ' 73 per cent of the D stream supplied a negative answer, whilst only 10 per cent of the A stream did so. They correctly perceived their lack of status in the eyes of the teacher. In short, members of the low streams were aware of the discrimination against them and their self-esteem was low relative to that of high stream pupils.

If one of the key values of our society is achievement, then the school becomes a central focus and means by which individuals can achieve. Its stress on academic achievement, which is a major determinant of future occupation, represents an embodiment of these societal values. In England the influence of academic achievement is revealed in the distinction between the Grammar Schools and the Secondary Modern Schools, for which children are selected on their 'success' in the competitive eleven-plus examination. That the nation has accurately perceived that entry to a Grammar School offers greater opportunity for academic and therefore social advancement and success is evidenced by the growing amount of parental concern over the child's results in the eleven-plus examination, and by the predominantly middle class opposition to the re-organization of secondary education on comprehensive lines. The fact that the eleven-plus examination is seen in terms of 'success' and 'failure' indicates that academic and social aspirations have undermined the somewhat unrealistic concern in England to provide a variety of secondary schools appropriate to the abilities and aptitudes of their pupils and that such schools should have, in the eyes of the public, 'parity of esteem'. The educational system selects and differentiates its pupils in a further manner, for the vast majority of secondary schools whether Grammar, Modern or Comprehensive, stream pupils by their achievement relative to one another. Though there may be good educational grounds for so doing − a question which cannot be answered here − we cannot ignore that the effect of streaming is to separate children with relatively greater academic achievement into 'higher' streams; and to most of the public 'higher' is synonymous with 'better" To succeed at school is to succeed in society. To divide our children in this way means that we must also have children who 'fail', by not obtaining entry either to a Grammar school and/or to a high stream.

In the low streams boys are deprived of status in the sense that they are *double failures* by their lack of ability or motivation to obtain entry either to a Grammar school or to a high stream in the Modern School. At Lumley school members of the low stream were very rarely allowed to enter for external examinations. This meant, in practice, that their chances of obtaining a non-manual or skilled manual job with the concomitant social status and future monetary rewards were extremely limited. In other words, low stream boys are subject to status frustration and deprivation by their inability to gain any sense of equality of worth in the eyes of the teachers, but in addition their occupational aspirations for their future lives in society are reduced in scope. When a low stream boy attempted to obtain a good job without a formal qualification, his dependence on supportive references from the Headmaster increased. The negative attitude and behaviour displayed in school by such boys did not help them to enlist the Headmaster's aid. Compare the following references from the Headmaster to prospective employers. For the A stream boy:

His attendance has been regular and punctual. He is a boy of very good appearance and of pleasant disposition, performing his work cheerfully and thoroughly. During his final term he has been Head Prefect of the school and his duties in that connection have been carried out in a most efficient and responsible manner.

For the D stream boy:

He has been an unsatisfactory pupil in all respects and I cannot recommend him for a post with your company.

Occupational opportunity, a second and important way in which the low stream pupils were status deprived, is neglected in Cohen's theory but is of great importance in the work of Cloward and Ohlin (4), who seek to show that the opportunities available to the working class boy to achieve the dominant success goals which he has internalized are very restricted. By the fourth year at Lumley School, when the pupils perceive – often for the first time – the connection between stream position, eligibility for external examinations, and future occupation, the low stream pupil with aspirations is likely to find himself in a situation where only the unskilled jobs lacking in prestige, security and prospects are open to him. In terms of his future occupation, his school experience is not only irrelevant but also a positive hindrance. But many retain their financial aspirations. Consider the essay on 'My Ambition' written by Clint, the leading delinquent.

My ambition is to become a millionaire, because I have never had much money. If I ever did become a millionaire, here are a few of the things I would do. I would certainly buy my mother and father a new house in the country. Then I would emigrat to Australia or somwere like that, I

146

would have a brand new house built for me. I would also buy a set of antique furniture for the house. The house would be fitted with central heating and swimmin pool. I would employ a few servants and a buttler and a gardener and a chef. I would also have a Jaguar car. After a few months in Australia I would go on a cruise round the world.

Whilst the fact that lower stream pupils are not entered for external examinations must inevitably lead to a reduction in motivation to achieve, the tendency to assign teachers with poorer qualifications and weaker discipline to these forms reduces even further the pressure exerted on such boys towards academic goals. Once teachers remove the incentive of examinations from these pupils, provide greater opportunities for indiscipline, and begin to expect little from them, it is hardly surprising that they become progressively retarded and alienated from the school's values.

In short, the low stream pupil is status deprived in school in three ways. First, his lack of conformity to teacher expectation of hard work and good behaviour leads him to be evaluated negatively by the teachers and thus to develop a sense of inferiority and lack of personal worth. Second, he is the object of discrimination in that privileges open to high stream pupils are denied him. Third, the range of occupations accessible to him becomes increasingly restricted.

This status deprivation is, as Rose (5) has rightly noted, a form of *relative deprivation,* and as such requires us to specify the appropriate comparative reference groups, which are by definition bound up with the concept of relative deprivation. If it is claimed that the delinquent suffers from relative deprivation, it is essential to ask the crucial question 'with what persons or groups is the delinquent comparing and contrasting his own position?'.

Central to the argument of this paper is the view that the school plays an important part in the provision and selection of reference groups by the delinquent. The working class child does not feel status deprived relative to others *in vacuo* but relative to those with whom he has a legitimate right to compare himself. Schools bring together boys of different social backgrounds and values into a common social system and into a common position-role, that of the pupil. The adolescent boy perceives that, as an occupant of this position role, he enjoys equal status in certain areas with all other pupils. Some differentiations will be accepted as legitimate. Older pupils may be granted some privileges, but this is acceptable because they will some day be his too. Some pupils are put in different 'streams' because of their greater academic abilities. This is not a major concern of the majority since it makes little difference to the daily routines of school life. But when differential evaluations, privileges and opportunities are bestowed on high stream pupils, then the low stream pupil is likely to experience a sense of social injustice, since such differential treatment fails

147

to accord with his expectation of equality of status among pupils. (Even some of the high stream pupils felt that their preferential treatment by teachers was unfair.) The relative deprivation among low stream pupils at Lumley arose because they had learned to perceive high stream pupils as a comparative reference group within a common membership group. They did not appear to feel deprived relative to middle class children or Grammar school pupils, though objectively such is the case. It is only the high stream pupils who, when they entered the competition for attractive jobs, began to regard Grammar school boys as a comparative reference group.

The bitterness of status deprivation has two major consequences for the low stream boy. In the first place, he becomes increasingly negative on an individual level in his attitudes to school and teachers. The fun ethic of 'having a laugh' acquires a more serious undercurrent. The effect is to exacerbate his rejection by the teachers and thus a vicious circle is set in motion. Secondly, there is a group effect. These boys increasingly develop a set of values in which it is normative to exhibit negative attitudes and behaviour, which are a source of status with one's peers. The peer group promotes and supports negative behaviour. Thus the differentiation of norms and values between high and low stream peer groups is accelerated, and distinctive subcultures emerge. It then becomes possible for a low stream pupil to complain about the privileges of high stream pupils, because they form a comparative reference group, and simultaneously to be anxious to avoid being transferred into a high stream, because the high stream is a negative reference group in normative terms.

On the question of the group dynamics by which the delinquent subculture arises there appears to be some definite agreement among the theorists. Cohen, who places gang delinquency within the framework of a general theory of subcultures, states:

'The crucial condition for the emergence of new cultural forms is the existence, in effective interaction with one another, of a number of actors with similar problems of adjustment.'

In other words, the crucial condition for the emergence of the subculture is the existence of a *group* of persons with the same problem of adjustment, and Cohen points out the paucity of research which has investigated the factors influencing the creation and selection of solutions. It is our contention that the school is an influence both in the determination of the status deprivation and in the creation of conditions in which the subculture can form and define itself.

Cohen goes on to suggest some of the mechanisms by which a group solution can occur, especially in his discussion of 'exploratory gestures'. By this he means that persons with the same problem of adjustment, which cannot be solved legitimately in terms of the dominant culture, will

148

initiate solutions in a tentative way by probing gestures of mutual exploration. By a process of joint acceptance and elaboration of the exploratory gestures a solution is arrived at. Those elements which are most rewarding to the group and which most facilitate a solution form the basis of group culture.

The group dynamics of delinquent subcultures are similarly treated by Cloward and Ohlin. They also emphasize the need for consensual validation of a delinquent solution. It is important for the deviant to:

> 'gain the support of others who are in the same position and who share the view that their misfortunes are due to an unjust system of social arrangements. Collective support can provide reassurance, security and needed validation of a frame of reference toward which the world at large is hostile and disapproving.'

Since the initial acts of deviance are likely to elicit repressive counter-measures from the conventional community — from the teachers in school — the deviant urgently needs reassurance and encouragement. According to Cloward and Ohlin he finds these by:

> 'Searching out others who have faced similar experiences and who will support one another in common attitudes of alienation from the official system.'

It can be argued that the school plays an important part in providing the conditions necessary for the emergence of a group solution. The school contributes to the genesis of the delinquent's 'problem of adjustment' because it exposes the pupils to the ideology of 'getting on', of social mobility of hard work and middle class behaviour. The teachers are the propogandists of the values required to succeed. For low stream boys, the school both exposes them to the ideology and simultaneously frustrates and deprives them because they lack the values, attitudes and abilities to succeed in that ideology. It penalises them by denying them privileges and by inducing a sense of failure and personal worthlessness.

Further, the boys facing such a problem of adjustment do not have to *seek out* other boys with the same problem, as Cloward and Ohlin suggest. The school in its streaming system provides a mechanism by which potential delinquents are brought together. At the end of each term two or three boys are promoted to a higher stream or demoted to a lower stream. Promotions and demotions are made on the basis of each boy's achievements and attitudes. Over four years, boys who lack the motivation to work hard and behave well are demoted to the lower streams. Thus the boys with negative attitudes and resentment against the system are concentrated together in the lower streams and the development of a group solution is considerably facilitated. In their common environment where they can interact together during the full school day they can explore their common problems and the possibility of a joint delinquent solution is enhanced.

When a delinquent or delinquescent group forms at school, it is within the school itself that the group is most likely to meet regular opposition and attempts at suppression by middle class agents. Out of school the delinquent can avoid such adults, for the degree to which he associates with middle class adults is under voluntary control. He can refuse to join clubs supervised by these adults and low stream Lumley pupils did so. As Downes (6) points out, the delinquent is likely to dissociate himself from middle class institutions since they threaten his self-image, either because he cannot meet their criteria for positive evaluation or because they oppose the emergent delinquent value system.

But as long as the boy is at school, he cannot (except by truancy) avoid and dissociate himself from the middle class teachers. They are an ever present and inescapable reality, however involuntarily the delinquent may come into contact with them. Moreover the enormous power differential between teacher and pupil and the ability of the teacher to invoke sanctions means that in general it is the teacher who decides the rules of the game of life in school — though in practice there is a certain amount of mutual adaptation. At root the situation is one of heads-I-win-tails-you-lose, for the delinquent lacks the qualities and abilities to succeed by becoming the 'good pupil' and his alternative status and value system or desire for withdrawal are regarded by the teachers as illegitimate solutions to his problems.

As part of the solution to his problems the delinquent rejects the pupil role, initially because it represents a role in which he cannot succeed and later because it represents the antithesis of delinquent values and norms. Members of the delinquescent subculture seek to find alternatives to the pupil role and aspire to roles outside the terms of the school. The rejection of the pupil role is accompanied by admiration of and imitation of teenage and adult roles which is expressed in the exaggerated display of aspects of behaviour associated with older teenage and adult status. He rejects school uniform for jeans and long hair, he admires the pop stars who most obviously symbolize the permissive society, he smokes and drinks openly, and dreams of the freedom and independence of life beyond the school.

At the same time the developing delinquent has to come to terms with his life in school. He cannot sustain a continuous open rebellion against the system, for to do so would be to provoke the teachers into calling into force the most severe penalties at their disposal, including corporal punishment. The situation is not so much one of pitched battle but of intermittent skirmishes in which the occasional flouting of the school rules is detected and punished. The delinquent spends much of his time responding to school in terms of a sullen compliance to the rules of the game because although he does not accept or internalize the rules he does fear the sanctions. Such compliance to the rules is regarded as legitimate by delinquescent group members, who do not expect their friends to become martyrs. But from time to time the delinquent will openly flout the rules when apprehension and punishment seem certain and this will command the admiration of his fellows and enhance his peer group status. More commonly the overt expression of the rejection of the system occurs in situations where the probability of severe punishment is relatively low, for example in the class of a teacher with 'weak' discipline. The teachers form a convenient target against which the delinquent can direct his resentment and mobilize the group, as Webb (7) points out. Attempts by the teacher to suppress such behaviour increase the status of the offender and strengthen the cohesion of the group. So the delinquent does not deviate from school norms indiscriminately. Rather he takes a calculated risk. With luck he may be able to express his resentment and rejection with very little personal cost. The occasional severe punishment still remains a small cost relative to the high rewards that have accrued to him in the interim.

When the delinquent complies with the rules, he is still distinguishable from non-delinquents to some degree, since he conforms only to the very minimal requirements of the teacher. This is because his object is to avoid punishment, not to obtain approval. Indeed, compliance is a very dangerous state precisely because if he conforms beyond the minimal requirements he is in danger of receiving some sort of reward from the teacher – who may be intending to encourage the boy. But for the delinquent to receive approval from the teacher is to have his peer group status undermined. This arises only occasionally in practice, partly because the boys learn how to conform minimally without risk of receiving approval, and partly because if a boy mistakenly or accidentally oversteps the minimal requirement, his friends will warn him by 'kidding' him about working too hard or being too friendly with the teachers.

The teacher, whilst he is usually aware that anti-academic boys in high streams are deviant from the group norms, often fails to take adequate account of the fact that academically orientated boys in lower streams are also deviant from group norms. Deviance and conformity are defined in terms of the teacher's own definition of the pupil role, not in terms of peer group values. Because academic low stream boys conform to his expectations, he does not recognize their deviance from the group. To the teacher, it is the high status boys in the low streams who are deviant, yet it is in fact these very boys who are most integrated on a peer group level.

When the teacher rewards boys in high streams for good work or behaviour, he is confirming the dominant values amongst the boys. But when he does this to boys in lower streams, he is confirming the minority norms. In other words, teacher rewards demonstrate the *unification* of teacher and peer group values in high streams; but the same teacher rewards in low streams reveal the *disjunction* between teacher and pupil values. Teacher rewards thus confirm both subcultures, but in the lower streams this is the reverse of what the teacher intends, for by rewarding the deviant academically orientated boy he reinforces the dominant group values. Teacher rewards cannot have their intended effect in low streams at Lumley until the boys as a whole accept the validity of his definition of teacher and pupil roles.

In the academic subculture, because the boys behave in conformity to teacher expectations, and because the two sets of values are consistent, the teacher is able to exert considerable control over the peer group. In the delinquescent subculture, the teachers have little power of social control, because of the conflict which exists between teacher and pupil values. Attempts to change the culture of low streams must thus begin with the conversion of the leaders or high status boys. When teachers regard the high status low stream boys as 'worthless louts' with whom they cannot afford to 'waste time', they are in fact discarding not only these few boys, but also their only means by which group change might be effected.

The implication of this analysis is that there is a real sense in which the school can be regarded as a generating factor of delinquency and this study supports the suggestions of Johnson (8), Bordua (9) and Clegg (10). Research on a single school does not permit wide generalizations but detailed participant-observation studies of schools like Lumley may well expand and substantiate the broader investigation of McDonald (11) and the dramatic work of Power *et al* (12) on the significant role of the school in the generation of delinquency.

1. S. Glueck and E. T. Glueck Unravelling Juvenile Delinquency Boston, Harvard University Press (1950)
2. M. Gold Status Forces in' Delinquent Boys University of Michigan, Institute of Social Research (1963)
3. A. K. Cohen Delinquent Boys: The Culture of the Gang New York, The Free Press (1955)
4. R. A. Cloward and L. E. Ohlin Delinquency and Opportunity: A Theory of Delinquent Gangs London, Routledge & Kegan Paul (1961)
5. G. Rose 'Anomie and Deviation — A Conceptual Framework for Empirical Studies' British Journal of Sociology Vol. 17 (1966) pp. 29-45
6. D. M. Downes The Delinquent Solution London, Routledge & Kegan Paul (1966). See also the previous paper in this section
7. J. Webb 'The Sociology of a School' British Journal of Sociology Vol. 13 (1962) pp. 264-72
8. A. C. Johnson 'Our Schools make Criminals' Journal of Criminal Law and Criminology Vol. 33 (1942) pp. 310-15
9. D. J. Bordua 'Delinquent Subcultures: Sociological Interpretations of Gang Delinquency' Annals of the American Academy of Political and Social Science Vol. 338 (1961) pp. 119-36
10. A. B. Clegg 'Delinquency and Discipline: The Role of the School' Education Vol. 119 (1962) pp. 1239-40
11. L. McDonald Social Class and Delinquency London, Faber & Faber (1969)
12. M. Power, M. R. Alderson, C. M. Phillipson, E. Schoenberg and J. N. Morris 'Delinquent Schools?' London, New Society (19th October 1967). See also the paper by C. M. Phillipson in the final section of this book

Social Action and Subcultural Theories: A Critique
by Robert Witkin

The student who essays for the first time into the field of delinquency in pursuit of the sociological perspective is likely to be embarrassed by riches. However, although sub-cultural theorisation has been dominant in recent years it is increasingly apparent that there are no adequate bases for choosing between the various alternatives available. There is little possibility of eliminating theories by any empirical test because of the difficulty of drawing testable inferences from one theory which are inherently incompatible with the inferences drawn from another. Attempting to adjudicate on the basis of which theory has been more fruitful in terms of empirical research is also unlikely to yield much joy. All of the theoretical perspectives have been heavily researched and we have to admit that empirical findings have tended to confuse rather than illuminate (1). Furthermore, since that empirical evidence which supports one theory does not actually contradict others, the likelihood is that the family of variants on a sub-cultural theme will continue to grow provided that the approach itself remains a fashionable one.

It is hardly surprising, therefore, that in recent years attention has been directed in critical fashion to problems of conceptual clarity, particularly that of delimiting the concept of 'sub-culture' (2). This paper pursues the problem of conceptual clarity by asking questions about the assumptions both analytical and behavioural that are implicit in sub-cultural theories and the consequences that these assumptions have for our entire mode of conceptualising the delinquent process. Far from being confined to sub-cultural theories, the behavioural and analytical assumptions referred to are a generic feature of the sociological perspective as it is reflected in modern sociological theory. They are a feature too of the conceptual architecture of much psychology and anthropology. Research in delinquency has· been carried out within the context of theoretical perspectives formulated at quite a high level of generality. We should not be surprised therefore if this research exposes the inadequacy of certain tenets of our more general theories about human behaviour. Our concern must be to locate the theoretical inadequacies and to modify our approach accordingly.

The 'sociological man' as we understand him today has grown to maturity in a very definite form. He is socialised by means of a process whereby he 'internalises' or 'introjects' a pattern of norms and values which constitutes his cultural environment and he functions within a system of role relationships which, if he is socially adjusted, are compatible with the pattern of culture he has introjected. These two assumptions about the socialisation and functioning of human beings have given rise to a mode of conceptualising the relationship of the individual to his socio-cultural environment that is now so commonplace it is hardly ever questioned. In this paper, however, I am concerned to question this approach and to propose an alternative mode of conceptualising the relationship between the individual and his socio-cultural environment.

Despite his protestations to the contrary, the sociologist's analysis of social action within any particular action context tends to treat the personality, cultural and social systems as if they possessed the same form or structure as each other, variations in one paralleling variations in the other. From the point of view of the action situation therefore, the three systems may be said to be 'isomorphic' with one another. Our sociological man is constructed out of these three sets of variables: he is presented as being in normal health when they are isomorphic and as being in a pathological condition when they are not.

This paper seeks to establish that this sociological treatment of patterns of culture, personality types and social structures as possessing the same organisation and variability, is an inevitable consequence of the almost universal 'pattern introjection' approach to socialisation. It further seeks to argue that this isomorphism is an unintended, even undesired consequence from the point of view of the sociological theorist. This latter point is important because most sociological theorists do insist upon the independent variability of the three sets of variables and, as a rule, note this possibility in their analysis of social action. However, it will be argued that these 'allowances' can only ever have the status of a residual category given the mode of conceptualising social action that is being criticised here. When patterns of norms and values are 'introjected' in personalities and 'institutionalised' in social systems, the basis of independent variability is destroyed. So too, is any possibility of providing an adequate theoretical framework to guide substantive research in real social situations where the problem is to delineate the all important relations obtaining between culture, personality and social systems. Any framework which treats them as isomorphic within the action situation can only hinder the analysis of these relationships. The pattern introjection framework does just this. This paper seeks to make some small contribution to the solution of the problem by proposing an alternative framework preserving the independent variability of the three systems. It will be argued that this way of conceptualising the relationship between them — what I call 'sampling of structure' — overcomes the problems inherent in the prevalent notions of 'introjection' and 'institutionalisation'.

The establishment of independence between three 'systems' — culture, personality and social systems — is considered by Talcott Parsons to be of paramount importance. Writing of the relationship between personality and culture he says:

'Though there is a direct parallel between this classification of value-orientation patterns and the classification of motivational orientations it is very important to be clear that these two basic aspects, or components of the action system are logically independent . . . in the sense that the content under the two classifications may be *independently variable*.' (3)

On the following page Parsons is even more insistent:

'The clear recognition of the independent variability of these two basic modes of orientation is *at the very basis* of a satisfactory theory in the field of "culture and personality". Indeed it can be said that failure to recognise this independent variability has underlain much of the difficulty in this field, particularly *the unstable tendency of much social science to oscillate between "psychological determinism" and "cultural determinism".'* (4)

Two things are necessary if we are to achieve the 'independent variability' of which Parsons speaks. The personality must be described in terms of units that are distinct from, and of themselves neutral, with respect to the units in which social and cultural systems are described. Secondly, processes that are held to relate one system to another must be described in terms of the processes of the variability in one system in relation to the processes of variability in the other. In short, the structure and functioning of each system must be reflected both in the terms chosen to describe each system, (cultural, social, psychological) and in those chosen to relate them one to another. These structures are intended to apply to the relating of systems at different levels of analysis, such as the ones we are concerned with here. Without them it is difficult to see how interdependence can be established on a theoretical level without undermining the basis of independent variability.

If we consider the personality as a system in general action theory we are forced to conclude that neither of the two conditions mentioned above obtains at all. It is important to note we are concerned here only with the personality insofar as it enters sociological theory as a 'system of action'. Psychological theories frequently do go some way towards satisfying the first condition though rarely the second. In view of Parsons' insistence on the need for independent variability, it is instructive to consider his own approach to describing the units of personality. In his pre-war book 'The Structure of Social Action' he states:

'. . . a personality is nothing but the totality of observable unit acts described in their context of relation to a single actor.' (5)

At that time the unit of Parson's social system was also the unit act. In his post-war book 'The Social System' the unit had changed to that of the social role. Speaking of the personality he says:

155

'The system of social relationships in which the actor is involved is not merely of situational significance, but is directly constitutive of the personality itself.' (6)

Personality is described by Parsons *in terms of social system units*. He seems to base his concept of independence on the fact that each individual has a role set that differs in some degree from that of every other individual and also on certain vague references to the 'hereditary basis of personality'. Social structure is not simply related to personality, it is, to use his own phrase, 'constitutive of it'. In 'Family, Socialisation and Interaction Processes' and elsewhere, Parsons does deal with personality on a psychological level and puts forward his own variant of Freud's psychoanalytic theory. His concern, however, is chiefly with the theory of identification and the introjection of cultural patterns. This brings us to the second condition of independent variability, that concerning the relationship between systems. Just as the social system is constitutive of the individual's personality by virtue of his functioning within it, so the cultural system is also constitutive of his personality by virtue of his socialisation into it. The socialisation process is conceived of in terms of the 'internalisation' or 'introjection' of a pattern of culture. Personality is thus the raw material out of which culture fashions behaviour, or what is more extreme but in this case more accurate, the tabula rasa on which culture writes its pattern. Not only are culture and social structure constitutive of personality in Parsons' theory but they are, as a result of this, indistinguishable from one another. Social structure is cultural pattern manifest in the form of an action system, notwithstanding Parsons' attempt with Kroeber to distinguish between the two (7). Because cultural pattern and social structure are each isomorphic with personality, so they are with each other. The link is the personality, the functioning individual. Within the context of Parsons' theory at any rate social structure and cultural pattern are not merely compatible they are isomorphic.

'... the structure of systems of action is conceived as consisting in patterns of normative culture. The ways in which these types of action systems are differentiated, then, means that these patterns may be conceived as internalised in personalities and behavioural organisms, and as institutionalised in social and cultural systems.' (8)

Talcott Parsons has been singled out because his work illustrates the problem so well but in fact it is a general feature of the sociological perspective. The problem is that it is simply not possible to maintain a genuine analytical distinction between personality, culture, and social systems while maintaining assumptions that are completely incompatible with such a distinction. So long as we describe personality in terms of social system units and relate it to culture by means of the concept of

156

pattern introjection our analysis will be confined to one set of variables called by three different names.

The pattern introjection model has been with us for a long time and it! constitutes a deeply ingrained way of thinking about social behaviour. It is a central feature of the social psychology of Weber and Durkheim and it received its most explicit formulation in Freud's theory of the development of the Superego. It has a strong appeal for us as a solution to the problem of social order. Nor does it depend on some unitary notion of introjection or a psychological theory of identification à la Freud. A behaviourist view of personality and culture would lend itself even more to description in terms of pattern introjection. The laws of conditioning would then become the psychological means whereby personality was shaped by cultural pattern. One only has to look at the anthropologists' excursion into the field of personality and culture to find that assumptions about pattern introjection led them to confuse culture with personality (9). Even in the case of the most famous personality study of all, that on 'The Authoritarian Personality' (10), some critics were led to ask whether the co-varying traits constituted a personality at all or whether they were in fact the norms of a lower class sub-culture.

So widespread is the concept of the 'sociological man' as I have outlined him above, that it is not surprising to find him dominating the field of delinquency. Here, as elsewhere, of course, there are signs that researchers are impatient with him to an ever increasing degree. Signs of this impatience appeared in George Homans' 1964 Presidential address to the American Sociological Association (11). The so-called phenomeno-logical revolution has its adherents within the field of delinquency, notably Matza (12) and Becker (13), and it too represents an attempt to bring a real psychological man back into sociology. The psychological component of sub-cultural theories has fallen into disrepute. It consists of an hypothesised 'state of mind' that is the consequence of a breakdown in the isomorphism of the three sets of 'variables' comprising our 'sociological man'. The delinquent sub-culture solves the problem since it is the means whereby isomorphism is restored. This is the case for Cloward and Ohlin (14), and Cohen (15). With Miller (16), the only difference is that deviant behaviour is the product of the isomorphism between lower class social structure, culture and personality. He does not conceive of delinquency as arising from a break in this isomorphism. As a result of the pattern introjection model our 'sociological man' exists psychologically either as the embodiment of a system of roles and a culture pattern or as a state of tension or discomfort reflecting the disjunction between the two. Needless to say his existence is unlikely to be confirmed by empirical research. This theoretical weakness on the psychological level is repeated on the social and cultural levels. Again, because of the isomorphism between social structure and cultural pattern, questions are simply not framed about the independent variability of each and their relationship

157

one to another. Empirical research is unlikely to confirm the existence of our 'sociological man' in his social or cultural guises either. In reality, personality, social and cultural variables interact with each other in such a way that they are rendered mutable and new 'organisations' and the possibility for 'further organisations' are created at each level. This process is a continuing one and whether we locate our 'sociological man' in the garb of a delinquent, an automobile worker or a political boss, isomorphism is precisely the condition we would not expect to find unless it be within the context of an Orwellian nightmare. A sociological description would entail identifying the factors independently determining the structural organisation on each level and analysing the processes of 'constraint' or 'interaction' between the three structural organisations. The point is that a truly sociological description is indeed possible. The writer of this paper explicitly rejects the more fashionable critiques of the sociological perspective which go under various names such as 'phenomenology', 'symbolic interactionism' or 'social behaviourism'. They point out a serious problem concerning the sociological approach in its present form but they are an abdication rather than a solution, and in this case what is clearly psychology's gain is sociology's loss. Even worse is the abandonment of theory altogether in favour of some kind of atheoretical empiricism. It is instructive to note that following similar difficulties within psychology itself, the field was split into an arid and sterile division between an obscurantist phenomenology and an empty empiricism. Some might argue that psychology is only now emerging from this stage and rediscovering its interest in real psychological theory. The choice is the same for the sociologist. If he does not wish to abandon the sociological perspective then he must set about the process of development and modification necessary to put right the ills to which the various 'critiques' are reactions.

A first step in this direction would be to establish a real basis for differentiating on a theoretical level between the systems of personality, culture, and social structure, as three independently variable systems. This is exactly what is perceived to be essential by sociological theorists but it is precisely what they fail to achieve. It is argued here that the 'pattern introjection' approach to socialisation is largely responsible for this. To establish a real basis for independent variability we must endeavour to meet the two conditions stated earlier. The first is that the personality as a system (within sociological theory) must be described in terms of units that are distinct from, and of themselves neutral, with respect to the units in which social and cultural systems are described. It is important to stress that what we are concerned with here is the personality as it is of interest to the sociologist. Unlike the psychologist he is concerned with it only in so far as it enters into relationship with culture and social structure. A psychological description of personality is therefore sociologically inappropriate if the focus around which such a description is organised is purely

158

psychological. While it is quite beyond the scope of this paper to develop a concept of personality as it is called for here, a few highly tentative suggestions may be in order even at this stage. An extraordinarily useful concept from the point of view of the social psychologist is that of the 'attitude'. Unfortunately many writers treat the attitude concept as a lesser cousin to the cultural term 'value'. It is maintained here however that this is an entirely unhelpful procedure. Cultural terms, properly considered in abstraction comprise systems of rules. An attitude is not a rule. It is a disposition to function in a given way in respect of some 'object'. 'Disposition' in this sense is fully psychological in that it is an hypothetical construct used to describe the behavioural 'tendency' or 'posture' of an individual actor in relation to an object and is compounded of those aspects of the cognitive and motivational organisation of the individual which are the concern of the psychologist. It is more appropriate to say that one holds an attitude towards a value than to say simply that one holds a value. Even then an individual's attitude towards a value does not tell the whole story by any means. I may hold an extremely positive attitude towards honesty, deeming it to be the highest virtue, and at the same time hold dishonest attitudes in respect of all kinds of objects. The prisoners of San Quentin who comprised a part of the sample used in the Authoritarian Personality Study held positive attitudes towards values associated with obligations to parents, authority and society which were certainly not reflected in their attitudes defining their relationship to the world of social objects. Attitudes in this latter context are the determinants of behaviour in social systems in the immediate sense although they themselves are of course modified by attitudes held towards cultural objects. The process of modification between the two types of attitudes, those held in respect of cultural items and those held in respect of social objects, is a reciprocal one, although the extent to which they are consistent with one another is entirely problematical as was observed in the case of the San Quentin prisoners and also, incidentally, in a number of studies of delinquents (17). An attitude is an ideal unit with which the sociologist can describe the personality system as it is of concern to him. As a 'disposition' it is psychologically real and at the same time it is a relational term in that it is a statement of relationship between individuals as functioning units on the one hand and items of culture and social objects on the other. It is with what may be loosely termed the sociological end of the attitude construct rather than the psychological end that we are here concerned. It is the attitude as a relational term. In its structural aspect then, the personality is a system of attitudes (from the sociological point of view). Its mode of functioning is the establishing and organising of attitudes towards cultural and social objects. New organisations occur in so far as there is a basis for them within older organisations. The socialisation process is not the introjection of cultural patterns by the individual but *the process whereby certain organisations of attitudes are rendered more adaptive than others*, in the psychological sense. The stress here is on the word 'organisations'. Many differing organisations of attitudes are viable or adaptive in a given social situation. All that is required of such organisations is that, taken as a whole, they promote the proper functioning of the individual within the social contexts in which he acts. Whether or not particular attitudes towards cultural items or social objects are viable or adaptive is a matter of whether their inclusion within a given organisation of attitudes renders the individual's behaviour non-adaptive. Organisations of attitudes are able to tolerate quite wide variations as to the 'members' included in their composition. As systems they undergo compensatory changes which serve to maintain their level of adaption. Individuals hold all kinds of attitudes towards social objects and cultural items which are irrelevant or even negative with respect to the social situations in which they act. Provided that these are compensated for, within their organisation of attitudes, by the presence of attitudes that are positive with respect to the social situations in which they act, these organisations, so variable between individuals, will nevertheless be adaptive. However unlikely, provided the delinquent's physical prowess is established beyond doubt, there is no reason why he should not attend poetry readings; under certain circumstances it might even enhance his 'rep'.

The task of the sociologist is to analyse the components of the action situation. These are the product of the interaction between the three systems, personality, culture and social structure. To fulfil the second of the two conditions mentioned earlier, this interaction must be described by relating the processes of variability in one system to the processes of variability in the other. It is suggested here that it will be helpful to conceive of these processes in a particular kind of way. If we take two of the systems, culture and personality for example, then one can conceive of their contribution to the action situation in the following manner: the pattern of culture "partakes" of the attitudes of an individual in an entirely selective manner. Its particular organisation makes certain 'demands' in terms of attitudes. The culture pattern may be said to 'sample the structure' of the culture pattern. The product is a particular not exhaust the culture pattern. Its particular organisation makes certain 'demands' in terms of cultural items. The personality may be said to 'sample the structure' of the personality. Similarly the personality does organisation of attitudes/values that is inevitably very different from the cultural pattern and the personality system. Furthermore, there are qualitatively and quantitatively many different combinations of values/attitudes making up this organisation which constitutes the action situation. For each individual a different combination will provide the same level of adaptation in a common situation. Thus an individual with one type of organisation of attitudes may require to sample a great deal more of a particular culture pattern, or one part as opposed to another,

160

than an individual with a different organisation of attitudes *in order to achieve the same level of adaptation within the same situation*. If the third term is added, that of social structure, the components of the action situation are capable of full description. The relationship between social structure and the other two systems is the same as their relationship to one another. That is to say, the social system may be regarded as 'sampling the structure' of the personality system and vice versa, and as 'sampling the structure' of the cultural pattern and vice versa. The action situation is thus the emergent of the interaction between the three systems and is never a reflection of any one of them. Still less is it the reflection of a single system (usually cultural) masquerading as three different systems. The individual in relation to the socialisation process must be seen in a radically different way. He is not some kind of 'sponge' for social values or a repository for a cultural pattern. His relationship to social reality is essentially a creative one. Within the basic socialisation agencies, the family and the school, etc., he is placed in situations where some organisations of attitudes towards cultural items and social objects are more adaptive than others. Within the action situation itself we discover the real 'sociological man'. He is the composite reality of attitudes/values/roles emerging from the reciprocal sampling of personality on culture on social structure. Analysing the constraints on that sampling process and the action situation is the task of the sociologist when he confronts a social phenomenon which he intends to investigate.

The situation of delinquency, which is the 'sociological man' with which this book is chiefly concerned, could not (within the context of the view presented here) be described in terms of a 'sub-culture'. To analyse the situation of delinquency we would require to delineate both the 'sub-structure' and the personality system and develop a theory of the process of sampling of one structure on another. We would also need to isolate the determinants of 'sub-structures' and 'sub-cultures' within the context of the wider system. It may well be that the social and cultural determinants of 'sub-cultures' (i.e. cultural patterns) are relatively independent of the determinants of 'sub-structures' (i.e. gangs, cliques, near-groups). Perhaps some of the English findings that contradict or are inconsistent with American perspectives may be due to the fact that the determinants of 'sub-structures' are different in England. Even if the gang is a sub-structural form that is not found in England (in the American sense), this need not mean that the cultural patterns generated among delinquents are essentially different to their American counterparts. They probably are (for quite different reasons), but the point is that *whether this is true or not*, the situation of delinquency would still be different because in the process of sampling structure on structure the 'emergent' would be the product of inter-action between three systems, one of which was initially different (namely the sub-structure). It is not difficult to see how, using a framework of this kind, it should be possible to develop a theory of

161

delinquent and non-delinquent situations of action, emerging from the generation of particular social structures, culture patterns and personalities, and from the reciprocal sampling of personality on culture on social structure.

It has been argued throughout this paper that the 'sociological man' that has developed within sociological theory is a pattern of culture internalised in a personality and institutionalised in a social system. He bestrides the entire discipline and is very much in evidence in the field of delinquency. The widespread acceptance of what I have called the pattern introjection view of the socialisation process is responsible for this. Disillusionment with the sociological perspective has grown with the failure of substantive sociology to confirm the existence of this 'sociological man' while at the same time the phenomenologists are busy trying to free him from his cultural straight-jacket. This paper has taken a different approach. It has argued that the solution to the problem cannot lie in an abdication of the sociological perspectives in favour of some psychological approach. It must lie within sociology itself. It has been suggested here that if the bases for independent variability of the three systems of action can be satisfactorily established on a theoretical level and the processes of interaction between them analysed, then a 'sociological man' of real use in empirical research can emerge. It is to this end that the tentative suggestions concerning the organisation of the personality as a system of attitudes and the process of 'sampling of structure' have been put forward. Our perennial problem in social science is that anything that is inherently testable is usually not worth knowing and anything that is really worth knowing is usually untestable. Pure empiricism leads so frequently to the testing of the inconsequential and phenomenology so often makes consequential but unverifiable statements, that the best hope for progress within the discipline lies in the development of adequate sociological theory guiding substantive research.

1. J. F. Short and F. L. Strodbeck Group Processes and Gang Delinquency Chicago, University of Chicago Press (1966)
2. M. Yinger 'Contraculture and Subculture' American Sociological Review 25 (5) (1960) pp. 625-35
3. Talcott Parsons The Social System New York, Free Press (1951) p. 14
4. Ibid. p. 15
5. Talcott Parsons The Structure of Social Action New York, McGraw Hill (1937) p. 746
6. Talcott Parsons The Social System New York, Free Press (1951) p. 17
7. Talcott Parsons and A. L. Kroeber 'The Concepts of Culture and Social System' American Sociological Review 23 (1958) pp. 582-83
8. Talcott Parsons 'Pattern Variables Revisited: A Response to Robert Dubin' American Sociological Review 25 (1960) pp. 467-83
9. M. Singer 'A Summary of Culture and Personality Theory and Research' in B.

Kaplan (ed) <u>Studying Personality Cross-Culturally</u> Evanston, Row Peterson (1961)
10. H. H. Hyman and P. B. Sheatsley 'The Authoritarian Personality: a Methodological Critique' in R. Christie and M. Jahoda (eds) <u>Studies in the Scope and Method of the Authoritarian Personality</u> New York, Free Press (1954)
11. George C. Homans 'Bringing Men Back' <u>American Sociological Review 29</u> (1964) pp. 809-18
12. David Matza <u>Delinquency and Drift</u> New York, John Wiley (1964)
13. H. S. Becker <u>Outsiders</u> New York, Free Press (1964)
14. R. A. Cloward and L. E. Ohlin <u>Delinquency and Opportunity</u> New York, Free Press (1960)
15. A. Cohen <u>Delinquent Boys</u> New York, Free Press (1955)
16. W. B. Miller 'Lower Class Culture as a Generating Milieu of Gang Delinquency' <u>Journal of Social Issues 14</u> (1958) pp. 5-19
17. J. F. Short and F. L. Strodbeck op. cit.

C: Crime, Delinquency and Control

Introduction

Most modern British criminologists would probably accept the philosophical proposition that different effects have different causes. Not surprisingly, therefore, many of them adhere — at least implicitly — to the view that criminals and delinquents must differ distinctively from their law-abiding fellows in other respects than their behaviour. Based on this assumption, many contemporary investigations into the causes of crime and delinquency are aimed at identifying the characteristics that distinguish the offending population and, more difficult, at isolating those which play some causal role in the emergence of unacceptable conduct. The result is probably as well-known as it is baffling to many students: a plethora of conflicting theories has emerged, attaching aetiological significance to a wide variety of factors ranging from the individual's position in the social and cultural structure, through his family background and childhood experience, to his neurological functioning and genetic composition.

Arguable, or indeed defensible as the assumption underlying this approach to crime and delinquency may be, protracted discussion of its merit is not the purpose of this concluding section. Rather, we are here concerned with one of its more important side-effects, namely, the curiously attenuated view of formal social control that has resulted from this emphasis upon the investigation and analysis of offenders and their backgrounds. This is not to say, of course, that British criminologists have totally ignored society's formal provisions for dealing with its law-breakers — a substantial literature about methods of reasserting control through punishment and treatment testifies to the contrary. But as far as the causes of crime and delinquency are concerned, we have been slow to recognise the full significance of such provisions. Acknowledging the existence of doubts about the reliability of statistics collected by agencies such as the police, we have shied away from admitting the full extent to which the facts upon which we base our theories may be consistently distorted; conceding that crime is defined by law, we have hesitated to admit that legislation could be consistently selective in the kind of person that it designates as criminal; believing that treatment, if not punishment can

164

have some effect upon offenders, we have been reluctant to recognise that the consistent impact of formal social control could be anything other than good at its best or inconsequential at its worst.

Inevitably, there have always been some researchers who do not conform to this caricature of the British criminologist, and in recent years the number of such dissenters has been swollen by the addition of those sociologists who espouse what is usually referred to as an 'interactionist' perspective (1). Dissatisfied with many aspects of our traditional approach to deviance in general, those of the latter persuasion see the analysis of formal social control and of the offender's interaction with its agents as an indispensible part of any adequate description or explanation of deviant careers. As with all antidotes, there is here, of course, a remote danger of administering too much and thus arriving at a position which proclaims society's reaction to crime and delinquency as the only significant variable. But even among the critics of this perspective there can be few who really believe that this is what its adherents intend, and among the latter themselves, there are even fewer who would maintain such an extreme position (2). Rather, in common with traditional sceptics and with other sociologists intent upon reviving the sociology of law as a criminologically relevant discipline, the objective is merely to redress the balance after a century of investigation dominated by the uncompromising axiom that justice should study men rather than men study justice. This section brings together a number of papers representing the interactionist and other points of view which agree on the benefits that might accrue to our understanding of crime and delinquency from a better understanding of formal social control.

Criminological theory, like any other, must ultimately be consistent with the parameters of the phenomena that it studies. Theories about the causes of crime and delinquency must, in other words, fit the facts. It is in gauging the reliability of these very facts, however, that criminology confronts one of its most acute problems. Apart from findings based upon the use of self-reporting techniques, nearly all of the known or ascertainable facts about criminals and delinquents relate solely to those who have been apprehended, prosecuted and convicted. Comprising an unknown proportion of all offenders, these are the 'official' law-breakers in the sense that they have been designated as such by the formal agents of social control. In the same sense, the facts derived from studying them are also 'official', being generated through a joint, though not necessarily cooperative enterprise involving the offender, himself, and those who report, arrest, prosecute and convict him. All of the latter outcomes and the concomitant ascription of 'official' status are things which may or may not happen. They are contingencies in which society's reaction to illegal behaviour, from the unorganised response of the casual witness to the

165

more highly organised activities of bodies such as the police, plays no small part. Indeed, Goffman's comment about mental illness might be said to be at least equally true of crime and delinquency:

> '... in the degree that the "mentally ill" outside hospitals numerically approach or surpass those inside hospitals, one could say that mental patients distinctively suffer, not from mental illness but from contingencies.' (3)

If these contingencies were known to be random and constant, the ramifications for theoretical criminology would not be particularly far-reaching. The official rates of phenomena such as crime could safely be utilised in the construction of macro-sociological theories based on comparative analysis, and hypotheses postulating a radical aetiological differentiation between offenders and non-offenders could be tested by extrapolation from the official facts. Unfortunately, however, there is an abundance of evidence, particularly American, to indicate that such an assumption is both ill-founded and dangerous. The work of Douglas, Kitsuse, Cicourel, Skolnick and Sudnow — to name but a few of the better-known authorities on this subject — suggests that in addition to the obvious possibility of systematic variation in the reporting of offences, the way in which officials such as policemen, lawyers and social workers set about their routine tasks has an effect that is anything but random (4). Heavily dependant upon shared assumptions about the meaning of signs and events that are encountered, the implicit logic utilised by these decision-makers in arriving at appropriate modes of action plays a crucial role not only in generating but also in shaping the official pattern of crime and delinquency (5). From the offender's point of view, conviction is not only a contingency but also one which is systematically affected, at least to some extent, by the patterned beliefs and the organised activities of the agents of control. From the criminological perspective, these same systematic influences must call into question the use which may legitimately be made of official statistics in any theoretical context.

Although, as Paul Wiles points out in the first paper in this section, the existence of defects in the official statistics has long been recognised by criminologists in Britain as elsewhere, the theoretical implications of this situation often receive nothing more than cursory attention. While most of us, if pressed, would concede that the ostensible age-distribution of drug offenders or, indeed, the social class distribution of thieves could conceivably emanate from selective social control as much as from any particular propensity towards these offences on the part of certain groups, we nonetheless persist in attempting to use these official parameters as measuring rods for our theories. Conversely, we fail to pursue the logic of our own misgivings to the point where we admit that any theory of official crime which does not take account of the part played by formal social

166

control is at best incomplete and at worst totally misleading. The same point has been cogently expressed by Cicourel in relation to juvenile delinquency:

'Law-enforcement officials, statisticians attached to rate producing agencies, criminologists and sociologists have long known and commented on official statistics as misleading. Many corrections and refinements have been suggested and used. But regardless of whether corrections have been used, the official statistics are utilised nevertheless as indicators of the prevalence and significance of delinquency, and the net result has always been to use the findings (the "social facts") as documenting the theoretical position derived from commonsense or lay conceptions. An understanding of how official statistics are assembled informs the researcher as to how "delinquents" are produced by the socially organised and socially sanctioned activities of members of the community and representatives of law-enforcement agencies.' (6)

The theoretical framework most frequently utilised in investigating how criminals and delinquents are produced in Cicourel's sense is one which, as Wiles observes, places great emphasis on how individuals construct and in constructing, transform reality. Moreover, it is one which poses considerable methodological problems since appreciation of the officials' 'logic in use' ideally requires that the observer should get very close to the process of law-enforcement as it is happening, without himself transforming the reality of what takes place, How the sociological sophisticate can successfully immerse himself in the processes which he is studying and, at the same time, present them unviolated by his own frame of reference is thus a continuing problem in this kind of research (7).

These difficulties apart, however, there is in the present context another danger of at least equal significance, namely, that being absorbed in describing the systematic variation in formal social control from such close quarters, we may neglect the existence and indeed the impact of broader structural determinants. Nowhere is the possibility of systematic variation at this higher level more apparent than in the contrast between the enforcement of 'ordinary' criminal laws and society's response to what is usually called 'white-collar crime'. Focussing on those laws and other regulations which relate primarily or exclusively to white-collar groups and particularly to their occupational behaviour (8), this field is one which reflects some of the major structural differentiations in an industrialised society. As Aubert has pointed out, its theoretical significance lies in the fact that it is 'one of those phenomena which are particularly sensitive to — and therefore highly symptomatic of — more pervasive and generalisable features of the social structure' (9). If, as seems probable (10), the enforcement of these socially circumscribed laws and regulations is characterised by what the same author describes as 'slow, inefficient and highly differential implementation' (11), then the systematic variation in contingent control takes on a much broader dimension. The crude theoretical ramifications of such selectivity on the grand scale remain as relevant today as they were more than twenty years ago when Edwin Sutherland first pointed them out:

'Much more important is the bias involved in the administration of criminal justice under laws which apply exclusively to business and the professions and which therefore involve only the upper socio-economic class. . . . The sample of criminal behaviour on which the (criminological) theories are founded is biased as to socio-economic status, since it excludes these business and professional men. This bias is quite as certain as it would be if the scholars selected only red-haired criminals for study and reached the conclusion that redness of hair was the cause of crime.' (12)

The second paper in this section deals with the occupational behaviour and with the formal control of one extremely important white-collar group, that comprising the owners and occupiers of industrial premises. Here, where the legislation in question is explicitly criminal, the pattern which emerges is consistent with predictions derived from the theory of white-collar crime. While the amount of violation known to the relevant authorities is substantial, to say the least, prosecution is so infrequent that offenders might understandably deem it a contingency unworthy of consideration. True, there was nothing to suggest that this pattern of differential enforcement emanated from a conscious bias in favour of the upper socio-economic classes on the part of the officials involved; but in terms of outcomes rather than causes, this does not invalidate the conclusion that factory-occupiers are grossly under-represented in our population of officially defined offenders. Nor, indeed, does it preclude the possibility that some historical significance attaches to such a bias.

Examination of the enforcement of explicitly criminal laws does not, however, exhaust the potential contribution that the study of white-collar crime can make to our understanding of how contingent control may be differentially distributed throughout the social structure. There remains a further and no less significant possibility that the role-specific behaviour of white-collar groups is systematically more immune from criminal legislation, itself. Ironically, as the paper on white-collar crime suggests, the realisation of this was probably one of Sutherland's most perceptive insights into the nature of crime, even if the prevailing emphasis upon the study of the criminal diverted him from developing its full theoretical significance. Historically, his popularisation of the notion that substantial areas of criminal behaviour cannot be explained by factors such as poverty may well be overshadowed by his less intentional contribution to the development of the idea that crime cannot be understood in isolation from the sociology of law. Viewed within this framework, the skewed class distribution of 'official' criminals and delinquents might arise as much from differential law-making as from anything else. As Hermann Mannheim has observed, 'the history of criminal legislation in England and many other countries, shows that excessive prominence was given by the law to the protection of property against comparatively minor depredations, which of course means that the types of offences likely to be committed by members of the lower social classes figure more predominantly than others in criminal statutes and, therefore, also in the criminal courts and criminal statistics' (13).

This extension of the idea of contingent control to include differential legislation as well as law-enforcement need not be restricted, of course, to analysis based on social class. Inevitably, however, it does involve the criminologist in examining political processes and their relationship to social structure (14). This is an approach that sometimes excites adverse comment from those who assume that criminological analysis of such processes must involve some ideological stance while, paradoxically, to leave them unscrutinised does not. These ill-founded fears apart however, it is apparent that our understanding of crime as distinct from criminal behaviour can benefit from this kind of analysis (15). As even the most legalistically minded criminologist must concede, no mode of criminal conduct derives its essential criminality from any source other than the law, and if this is so, the study of how this legal definition is conferred comes to be an integral part of a discipline which purports to study crime:

'The absence of precise causal knowledge of many social phenomena is one of the reasons why the study of social correlations results in rather negative or indeterminate statements. Especially in criminology, where knowledge of the factors correlated with crime is essential, ... without a scientific knowledge of legal behaviour and of its factors, scientific statements concerning the genesis of crime are almost impossible.' (16)

Acknowledged as crucial by the authors of several eminent textbooks (17) and central to more than one currently popular perspective on crime (18), the study of legislative processes also, of course, concerns the sociologist of law. Indeed, the above statement about the criminological relevance of legal behaviour was taken from one of the pioneers in the latter field. From this tradition too, comes the paper which W. J. Chambliss has contributed to this section, relating the emergence and development of the law on vagrancy to structural changes over several centuries and, more specifically, to the interplay of status groups and vested interests. From this paper we not only obtain an interesting insight into the legislative background of what was once the crime that caused this country more concern than any other, but also into the benefits which might accrue to criminology from a revival of interest in the mainstream of sociological thinking about law rather than about the law-breaker.

Thus far, the main thrust of the argument in this section has been that the 'official' facts of crime and delinquency must frequently be treated as variables which may be dependent upon organisational and legislative processes. We come now to consideration of the direct impact which formal social control may have upon the groups and individuals with whom it deals. More specifically, we come to the controversial possibility that society's formal reaction to crime and delinquency may often play a dynamic role in sustaining and, indeed, in exacerbating the very phenomena it purports to control.

The theoretical perspective from which this somewhat paradoxical hypothesis emerges is one which sees the individual's concept of himself as an important part of his symbolic world and as a crucial component in his organisation of and motivation towards roles (19). The mental dialogue involved in thus viewing himself as object enables the individual to direct as well as to control his behaviour; indeed, the primary function of the latter may often be that of 'affirming in the language of gesture and deed, that one is a certain kind of person' (20). Arriving at this self-reflective definition as 'a certain kind of person' is not, however, something that occurs in complete isolation from social determinants. Rather, through an ability to take the role of others, or in C. H. Cooley's language, to imagine the effect of our reflection upon another's mind (21), it becomes a process which ultimately involves the incorporation of perspectives held by other people. The concept of self is socially anchored:

'There is a common attitude, that is, one which all assume under certain habitual situations. Through the use of language, through the use of the significant symbol, . . . the individual does take the attitude of others, especially (these) common attitudes, so that he finds himself taking the same attitude toward himself that the community takes.' (22)

Thus, when society reacts in a punitive and stigmatising fashion to offenders, this may lead them to redefine themselves as invidiously different (23). Negative evaluation by the community may accelerate commitment to criminal or delinquent roles.

Sociological investigation of these subjective processes arising out of formal social control can, however, lead to misunderstandings. In particular, it involves an appreciation of events as they appear to the people concerned, and in empathising to this extent, researchers may run the risk of seeming too closely identified with the groups they are studying. Indeed, some such suspicion may well be in the minds of those who charge that the adherents of this perspective sometimes come close to

170

laying the blame for crime, delinquency and deviance solely at the feet of the agents of control (24). Whatever its origins, however, this accusation does seem to involve a fairly basic misinterpretation. For there is no question here of simply replacing one uni-directional model of causation with another, nor indeed, of merely formulating a theory which is different but which, in the words of Albert Cohen, is still couched 'in terms of variables that describe initial states, on the one hand, and outcomes on the other' (25). Rather, the emphasis is upon the ongoing process of becoming deviant, delinquent of criminal — a process in which 'all causes do not operate at the same time' (26), and one in which community reaction may play a progressively more significant but not a totally exclusive part. Even the strongest and most systematic statement of this part, E. M. Lemert's formulation of 'secondary deviation' (27), still alludes to 'original' as well as 'effective' causes:

> 'Primary deviation is assumed to arise in a wide variety of social, cultural, and psychological contexts, and at best has only marginal implications for the psychic structure of the individual; it does not lead to symbolic reorganisation at the level of self-regarding attitudes and social roles. Secondary deviation is deviant behaviour, or social roles based upon it, which becomes means of defense, attack, or adaptation to the overt and covert problems created by the societal reaction to primary deviation. In effect, the original "causes" of the deviation recede and give way to the central importance of the disapproving, degradational, and isolating reactions of society.' (28)

This section concludes with three contributions underlining the relevance of the above perspective for British criminology. In the first of these, we reprint L. T. Wilkins' well-known formulation of the 'deviance-amplifying system'. In this model of the interaction between deviance and control, a small initial stimulus originating on either side can generate a disproportionate impetus towards non-conformity as a result of the constant feed-back between public definitions, self-perception and deviant behaviour. It is ironic that writing over half a decade ago, Wilkins should have chosen the possible effects of any attempt to tighten up our drugs regulations as a hypothetical example of how increased control might exacerbate the problem.

Using Wilkins' model and a number of concepts derived from the wider 'transactionalist' tradition, Stanley Cohen's paper on 'Mods and Rockers' provides an interesting case-study in community reactions to juvenile delinquency. More specifically, it shows how generalised beliefs about such social phenomena may sensitize the community to relatively insignificant events and may legitimate escalation in the methods of control adopted by the relevant authorities. Careful to acknowledge the limitations of his perspective, the author successfully justifies his conclusion that, at the

171

very least, the behaviour in question did not develop independently of the reaction it provoked.

Finally, in an original contribution prepared for this book, C. M. Phillipson examines delinquency in the setting of the school. Here, in a social context which has hitherto received relatively little attention from students of 'labelling' processes, the author sees social typing and stigmatisation playing a crucial role in the development of a delinquent self-concept and, more generally, in the emergence of differential rates of delinquency between schools. An important complement to the material on the school which was presented in the preceding section, this paper underlines the need to include agencies other than the most obvious ones in our analysis of the interaction between offenders and formal social control.

1. Usually referred to more fully as 'symbolic interactionism', this perspective has generated a substantial literature which cannot be listed in full. Useful selections may be found however in the following books: H. S. Becker Outsiders New York, Free Press (1963), H. S. Becker The Other Side New York, Free Press (1964); E. Rubington and M. S. Weinberg Deviance: The Interactionist Perspective New York, Macmillan (1968); J. G. Manis and B. N. Meltzer Symbolic Interaction: A Reader in Social Psychology Boston, Allyn & Bacon (1968) and Arnold M. Rose Human Behaviour and Social Processes: An Interactionist Approach London, Routledge & Kegan Paul (1962). For a selection of British work that views deviance from this perspective see S. Cohen (ed) Deviants and Others London, Penguin (forthcoming)

2. For criticisms of this extreme order see J. P. Gibbs 'Conceptions of Deviant Behaviour: The Old and the New' Pacific Sociological Review 9 (1) (Spring 1966) pp. 9-14 and R. L. Akers 'Problems in the Sociology of Deviance: Social Definitions and Behaviour' Journal of Social Forces 47 (1968). For a more balanced view see Edwin Schur 'Reactions to Deviance: A Critical Assessment' American Journal of Sociology 75 (1969) pp. 309-322

3. E. Goffman Asylums: Essays on the Social Situation of Mental Patients and Other Inmates London, Penguin (1968) p. 126

4. J. D. Douglas The Social Meanings of Suicide Princeton, Princeton University Press (1967); A. V. Cicourel The Social Organisation of Juvenile Justice New York, John Wiley (1968); J. H. Skolnick Justice Without Trial New York, John Wiley (1967); A. V. Cicourel and John I. Kitsuse 'A Note on the Use of Official Statistics' Social Problems 11 (Fall 1963) pp. 131-139; D. Sudnow 'Normal Crimes: Sociological Features of the Penal Code' Social Problems 12 (Winter 1965) pp. 255-276

5. One of the best examples of how this happens is described in I. Piliavin and S. Briar 'Police Encounters with Juveniles' American Journal of Sociology 69 (September 1964) pp. 206-214. For an example of a similar effect in another area of law-enforcement see W. G. Carson 'Some Sociological Aspects of Strict Liability and the Enforcement of Factory Legislation' Modern Law Review 33 (4) (July 1970) pp. 396-412

6. A. V. Cicourel Op. Cit. p. 27

7. For the problems involved in this kind of 'ethnomethodology' see H. Garfinkel Studies in Ethnomethodology Englewood Cliffs, Prentice-Hall (1967) and A. Schutz Collected Papers 1: The Problem of Social Reality The Hague, Martinus Nijhoff (1967)

8. H. L. Ross has proposed that this emphasis on occupational behaviour and white-collar status is misplaced. Along with traffic law violations he would define white-collar crime as a sub-species of folk crime — 'violations of laws that are introduced to regulate the novel kinds of behaviour that an increasingly advanced technology and an increasing division of labour generate.' H. L. Ross 'Traffic Law Violation: A Folk Crime' Social Problems 8 (3) (Winter 1960-61) pp. 231-240

9. V. Aubert 'White Collar Crime and Social Structure' American Journal of Sociology 58 (November 1952) pp. 263-71

10. See, for example, E. H. Sutherland White Collar Crime New York, Holt, Rinehart & Winston (1949); D. R. Cressey 'The Criminal Violation of Financial Trust' American Sociological Review 15 (1950) pp. 738-43; M. B. Clinard 'Criminological Theories of Violations of Wartime Regulations' American Sociological Review 11 (1946) pp. 258-70 and F. E. Hartung 'White-Collar Offences in the Wholesale Meat Industry in Detroit' American Journal of Sociology 56 (1950) pp. 25-34

11. V. Aubert Op. Cit. p. 265

12. E. H. Sutherland Op. Cit. p. 8. See also his earlier papers 'White Collar Criminality' American Sociological Review 5 (February 1940) pp. 1-12 and 'Is "White Collar Crime" Crime?' American Sociological Review 10 (1945) pp. 132-139

13. H. Mannheim Comparative Criminology Vol. 2 London, Routledge & Kegan Paul (1965) p. 460. See also P. Wolf 'Crime and Social Class in Denmark' British Journal of Criminology 3 (1) (July 1962) pp. 5-17

14. For a general discussion of the need to examine crime in its political context see R. Quinney 'Crime in Political Perspective' American Behavioral Scientist 8 (1964) pp. 19-22. Donald Newman has also pointed out that, as far as white-collar crime is concerned, the researcher 'must be able to cast his analysis not only in terms of those who break laws but in the context of those who make laws as well.' D. Newman 'White Collar Crime' Law and Contemporary Problems 23 (1958) pp. 735-753

15. See C. R. Jeffery 'The Structure of American Criminological Thinking' Journal of Criminal Law, Criminology and Police Science 46 (1956) pp. 658-672. C. R. Jeffery 'An Integrated Theory of Crime and Criminal Behaviour' Journal of Criminal Law, Criminology and Police Science 49 (1958-59) pp. 533-552. For a discussion of the wider issue of value free sociology see J. Douglas (ed) The Relevance of Sociology New York, Appleton-Century-Crofts (1970)

16. N. S. Timasheff 'What is "Sociology of Law"?' American Journal of Sociology 43 (1937) pp. 225-235

17. See, for example, E. H. Sutherland and D. R. Cressey Principles of Criminology (Sixth Edition) Chicago, Lippincott (1960) p. 3. George Vold Theoretical Criminology New York, Oxford University Press (1958) p. vi. H. Mannheim Op. Cit. Vol. 1. p. 14

18. The need for explanation on this level is implicit, of course, in the interactionist perspective which regards the social audience as a 'critical variable' in the study of deviance. See K. T. Erickson 'Notes on the Sociology of Deviance' in H. S. Becker The Other Side New York, Free Press (1964) pp. 9-21. It is also central to the conflict perspective on crime, see, A. T. Turk Criminality and Legal Order Chicago, Rand McNally (1969)

19. See footnote 1. Other books of importance in this context are: G. H. Mead Mind, Self and Society Chicago, University of Chicago Press (1934); Anselm Strauss George Herbert Mead on Social Psychology Chicago, Phoenix Books (1964); C. H. Cooley Human Nature and the Social Order New York, Charles Scribner's (1902); C. Gordon and K. J. Gergen The Self in Social Interaction Vol. 1, New York, John Wiley (1968); E. Goffman The Presentation of Self in Everyday Life New York, Doubleday (1959) and E. Goffman Stigma London, Penguin (1968)

173

20. A. Cohen 'The Sociology of the Deviant Act: Anomie Theory and Beyond' American Sociological Review 30 (1965) p. 13
21. C. H. Cooley Op. Cit. p. 183 ff
22. Anselm Strauss Op. Cit. p. 35. Edwin Schur emphasises the same point: 'The self-conceptions of the deviating individual should be considered a crucial dependent variable, to which we should pay more attention than to the deviating behaviour itself.' Op. Cit. p. 311.
23. See E. Goffman Stigma London, Penguin (1968); H. Garfinkel 'Conditions of Successful Degradation Ceremonies' American Journal of Sociology 61 (1956) pp. 420-424; A. Strauss 'Transformations of Identity' in Arnold Rose Op. Cit.; E. M. Lemert Social Pathology New York, McGraw Hill (1951) and E. M. Lemert Human Deviance, Social Problems and Social Control Englewood Cliffs, Prentice-Hall (1967)
24. R. Akers Op. Cit.
25. A. Cohen Op. Cit. p. 9
26. H. S. Becker Outsiders New York, Free Press (1963) p. 23
27. E. M. Lemert Human Deviance, Social Problems and Social Control Englewood Cliffs, Prentice-Hall (1967) Chap. 3
28. Ibid. p. 17

Criminal Statistics and Sociological Explanations of Crime.
by Paul Wiles (1)

1. The Historical Development of the Collection of Social Statistics about Crime in England

The idea of experimental reasoning was being tentatively applied to the examination of social problems in England as early as the seventeenth century. Probably the best known work in this context was that of William Petty (1623–1685) and John Graunt (1620–1674) both of whom suggested the collection of social statistical data and carried out analyses of the early bills of mortality. In his sketches of the kind of data that should be collected, Petty mentions statistics of crime and suggests that they might help in the making of policy decisions and in judging the 'moral health' of the nation:

'By the number of Decrees, Verdicts and Judgements in all courts, to know the number of Judges and Lawyers necessary. And by the number of writs and bills to know who is vexatious.

By the number of people, the quality of inebriating liquors spent, the number of unmaryed persons of between 15 and 55 yeares old, the number of Corporall sufferings and persons imprisoned for Crimes, to know the measure of Vice and Sin in the Nation.' (2)

In his plan for 'Mercurius Londinensis' — a statistical gazette — he further

174

suggests that the monthly figures of those 'committed to Prison: for debt, crimes, small matters and Tryalls at Law' should be included. But while he saw the possibility of using statistical data as a guide to policy making, he also realised that at that time the means of collecting such data were inadequate:

'The method I take to do this [to improve the lot of England] is not yet very useful; for instead of using only comparative and superlative Words, and intellectual arguments I have taken the course [as a specimen of the Political Arithmetic I have long aimed at] to express myself in Terms of *Numbers, Weights*, or measures; to use only Arguments of Sense, and to Consider only such Causes, as have visible Foundations in Nature; leaving those that depend on the mutable Minds, opinions, Appetites and Passions of particular Men, to the Consideration of other. . .' (3)

By the late eighteenth and early nineteenth centuries in England, Petty's hope that his 'Numbers, Weights, or Measures' would make 'intellectual arguments' about the nature of government superfluous, had become a cardinal part of the ideas of the political economists. Philip Abrams has traced the influence of these ideas on the development of British sociology, summing up the ideas of the political economists about government as follows:

'The most general theory of society implicit in political economy was then, to borrow Dahrendorf's term, an integration theory. It postulated a fundamental consensus and community of interests among individuals and classes. . . . Conflict had to spring from ignorance or unreason, since it would not spring from real incompatibilities. . . . Only when the natural laws of society were properly known would political legislation be appropriate. The first task was research. . . . Within the frame of reference of political economy the proper response to doubt and dissension was to mobilize empirical information.' (4)

Nowhere was the influence of fact-gathering to aid policy of more paramount importance than in the area of crime. Crime and its attendant conditions of poverty and drunkeness were a cancer of moral depravity disfiguring the otherwise triumphant face of Britain's new industrial success and if they were not ameliorated by prudent social policies, might well lead to the overthrow of the political and social structure. Coaxed on by a desire to remove a disfunction in a social machine which seemed historically almost unbelievable in the speed of its progress, driven on by a fear that the problem might burst out into revolutionary insurrection, the need to correct the situation by a careful empirical charting of its nature became of central concern. But this approach was not to provide the basis

175

for developing wider theoretical perspectives of society, for, as Abrams suggests, the further influence of Utilitarian Christianity atomised the focus and provided a ready-made theory of social causation the uncritical acceptance of which hindered the development of more complex theories.

However, the first task necessary to implement these ideas was the systematic collection of empirical data. Although the bills of mortality for London were available in Petty's time, it was not until the nineteenth century that machinery was set up for the systematic collection of national demographic statistics. In 1778 Bentham had suggested that a start should be made on the systematic collection of data about crime, and in 1810 prison statistics (although of a more limited kind than Bentham had suggested) were published. Bentham's suggestion however, was much broader than a simple collection of material and reflected a growing interest in the use of data-collection as an integral part of the decision-making processes of government:

'The ordering of these returns is a measure of excellent use in furnishing data for the legislator to go to work upon. They will form altogether a kind of *political barometer*, by which the effect of every legislative operation relative to the subject may be indicated and made palatable. It is not till lately that legislators have thought of providing themselves with these necessary documents. They may be compared to the bills of mortality published annually in London; indicating the moral health of the community (but a little more accurately, it is to be hoped) as these latter do the physical.

It would tend still farther to forward the good purposes of this measure, if the returns, as soon as filed, were to be made public, by being printed in the Gazette, and in the local newspapers. They might also be collected once a year, and published all together in a book.

A few years ago, I began sketching out a plan for a collection of documents of this kind, to be published by authority, under the name of *Bills of Delinquency*, with analogy to the *Bills of Mortality* above spoken of: but the despair of seeing anything of that sort carried into execution, soon occasioned me to abandon it. My idea was to extend it to all persons convicted on criminal prosecutions. Indeed, if the result of all law proceeding in general were digested into tables, it might furnish useful matter for a variety of political speculations.' (5)

But this view of the relationship between empirical information and government influenced more than just the collection of official statistics, for it was within this intellectual framework that the development of sociology as a separate discipline took place in this country. English sociology has tended to be characterised by an essential pragmatism and a continuing interest in matters of policy and welfare, a preoccupation which — as we have seen in the introduction to the historical section of

176

this book — is nowhere more apparent than in criminological studies. No important sociological theory of crime is associated with English criminologists. Instead, English criminology has been much more concerned with questions of policy and treatment. But the early interest in empirical information about crime did mean, however, that the English criminal statistics developed relatively fully and quickly — much more so than in the United States, for example — so that by the mid-twentieth century there are a host of public reports by departments or agencies concerned with the administration of justice. (6)

In spite of this comparatively full collection of officially published statistics, the brave hopes of the nineteenth century have not been fulfilled. Crime in England has proved to be more than a technical problem of social policy. Although some still cling to the belief that this failure stems from methodological defects in the statistics themselves, the 'official' figures seem doomed to remain very imperfect as instruments of social engineering. To understand why this should be so, it is necessary to examine the statistics themselves, as well as what they purport to measure. The rest of this essay will be devoted to doing this in three different ways. It will first examine what the criminal statistics indicate about the scope of crime in our society and also the way in which such information is subsequently used. It will then discuss one of the major methodological problems concerned with these statistics and finally, it will briefly examine their social meaning.

2. The 'Official' Statistics of Crime and their Use

In popular debate about crime as a social problem one question always dominates all others: how much crime is there in our society and is it increasing or decreasing? To answer these questions people usually turn to the criminal statistics and, indeed, the publication of these has become an event to be commented upon by the press as an indication of the nation's moral health:

The SKETCH says
Society in the Dock

THE BRUISED face of Britain is no longer a very pretty sight. Especially after dark.

"Queer-bashing" ... "Paki-bashing" ... "Mobbing and mugging" "Aggro and bovverboots."

UGLY WORDS FOR AN UGLY AGE. AND IT'S GETTING UGLIER BY THE MONTH.

FACT: For every 100 crimes of violence against the person in 1968, there were 117 last year.

FACT: For every 100 woundings and cases of assault in London in 1968, there were 128 last year.

Violence in this country — especially among the young — is spreading like a contagion.

On the hustings the Tories paraded as the party of "Law and Order." Now they're in power what are they going to do about it?

The best deterrent to crime is the certainty of being caught. That means more, better trained, better equipped police.

However, it's not much use the police catching the thugs if the courts let them off too lightly.

So punishment for crimes of violence must be made surer, swifter and sharper.

But, more police and stiffer sentences only provide part of the answer.

Somehow, in the home and at school, we have to restore in the young a respect for authority. And that's not going to be easy. For the values of our adult world today are tarnished and shaky.

If the young look around them for an example, what do they see?

Tax evasion and fiddling of expense accounts made into a virtue. Anarchy on the shop floor. Double-dealing in politics. AND nightly on the Box, opinion formers preach the fashionable message: *Freedom is the prize and self-discipline is at a discount.*

The grim crime statistics published yesterday are not an indictment of the young alone. The whole of British society, complacent and permissive, is in the dock. (7)

The statistics probably quoted most often in the press and in other discussions about crime are the number of 'indictable crimes known to the police' (8) — 'indictable' because these are often thought to be the more serious offences, and 'crimes known to the police' because these are thought to give the fullest measure of the problem unbiased by variations in the efficiency of the police. Figure 1 shows the upward trend in indictable offences known to the police during this century. In 1900, there were 77,934 such offences but by 1968 this figure had risen to 1,289,090, an increase of over sixteen-fold in just under seventy years. The rate of increase also displays an accelerating trend: between 1900 and 1935 crimes known to the police trebled; between 1935 and 1968 they increased five and a half times. In the eighteen years between 1950 and 1968, they almost trebled — the same rate of increase as for double the period in the earlier part of the century. (9) It is this trend of constant and accelerating increase that lends weight to popular fears that, at best, our

178

FIGURE 1. Indictable Crimes known to the Police 1900-1968

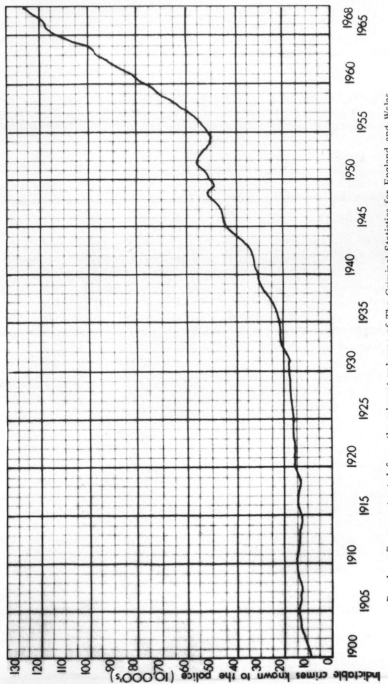

Based on figures extracted from the relevant volumes of The Criminal Statistics for England and Wales

society is suffering from a sharp decline in moral standards and, at worst, is destroying itself in a final anarchic tumult. Even when the figures are recalculated to give a rate per million of the population at risk – thus allowing for the argument that there is simply a growing number of people available to commit crimes – there is an increase from approximately 2,557 indictable offences per million in the period 1900–1904, to 29,914 per million for the years 1965–1968.

When the American National Commission on Law Observance and Enforcement examined the problem of criminal statistics provided by governments, it warned of the dangers inherent in giving 'official' status to statistics such as those quoted above:

'. . . . the greatest care should be taken to avoid publishing officially conclusions and interpretations based on partial data, but appearing to be official determinations on the basis of adequate information. . . .' (10)

Despite this cautionary note, however, criminal statistics produced by departments of government, both in the United States and in this country, are still often taken as indicating the 'official' picture of crime. This status has important implications for the meaning which comes to be attached to the statistics. First, it invests them with a degree of truth which, as will be discussed later, may not be justified. Equally important, they themselves become social facts irrespective of their accuracy and validity, in as much as they form the basis for political decision-making and debate. Because they are statistics emanating from the government of the day, they are ideally suited for use by opposition parties and pressure groups attempting to influence governmental policy:

'. . . criminal statistics over the past 10 years revealed a growth rate of 7 per cent and (that) crimes known to the police had more than doubled and drug addiction had increased sixfold.

Under the theme of "freedom under the law" (the speaker) was presenting a motion which asked the conference to take account of the rise in crime and the increase in public disorder. The Government, the motion stated, should not only take such measures as were necessary for strengthening the police force and improving the administration of justice, but should also embark upon a campaign of re-educating public opinion and introduce measures to restore a sense of social obligation in the community.' (11)

In political debate then, small percentage changes in the statistics of crime may be wielded as matters of momentous importance. For opposition parties, the statistics of crime resemble those for retail prices – almost always rising and therefore always weapons with which to attack

180

the government of the day. But just as price increases do not necessarily mean a rise in the relative cost of living, so an increase in the amount of official crime need not necessarily mean a decrease in moral standards or a need for tougher penalties. While a government may indeed resist policy proposals that claim foundation on the criminal statistics, however, it will experience great difficulty in denying the validity of the official picture as such.

For the various agencies involved in law enforcement and in the administration of justice this predicament is very similar. The statistics are inevitably construed as reflecting the activities of the organisation itself and, as such, may be used to draw conclusions about its efficiency and competence. Police officials may be well aware of the inadequacies and spuriousness of using arrest rates as a measure of police efficiency, but because of their obligation to produce statistics (12) they may be forced to defend themselves from criticism that assumes such rates to be adequate measures. This they will rarely do by denying the validity of the figures since these are, after all, a product of their own organisation. Indeed, many reports do little to discourage statistically groundless interpretations, preferring instead, to proffer other and organisationally external explanations for apparent trends:

'(The) sense of well-being in the service was marred by two disappointments. First, there was an increase in the amount of recorded crime in the provinces of 8.54% (though it is interesting to note that in the Metropolitan Police District the increase was only 0.08%). This was particularly disappointing because, after an average of some 7% during each of the previous ten years, in 1967 the increase was negligible and there were high hopes that the annual increase was at last being stemmed.

It is tempting to seek to see in this rise some failure in those responsible for the maintenance of the police, but this would be to over-simplify the matter. One possible reason is that the increasing urbanization of society may have encouraged the expansion of criminal activities into those parts of the country which were formerly of a rural and more law-abiding nature. Whatever the reasons, however, we cannot escape the fact that a greater proportion of the public is unfortunately becoming more dishonest each year and more and more people are prepared to break laws relating to offences against the person and against property. . . .' (13)

3. The Dark Figure and the Interpretation of Criminal Statistics

If the officially collected statistics of crime are to be used either as an aid to policy-making or for criminological research there are a great number of

181

methodological problems which must first be overcome. The literature abounds with detailed discussions of these difficulties, and for this reason no systematic examination of them all is envisaged here (14). There is, however, one paramount problem which must be considered since, on its own, it places very great restrictions upon the usefulness of the statistics and casts grave doubt upon criminological researches that fail to take account of its logical implications. Indeed, while it has probably been known to criminologists for longer than any other methodological problem, it is frequently ignored or merely mentioned and then quietly forgotten (15).

Often referred to as the 'dark figure' (16), this problem area comprises those social acts which are prohibited by the criminal law but which are not reported to the police and do not therefore appear in the official statistics (17). Thus what we are examining when we analyse 'crimes known to the police' is merely a selection of all the behaviour which would be defined as criminal if it were reported. But recognition of this fact does not mean that a solution has been found to the problem, nor indeed, that the logic of its existence is always accepted. The criminological literature still reports projects which espouse the axioms that individuals involved in criminal behaviour can be differentiated by variables other than their criminality and that this differentiation can be tested by comparing groups of convicted criminals with controls ostensibly without conviction. The contamination of control groups by dark figure crimes is all too frequently ignored.

Until the recent revival of interest in the processes of law enforcement, investigations into the nature of this dark figure have fallen into two broad categories: studies based on self-admissions of criminal behaviour and studies based on self-admissions of having fallen victim to such behaviour. Indeed, even though the latter technique has been discussed for a long time, it has only really emerged as a viable approach with the United States President's Commission on Law Enforcement and the Administration of Justice in 1967 (18). Self-report studies, on the other hand, have all too often been carried out on a small scale using convenient but unrepresentative samples of college students. But the more broadly based self-report studies (19) – together with the victim surveys – do support the idea that there is a dark figure of crime sufficiently large to render reported and recorded offences highly suspect as a basis upon which to make any inferences about criminal behaviour in general (20).

Two factors underlying variable reporting are whether or not the potential reporter perceives the action as criminal and, having so perceived it, whether or not the particular social situation in which the action takes place is conducive to reporting. An action may not be perceived as an offence either because of ignorance about the law's proscriptions, or because the real social situation makes it difficult to decide whether it falls within one of the ideal formulations of action upon which the law depends. The social situation within which the action takes place may affect the probability of reporting in several ways. The social relationships between the actors may be crucial since reporting the offence when the culprit is personally known to the observer may involve consideration of the likely consequences for the offender. Consequences considered tolerable or even necessary when the latter is a stranger may not be deemed so beneficial when he is closely related. Conversely, the offender's reaction to the reporter is much more likely to be perceived as sufficiently intolerable to preclude reporting when he is a close social contact. Invoking the processes of justice without traumatic conflicts requires a certain degree of social distance. At the same time, too much social distance may also lead to non-reporting: the behaviour has 'nothing to do with' the potential reporter and he therefore feels no obligation to report it to the police.

The social role of the potential reporter in relation to the offence may also be an important factor. Certain roles such as that of policeman involve an obvious obligation to report offences, while many others incorporate such an obligation to a greater or lesser extent. For example, caretakers who have a responsibility for property are under a strong obligation to report offences involving that property; similarly, as Rose found, shops that may not always report theft of their own stock will report minor thefts from charity boxes, since they feel responsible because the property is not their own (21). Sometimes, too, the definition of a formally or informally prescribed role may contain an element of conflict about reporting. Thus, Probation Officers have an obligation to report their clients' further offences to the court, but at the same time they also have a not necessarily compatible obligation to cope with his wider social welfare (22).

There are, then, contradictory cultural prescriptions as to whether offences ought to be reported in particular social situations, and some-times these contradictions may be formally incorporated into the social role of the potential reporter. But the problem of conflict in cultural prescriptions is not just one of contradictions within a homogeneous culture: cultural conflicts in a heterogeneous society are just as likely to produce systematic differences in reporting. A good deal of sociological research has been aimed at relating cultural diversity to systematic differences in the probability of being arrested and found guilty, and the same research is suggestive of systematic variations in the probability of an offence being reported in the first place. The development of contra-cultural ideologies which may encourage the commission of offences may also discourage the reporting of them (23). Sub-cultural norms which may encourage behaviour constituting an offence may, at the same time, remove the obligation to report such behaviour on the part of others. Thus, teenage gangs may perceive themselves as being in conflict with the police and hence may proscribe the reporting of any illegal activity to the authorities. Similarly, a recently arrived group of immigrants may have a normative system which does not proscribe the same behaviour as the law and which does not therefore include any normative constraints to report certain forms of conduct.

Sociological models of society which take cultural heterogeneity to the point of cultural pluralism make the determination of the probabilities of reporting even more problematic. The general point will, however, remain the same: the probability of an individual reporting an offence will depend upon the relationship between the cultural system to which he perceives himself as belonging and the cultural values embodied in the substantive law and its enforcement. Without a sociology of law that traces such relationships, without sociological theories that explain how they come about and how they effect law enforcement, we will be unable to predict the probability of an offence being reported except in crudest outline. Concepts such as 'subculture' and 'contraculture' are such crude outlines, but within the present limitations of our knowledge they provide us with some indication of how the reporting of criminal acts will be related to the wider social structure.

This does not mean, however, that the individual actor will only fail to report an offence when the law and his own cultural system are in conflict over the particular act which he observes. He may subscribe to a norm of his cultural system which is the same as that of the law, but still be in a social situation which places him in a deviant position in relation to other norms of that same cultural system. For example, a businessman who has his wallet stolen by a prostitute whilst at a conference may feel reluctant to report the loss. The advantage of sociological analysis which sees norms and values as structured variables is that it allows us to examine the interplay between conformity and deviation. It is this interplay in the real social situation which determines the actor's decision as to whether to report an act as criminal. Indeed, reportability as a variable could itself be used to study the relationship between legal norms and the diversity of norms within the wider social structure.

Our understanding of precisely why offences are not reported is at present rudimentary, but the existence of a dark figure has one crucial implication for the explanatory use of criminal statistics. It is possible that the variation in the reporting of offences could account at least partly for fluctuations in the recorded rates for offences. If this is so, then variations in the official rates demand a different kind of explanation. While no-one can prove that, for example, the increase in recorded crime is due to changes in reporting behaviour, such a hypothesis is not completely unrealistic. Conversely, the implication for the interpretation of changes in the crime rate is that their real significance cannot be understood unless the extent to which they emanate from changes in reporting behaviour is known.

184

4. Sociology and the Meaning of Criminal Statistics

The problem of what criminal statistics meant in a theoretical sense was not regarded as a pertinent question by criminologists until comparatively recent writers, mainly American, raised it as a fundamental problem. English criminology with its tradition of pragmatic empiricism had regarded criminal statistics as social facts *par excellence*. True there were problems, but these were almost exclusively seen as methodological in nature. The question of what the criminal statistics meant was to be answered by increasing methodological sophistication so that an exact charting of the nature and scope of the social problem of crime could finally reach its expected culmination in the eradication of crime as a problem. These methodological problems were formidable enough of course, and, whilst some of them could be dealt with by painstakingly detailed analysis, it was felt that the main difficulties could only be resolved by increasing the sophistication of the collection and presentation of data itself. As a result of this, in 1963, a Departmental Committee was set up under the chairmanship of Mr. Wilfred Perks, to suggest modifications in the collection and presentation of criminal statistics.

The way in which the committee defined the purpose of the collection of criminal statistics was within that traditional English view of the relationship between statistics and government:

'We are agreed that the purpose of collecting and publishing criminal statistics is to provide society with information, both as a matter of public interest and as a basis for action. . . . We should like to emphasise that in our view criminal statistics should serve not only to inform Parliament and the public; they should be capable of use as a basis for decisions by the authorities responsible for legislation, law enforcement and the treatment of offenders, and for research.' (24)

It was a view which Bentham, or even Petty, would have found perfectly intelligible. Even if fully implemented, the committee's report would not indeed overcome some of the more fundamental methodological problems, but it would nonetheless provide a welcome addition of precision to statistics which are notoriously lacking in that quality.

However, in the same period as the Perks' Committee was examining improvements in the collection and recording of data, sociological attention was being re-directed towards the problem of what criminal statistics meant; but this time as a theoretical problem. What various writers of the 1960's were doing was applying ideas from a wider sociological frame of reference, and in doing so bringing a fresh clarity of vision to what, for criminology, was a perennial problem.

The starting point for this reappraisal was that the definition of what

185

should be treated as criminal could not be taken for granted. In a sense, this was no more than an insistence that the sociological study of crime must be able to explain *how* people became criminal, as well as *why* they became criminal. The implications for criminal statistics were however profound, for it meant that rather than being seen as providing the parameters for the study, they now had to be seen as part of that problematic area comprising the processes by which people became criminals. Criminologists, of course, had not previously ignored the problem of what they meant by 'criminal'. Criminological textbooks have traditionally felt obliged to give some definition of what they were going to study, and this they have usually done by referring to the criminal law. For example: 'Provisionally, we can define crime as human behaviour which is punishable by the criminal law'. (25) However, the logic of this kind of definition was often curiously ignored: if we are to take crime as a variable dependant upon the criminal law, then the study of how, within a given social structure, the law comes to be made and enforced is an integral part of any attempt to understand crime. What we must examine in searching for an explanation of crime, in sociological terms, is the complex interrelations between the law and the agencies of its enforcement, and the wider social structure. Lemert summed up this view as follows:

'The task of sociology is to study not the theoretically conceived "stuff" of delinquency but the process by which a variety of behaviours in contexts are given the unofficial and official meanings that is the basis for assigning a special status in society.' (26)

The practical application of law depends very largely on bureaucratically organized agencies charged with its enforcement, and it is from information provided by these agencies that criminal statistics are produced. The scope of the data will therefore be bounded by the scope of a particular organisation's activities, and the quality of the data, by the efficiency of that organisation. The information will be above all else a record of the day to day activities of the agency concerned. What criminal statistics record therefore is not a direct transcription of the social reality of crime, but a refraction of that reality through the various processes involved in the collection and recording of data. To understand precisely what the criminal statistics mean we must have a detailed knowledge of the organisations involved in the collection process and how they relate to, and are influenced by, the wider social structure.

The wider social structure places a variety of constraints on the operations of the law enforcement process. Structural inequalities which influence the life chances of the individual in other areas of social life, will be no less influential in the field of law enforcement. What happens to the individual once he has been caught committing an offence will depend on

186

how much the process of enforcement is something which happens to him as an external event beyond his control, as opposed to an event which he is to some extent able to control and modify. The most complete control of the process will occur when the individual is able to completely extricate himself from the process; but at each succeeding stage the offender will have more, or less, ability to modify the results and so gain some control over the future stages. We know that the higher the social status of the individual concerned, the more likely he is to be able to control the enforcement process. The results of this differential will show itself in the statistical records of the process, and what should surprise us is not that persons of low social status are over-represented, but that a small proportion of high social status persons were unable to successfully modify the results of enforcement. In other areas of social life the question would normally be phrased the other way round: we don't wonder about the preponderance of middle class children receiving higher education, but rather we search for what is special about the small proportion of working class children in that position. For the legal system however, such a realisation is embarrassing, for it means that the formal notion of legal equality is practically unreal in a society whose social structure is based upon a stratification system of social inequality.

Not only does our social structure produce a differential ability to manipulate the agencies of control, it also produces what Chapman has called 'differential distribution of immunity' from involvement with agencies of enforcement. Chapman sees the differential ability to control privacy as one of the main determinants of this:

'The institutions of privacy have been little studied by the sociologists, yet the degree to which a person's life is spent in public rather than private places will have a quantitative effect on his liability to break the law and to be detected in breaking the law. . . . It would be possible to measure social status in terms of the ratio of time spent in public places (places to which the police have continued and unfettered access) to time spent in private places (places to which the police has access only in special circumstances and after due safeguards).' (27)

So far the structural differences examined are the unintended consequences of wider structural factors. Added however to the differential access by the police to scenes of action, is the differential presence of the police at those scenes to which they have access. This is an intended consequence of decisions about enforcement policy, but it does also produce some unintended consequences. Enforcement agencies cannot hope to exercise active control in all situations at all times, and decisions have to be made as to how scarce resources are to be employed. Historically the beginnings of policing in England are linked to a fear of the danger presented by the new urban proletariat, and the solution to the practical problem of control was a greater use of police patrols in those areas of the city where the danger was concentrated. The unintended consequence of this, however, was that the extra presence of the police produced extra knowledge of crime in those areas. The result was an over-representation in the statistics of crime of those areas most heavily policed, which in turn provided the necessary evidence to support a policy of differential patrolling. The pattern today is no longer a simple one of urban areas, but rather a differential police presence between different social situations, according to their perceived differences as criminogenically inducing — a judgement which in part draws upon the frequency with which these social situations appear in the statistics of crime. Here criminal statistics are no longer just factual reports of an agency's activities, but themselves come to play an active part in the process of law enforcement. Problems of interpretation and meaning become of theoretical importance in explaining crime, rather than just points of statistical methodology in getting to the facts.

Once the possibility of criminal statistics playing an active role in the process of enforcement is recognized, then it becomes necessary for any theoretical model which attempts to understand crime to be able to explain the nature and form of criminal statistics. To be able to do this we must examine the process by which an event becomes a statistic.

The organizational structure of the agencies responsible for the compiling of statistics will itself place certain limitations upon the nature of the statistics. A rigid, heirarchical organization such as the police, will need a flow of information up the heirachy to enable decisions to be made at the higher levels. The nature of this information will be constrained by the kind of decisions which have to be made. Policy changes relating to the work of the police will therefore effect not only the nature of their work, but also the nature of the information collected for practical implementation of those changes. An organizational structure designed to achieve specific goals will only be able to collect information which is gathered in the pursuit of those goals. Criminal statistics are based on data collected not by agencies designed to collect information about crime, but agencies designed to enforce the law. The statistics which result are a part of the attempt to achieve that goal. The nineteenth century political economists were correct in seeing the collection of statistics by such agencies as part of the process of government, but the implication of this for the sociological study of crime is that the statistics themselves must be explained, rather than that they provide data for the explanation.

Attempts to explain the statistics have recently taken the form of exploring different levels of meaning. This is part of a wider phenomenologically orientated, interactionist attempt to understand deviant behaviour (28). Stated briefly, the theory sees the social world as centred around the individual actor and his attempt to make the world meaningful. More than that, the social world only gains its meaning from the interaction of actors within the social setting and from their constructions of reality in this process. The social world then, can only be understood in terms of the differing individual constructions of social reality, for it will be within this reality that the individual will act, and within this reality his actions will be meaningful. To understand an individual criminal act we must understand the meaning of that act for the individual concerned. Criminal statistics, however, will not reflect the meaning of that action for the deviant concerned, but the ascribed meanings placed upon it by the observer. At a more general level, these theorists have explored the effect on future action of the changes in the individual deviant's construction of reality brought about by his interaction with enforcing agents, and their ascription of meanings to his action — meanings which may differ from his own. In interpreting criminal statistics, it is argued, the meanings which criminologists impute may be quite different from those intended when the data was collected. Indeed the collection process may involve a series of different meanings being ascribed, all of which will affect the kind of active role they may play in the enforcement process. Cicourel has made this point in relation to statistics of juvenile delinquency:

'The set of meanings produced by *ex post facto* readings of statistical records cannot be assumed to be identical to the situational meanings integral to the various stages in the assembly of the official statistics.' (29)

Douglas raises the same problems in what at first may seem to be the fairly unproblematic area of what is meant by 'suicide':

'What the term "suicide" means to the different groups of individuals including the different officials who categorize and tabulate deaths, can be decided only by a great deal of different empirical investigation of these official organizations.

... most importantly, we must recognise that the social imputation of a category such as suicide involves the *social imputation of causality of social action*, something which depends on many factors other than the "physical structure" of the events, which the positivistically inclined would have us believe are the only *significant* determinants of the imputations of the categories of "cause of death".' (30)

These ideas render untenable any conclusions about criminal statistics which assume that they reflect an indisputable reality of shared meanings. However, these explorations of the intersubjective meaning of criminal behaviour leave unexplored the structural boundaries of meaning which are available in the situation of legal enforcement, and these might be different from, and impinge upon, those of the individual's biographically determined reality. Explaining the meaning of his action to a court, an

189

accused person may wish to introduce 'impressions' which are, for him, a meaningful part of the reality of the event; but he may find that the boundaries of meaning proscribed by the legal system will make this inadmissable. What must be done to complete our understanding of the meaning of criminal statistics, is to explore the effects of formal law on the process. We need to know precisely how and why a particular law was made, how it relates to differences in the wider social structure, how it relates to the distribution of normative structures, and what kind of typifications of meaning it includes. Not only is this necessary for law but also for the different kinds of enforcement agencies which are created for the practical implementation of a specific law. We need as it were a map of the relationship between individuals and the various, and different, stages in the process of enforcement. Criminal statistics are a part of this process, and their meaning can only be fully intelligible in terms of this wider explanation. In the meantime, however, they provide us with one of the keys to that explanation.

1. This summary of some of the main points about the place of criminal statistics in sociological explanations of crime has been written by one of the editors to draw together a series of otherwise widely scattered points. In doing this, the indebtedness to many sources is freely acknowledged
2. H. C. K. Fitzmaurice (ed) The Petty Papers London, Constable & Co. (1927). For further information on the writings of both Petty and Graunt and on the disputed authorship between them see C. H. Hull (ed) The Economic Writings of Sir William Petty Cambridge, The University Press (1899)
3. Sir William Petty Political Arithmetic London, (1699)
4. P. Abrams The Origins of British Sociology 1834–1914 London, University of Chicago Press (1968) p. 9
5. J. Bentham 'A View of the Hard Labour Bill' (1778) in J. Bowring (ed) The Works of Jeremy Bentham Edinburgh, William Tait (1843) quoted in L. Radzinowicz History of the English Criminal Law since 1750 London, Stevens (1948) Vol. 1 p. 395
6. The most often used for criminological purposes are: The Annual Criminal Statistics for England and Wales, the reports of various chief constables, the Report of the Work of the Prison Department, The Report of the Children's Department of the Home Office, The Statistics Relating to Approved Schools, Remand Homes and Attendance Centres, and the Report of Offences Relating to Motor Vehicles
7. Taken from the Daily Sketch (25th June 1970) commenting on the Report of Her Majesty's Chief Inspector of Constabulary for the Year 1969 London, H.M.S.O. (1970)
8. For a succinct discussion of the distinction between indictable and non-indictable offences see N. D. Walker Crime and Punishment in Britain Edinburgh, Edinburgh University Press (1965) p. 14
9. For a detailed examination of the trends in the criminal statistics see F. H. McClintock and N. Howard Avison Crime in England and Wales London, Heinemann (1968)
10. National Commission on Law Observance and Enforcement (The Wickersham Commission) Washington D.C., (1931) p. 18

11. The *Guardian* (9th October 1970) reporting on the Conservative Party Conference
12. By the County and Borough Police Act (19 & 20 Vict. c. 69) Sec. 14, (1856)
13. Report of Her Majesty's Chief Inspector of Constabulary for the Year 1968 London, H.M.S.O. (1969)
14. For general reviews see T. Sellin and M. E. Wolfgang The Measurement of Delinquency New York, John Wiley (1964) and 'Criminal Statistics' in Information Review on Crime and Delinquency edited by E. Doleschal 1(8) (August, 1969). Most of the standard text-books also contain a chapter on this subject
15. For some acid comments on this criminological habit see J. D. Douglas The Social Meaning of Suicide Princeton, Princeton University Press (1967) p. 190
16. Discussions of the dark figure in criminology have a long history. For reviews of this see T. Sellin and M. E. Wolfgang Op. Cit. and L. Radzinowicz Ideology and Crime London, Heinemann (1966). For a very full discussion of the dark figure itself see F. H. McClintock 'Criminological and Penological Aspects of the Dark Figure of Crime and Criminality' Collected Studies in Criminological Research Vol. 5. Strasbourg, Council of Europe (1970)
17. Some writers include in the dark figure those acts which *are* reported to the police as offences but which, for one reason or another, the latter do not record as such. These, however, present different problems from the crimes which are not reported to the police
18. Although interest in crime from the perspective of the victim is not new and indeed, was given great prominence by Colquhoun, Mayhew and Booth, the idea of using sampling methods to discover the incidence of crime by victim-reports has only been carried out systematically by the President's Commission. See President's Commission on Law Enforcement and Administration of Justice Washington, D.C., Government Printing House (1967) Field Surveys 1, 11 and 111
19. See, for example, the following:
   W. A. Belson, 'Extent of Stealing by London Boys', Advancement of Science, 25 (124), (1968), 171-84; W. J. Chambliss & R. H. Nagasawa, 'On the Validity of Official Statistics: A Comparative Study of White, Black, and Japanese High-School Boys,' Journal of Research in Crime and Delinquency, 6(1), (1969), 71-7; N. Christie, J. Andenaes & S. Skirbekk, 'A Study of Self-reported Crime' in K.O. Christiansen (ed), Scandanavian Studies in Criminology, 1; K. Elmhorn, 'Studies in Self-reported Delinquency among School Children in Stockholm', in K. O. Christiansen (ed), Scandanavian Studies in Criminology, 1.; L. T. Empey & M. L. Erickson, 'Hidden Delinquency and Social Status,' Social Forces, 44 (1966), 546-54; M. Gold 'Undetected Delinquent Behaviour,' Journal of Research in Crime and Delinquency, 3, (1966), 27-46; F. I. Nye, J. Short & V. J. Olson, 'Socio-Economic Status and Delinquent Behaviour,' American Journal of Sociology, 63, (1958), 318-339; J. F. Short & F. I. Nye, 'Extent of Unrecorded Juvenile Delinquency: Tentative Conclusions,' Journal of Criminal Law, Criminology & Police Science, 49, (1958), 226-233; E. W. Vaz, 'Self-reported Delinquency and Socio-Economic Status,' Canadian Journal of Corrections, 8, (1966), 20-7; H. L. Voss, 'Socio-economic Status and Reported Delinquent Behaviour,' Social Problems, 13, (1966), 314-24.
20. For a review of the results of research into the dark figure see R. Hood and R. Sparks Key Issues in Criminology London, Weidenfeld & Nicolson (1970) chapters 1 & 2
21. G. N. G. Rose The Classification of Crime unpublished mimeograph, Institute of Criminology, Cambridge (1970)
22. Probation Officers are obliged by the 'Probation Rules' (made as Statutory Instruments) to report to the court any breach of the probation order, and a further offence must almost always constitute such a breach. However, by the

191

same rules the officer is obliged to take care of the long-term welfare of the client.

23. Yinger's distinction between 'contraculture' and 'subculture' is being followed here. See J. M. Yinger 'Contraculture and Subculture' American Sociological Review 25(5) (1960) pp. 625-35

24. Report of the Departmental Committee on Criminal Statistics (The Perks Report) London, H.M.S.O. (1967) Cmnd. 3448

25. H. Mannheim Comparative Criminology London, Routledge & Kegan Paul (1965) Vol. 1. p. 3

26. E. M. Lemert Human Deviance, Social Problems and Social Control Englewood Cliffs, Prentice-Hall (1967) p. 25

27. D. Chapman Sociology and the Stereotype of the Criminal London, Tavistock (1968) p. 56

28. For a useful review and critique of this school's work see E. Schur 'Reactions to Deviance' American Journal of Sociology 75 (1969) pp. 309-22

29. A. V. Cicourel The Social Organisation of Juvenile Justice New York, John Wiley (1968) p. 29

30. J. D. Douglas The Social Meaning of Suicide Princeton, Princeton University Press (1967) p. 189

White-Collar Crime and the Enforcement of Factory Legislation
by W. G. Carson
Reprinted from The British Journal of Criminology 10 (1970)

1. The Study of White Collar Crime

In one of his essays on 'Crude Criminology' George Bernard Shaw (1) attempted to dispel a common illusion about crime by pointing to the close similarities between the socially reprehensible behaviour of criminals and the ostensibly reputable behaviour of the military gentlemen of his day. The difference between the two was no greater, he suggested, than that between a jemmy and a bayonet or, more pointedly, than that between a chloroformed pad and a gas shell. Nor, apart from the wholesale and therefore more massive scale of the gentleman's depredations, were the results of the two kinds of behaviour distinguishable to Shaw's not unperceptive eye:

> 'Gild the reputable end of it as thickly as we like with the cant of courage, patriotism, national prestige, security, duty and all the rest of it: smudge the disreputable end with all the vituperation that the utmost transports of virtuous indignation can inspire: such tricks will not induce the divine judgment ... to distinguish between the victims of these two bragging predatory insects the criminal and the gentleman.'

At a more general level very similar views are frequently expressed by academic criminologists, though rarely with anything approaching Shaw's eloquence. Since the publication of Edwin Sutherland's controversial book on 'White Collar Crime' (2), a literature of growing theoretical and empirical sophistication has slowly accumulated around the central theme of the criminal behaviour of persons who, if not gentlemen, are at least members of the upper socio-economic class. Although a disagreement about basic definitions has continued unabated, degenerating at times into what one writer regards as 'a futile terminological dispute' (3), white-collar crime today usually takes its place alongside all the other standard topics in any criminological text-book.

In broadest outline Sutherland and his disciples argue cogently that the behaviour of persons of respectability and upper socio-economic class frequently exhibits all the essential attributes of crime but that it is only very rarely dealt with as such. This situation emerges, they claim, from a tendency for systems of criminal justice in societies such as our own to favour certain economically and politically powerful groups and to disfavour others, notably the poor and the unskilled who comprise the bulk of the visible criminal population.

Attempting to underpin these claims with the strongest possible support, Sutherland himself set a dangerous precedent when he expanded his definition of crime to include socially injurious behaviour which is legislatively proscribed under any kind of penalty as well as behaviour specifically prohibited by criminal law. His motives in doing so were to show that under such a definition the white-collar criminal would figure much more prominently and that legislatures, themselves, are not precluded from the possibility of bias in their determination of the limits of criminal justice. However defensible on these grounds, or indeed on grounds of social justice, this expansion of the concept came close to throwing the entire subject of white-collar crime into academic disrepute. Opponents were not slow to see here the intrusion of subjectivity into criminology:

'One seeks in vain for criteria to determine this white-collar criminality. It is the conduct of one who wears a white collar and who indulges in ... behaviour to which some particular criminologist takes exception. ... A special hazard exists in the employment of the term, 'white-collar criminal', in that it invites individual systems of private values to run riot in an area (economic ethics) where gross variation exists among criminologists as well as others. The rebel may enjoy a veritable orgy of delight in damning as criminal most anyone he pleases. . .' (4)

Another and a conceptually less problematic possibility than that of legislative bias is that even when the behaviour of the white-collared is defined as crime by 'the law in books', even when it is technically subject to criminal sanctions, it nonetheless enjoys substantial immunity at the operational level of 'the law in action' (5). Such immunity may certainly operate to some extent when white-collar people or their children engage in 'ordinary' criminal activities (6), but this nebulous form of bias, if such it is, has only a tangential relationship to the main argument about 'white-collar crime'. As Sutherland himself pointed out, a more crucial issue is the possibility of 'bias in the administration of justice under laws which apply exclusively to business and the professions and which therefore involve only the upper socio-economic class' (7). Restricted to the occupational activities of the allegedly favoured groups, the enforcement of these laws might reasonably be expected to display the most acute and most systematic form of bias if the theory of white-collar crime is correct.

As originally conceived, the theoretical significance of these ideas lay principally in their implications for the development of a general theory of criminal behaviour. For too long, Sutherland argued, criminologists had ignored the criminality so effectively though not conspiratorially concealed by the reluctance of legislatures and enforcement agencies to employ criminal sanctions in controlling business and professional behaviour. By accepting too blithely the modus operandi of the system the theorists had unconsciously colluded in perpetuating the myth that law-breaking is a primarily working-class phenomenon. As a result, their general theories had all too frequently been evolved on the basis of samples which were not truly representative of the behaviour they purported to explain. Thus, while Sutherland's avowed object was to reform criminological thinking, his ambition in this respect remained a comparatively modest one. He wished, indeed, to draw attention to the legislative and procedural differences between white-collar crime and ordinary crime, but only so that these conceptually false demarcations might be swept from the path of general theorisation about the causes of criminal behaviour. As C. R. Jeffery puts it, 'he accepted the Positivists' emphasis on the criminal while rejecting their definition of crime' (8).

Today, of course, criminologists tend to be much less concerned with seeking general explanations for criminal behaviour, having abandoned this ambitious quest in favour of more modest, if not notably more successful investigations into particular types of offence. This tendency to abdicate from generalisations about criminal behaviour is not, perhaps, to be regretted, but there is certainly one respect in which the potential of a generic approach to the socially homogeneous phenomenon of crime has by no means been exhausted. However wide the variety of behaviour which may be involved, all crimes possess the common denominators of proscription under the criminal law and the at least hypothetical possibility of a punitive reaction by the state. These formal characteristics of the phenomenon require explanation just as much as any others if our theories are not merely to rank as hypothetical statements about behaviour rather than about crime as such (9). They constitute a field in which valid generalisations can and should still be sought:

'We will have to scrutinise more carefully the process by which the criminal law is formed and enforced in a search for those variables which determine what of the total range of behaviour becomes prohibited and which of the total range of norms become a part of the law.' (10)

Such a perspective is slowly winning popularity among sociologists of deviance, particularly in the United States. In recent years a substantial literature has accumulated around the related problems of how society selects certain forms of behaviour – and subsequently some, but not all of the individuals engaging in them – to be 'labelled' as deviant or criminal. With regard to the specific issue of selection at the legislative level, it is ironic that recognition of these problems should have been implicit in Sutherland's approach even if he did not, himself, pursue their theoretical significance to its logical conclusion:

'. . . this newer emphasis on studying the law itself has (also) received major impetus from the theoretical issues raised by an interest in white-collar crime. The very differences between the set of laws regulating occupational behaviour and other statutes embodying legal proscriptions and sanctions have raised questions about how and why they were enacted – not just why they have been violated.' (11)

This is an area in which much remains to be done from a historical as well as a contemporary standpoint. It is an area, moreover, in which the student of white-collar crime may legitimately engage without arraignment for the apparent heresy of extending his basic definitions to embrace behaviour which is not contrary to the criminal law. Where necessary, he can accept such behaviour as 'non-crime' and with theoretical justification attempt to isolate the factors operative in keeping it outside the confines of the criminal law despite its marked similarities to 'real crime'.

In connection with the second major problem – that comprising the processes whereby subsequent to the enactment of criminal legislation some and not other law-breakers are formally designated as criminal – the study of white-collar crime is potentially just as fruitful. If the proponents of this subject are correct in their view it is an area distinguished by a peculiarly systematic form of 'non-labelling' at the operational level. Symptomatic of 'more pervasive and generalisable features of the social structure' (12), its investigation may serve to underline some of the crucial variables involved in this sifting process over a wider range of law-enforcement. Such research would focus primarily upon the specially constituted, administrative agencies to which the enforcement of criminal laws governing business and professional behaviour is frequently entrusted. Not only are these boards, commissions and inspectorates invested with an inevitable discretion about the use of prosecution, but also not infrequently with a range of administrative alternatives to enforcement through the criminal courts. In the exercise of these discretionary powers, however extensive, it is possible that a pattern of enforcement corresponding to what Aubert has characterised as the 'slow, inefficient and highly differential implementation' (13) of laws relating to white-collar crime may emerge.

Records pertaining to the enforcement of law by such agencies in this country remain almost totally uninvestigated by criminologists. Along with examination of legislative processes, scrutiny of these records is one of the more pressing items on the criminological agenda. In undertaking such research the criminologist can move further towards the sociology of law — a subject from which he has for too long been estranged — and also, perhaps a little lamely, towards recognition of his error in accepting too uncritically the aphorism that 'justice should study men rather than men study justice' (14).

2. The Enforcement of Factory Legislation

The remainder of this paper describes and interprets some empirical data concerning the enforcement of Factory Legislation. This is an area of social control which conforms in several respects to the broad configurations of laws relating to white-collar crime. Mainly, though not exclusively directed towards regulation of employers' occupational roles, the Factories Acts impose legal constraints upon one of the most important aspects of white-collar behaviour in an industrialised and highly differentiated society. Over a period of more than a century and a half the state has gradually increased the level of its intervention in the industrial sphere by stipulating the minimum standards of safety, health and welfare which factory-occupiers should observe. In doing so it has sought to ensure that the legitimate economic objectives of manufacturers are not pursued at the expense of the persons who are employed; to alter what R. W. C. Taylor called 'a method of economy which subordinated immediate human interests to the blind discretion of employers filled with the most pitiless of all passions, the pursuit of gain. . .' (15).

While discussion of the legislative background to these enactments lies beyond the scope of the present paper, there is one aspect of the statutory provisions which is particularly germane to the subject of enforcement. Factory Legislation expressly provides for its enforcement by means of criminal sanctions. Offenders can be tried summarily and may be fined up to £300 in instances where the contravention was likely to cause death or bodily injury. With a fine eye to the integrity of the law's administrative machinery and personnel, imprisonment for up to three months is permitted for offences such as personation, forgery of documents and making false declarations. In terms of 'the law in books' therefore, little difficulty attaches to the definition of violations as crime unless, of course, one ventures down the more tortuous paths of legal argument about mala prohibita and absolute liability.

Originally vested in 'visitors' appointed by the Justices of the Peace, responsibility for the enforcement of this legislation rests today with the Inspectorate of Factories. This body is immediately answerable to the Secretary of State for Employment and Productivity and has an authorised staff of inspectors numbering approximately six hundred. Its various enforcement activities involve around 380,000 premises of different kinds and in 1967, inspectors paid more than 170,000 visits to factories alone (16).

While this enforcement agency has received considerable attention from students of social and administrative history (17), it has received little or none from criminologists. Nor is the kind of information required by the latter very easily accessible. Although the reports submitted annually by the Chief Inspector give details of all prosecutions, they do not specify what proportion these constitute of the total violation which is known. Even more important in the context of white-collar crime, they do not provide any details about the Inspectorate's use of methods other than prosecution in its dealings with those factory-occupiers who are found to have offended.

To obtain information on these and related issues the Inspectorate's files relating to a randomly selected sample of two hundred firms in one district of south-eastern England were examined (18). The area chosen for the research was selected for its relatively wide range of different industries and different sizes of firm. The files which were examined contained data on all contraventions formally recorded against the firms, the means whereby the offences were discovered, the enforcement response which was made in each instance and a vast amount of less quantifiable information in the form of the written reports and comments of individual inspectors. Since the Department's programme was operating on the basis of a four year inspection cycle, data covering the four and a half years from mid 1961 to the beginning of 1966 were collected.

Analysis of the 'harder' among these data revealed a high level of offending among the firms in the sample. During the period covered by the survey, 3,800 offences were recorded against them, every firm contributing at least some violations to this total. The minimum number for any single firm was two; the maximum was ninety four. Detailed discussion of the nature of these offences lies beyond the scope of the present paper but, as can be seen from Table 1, the vast majority cannot be dismissed as trivial violations of the law's administrative requirements.

Knowledge of these contraventions reached the Department in several different ways. Chief among these and central to the entire system of enforcement was the Inspectorate's ongoing programme of general inspection. A relatively detailed examination of every factory operated by

TABLE 1 Nature of Offences recorded against 200 Firms during period of four and a half years

Type of Offence	Number	%
Lack of secure and properly adjusted fencing at dangerous machinery	1,451	38.2
Inadequate precautions against fire and explosion	460	12.2
Other safety requirements	380	10.0
Failure to examine, test or treat plant and equipment	162	4.3
Failure to provide proper training, supervision or medical examination for employees	108	2.8
Offences against health and welfare requirements	317	8.3
Offences against administrative requirements	917	24.1
Other	5	0.1
Total	3,800	100.0

firms in the sample was carried out under this programme during the 4½ years and these visits accounted, in all, for the discovery of around three-quarters of the recorded offences. A much smaller percentage — around 5% of the total — came to light in the course of investigations into complaints which emanated from a variety of sources, mainly employees or persons connected with them. Investigations consequent upon the obligatory reporting of industrial diseases, dangerous occurrences and accidents accounted for an even smaller proportion of the total. The last of these did reveal, however, a relatively high incidence of contravention, approximately two-thirds of the relevant visits resulting in the detection of at least one offence directly related to the occurrence of the accident. A final and by no means insignificant source of information about violation was a special type of visit paid with the express intention of following-up matters which had already come to light in any of the foregoing ways. Nearly 13% of the contraventions were discovered in the course of such visits.

With reference to the pivotal issue of the law's enforcement, the survey revealed the use of six major methods which can be arranged on a continuum running from 'no formal action', at one end, to prosecution, at

198

the other.* The procedures intervening between these self-explanatory extremes comprise formal and relatively standardised communications of differing forcefulness. Least threatening of these is a form which merely notifies the offender that at a recent visit to his premises it was observed that the matters mentioned required his attention. Barely more forceful, though clearly differentiated in the Inspectorate's standing instructions, is a letter which appends a rider to the effect that the matters in question require 'urgent' attention. In neither of these communications is any mention made of legal proceedings under the Factories Act. Reference to such action makes its first appearance in another type of letter which concludes by reminding the occupier that 'failure to comply with legal requirements can lead to prosecution.' Distinguishable as an 'indirect threat' since it explicitly mentions legal proceedings without suggesting that such action will necessarily result from further contravention, this procedure differs from a final type of communication which directly threatens the offender with prosecution. In its mildest form, the latter indicates that failure to comply will leave the inspector no alternative but to consider or institute proceedings; in its strongest form, the offending firm is given a very clear indication that prosecution has already been actively considered and that although no further action is being taken on this occasion, further violation will result in prosecution.

In processing the 3,800 recorded offences 663 specific enforcement

TABLE 2 Types of Enforcement Decision taken in Respect
of Recorded Offences

Enforcement Decision	Number	%
No formal action	36	5.5
Notification of matters requiring attention	494	74.5
Notification of matters urgently requiring attention	79	11.9
Indirect threat of prosecution	30	4.5
Direct threat of prosecution	12	1.8
Prosecution	10	1.5
Total	661*	99.7*

* There were two instances in which a seventh method − threat of issuing a certificate of unsuitability against underground rooms − was employed. (Sec. 69.) In neither case was the certificate issued and in these tables the two decisions are excluded.

decisions were made by the Inspectorate, all of the offences detected at a visit normally being dealt with by means of one communication. As can be seen from Table 2, these decisions displayed a pronounced tendency to concentrate around the least threatening procedures short of taking no formal action whatever.

All of the ten decisions to prosecute, shown in the above table, followed the occurrence of industrial accidents involving machinery in motion. Surprisingly, however, they did not represent the most serious accidents which were found to have involved contraventions. A plea of guilty was entered in every case and the average fine imposed after conviction was £50.

Another matter of particular relevance in the context of enforcement was the Inspectorate's response to those occupiers who either repeated specific contraventions (or failed to remedy defects) in spite of having received formal notification about them. Nearly 10% of the recorded offences fell in this category and although there was a noticeable trend

TABLE 3 Types of Enforcement Decision taken in Respect of
Recorded Offences, distinguishing those which
involved Repeated Offences from those which did not

| | Repeated Offences Involved | | |
Type of Decision	None %	Detected for Second Time %	Detected for Third or more Time %
No formal action	3.0	7.8	19.3
Notification of matters requiring attention	92.5	38.7	17.5
Notification of matters urgently requiring attention	0.9	35.2	43.9
Indirect threat of prosecution	1.9	11.3	8.8
Direct threat of prosecution	0.4	4.2	7.0
Prosecution	1.1	2.1	3.5
Total	(99.8 = 463)	(99.3 = 141)	(100.0 = 57)

towards greater severity in dealing with them, the concomitant enforcement-decisions still remained heavily weighted towards the less threatening forms of action. (Table 3)

The pattern which emerges from the above findings is one of substantial violation countered almost exclusively by the use of formal administrative procedures other than the prosecution of offenders. Superficially compatible with the findings of earlier studies in other areas of law relating to white-collar crime, this does not however point inexorably to the conclusion that the enforcement of factory legislation exemplifies a conscious bias in the administration of criminal justice. Such a conclusion would impute motives to the Inspectorate which would ultimately only be verifiable by reference to the intentions of its members both collectively and individually. Without corroboration of this kind motives could only be attributed on a 'post hoc' basis and need not bear any resemblance to those which were actually instrumental in generating the pattern of enforcement which was observed.

The crucial component in this motivational background is the inspector's interpretation of his own function, since it is from this that his decisions about how to enforce the law derive their immediate contextual meaning. In the course of the survey it quickly became evident that regardless of the role in which they might be cast by the sociologist, the inspectors in the District did not see themselves as members of an industrial police force primarily concerned with the apprehension and subsequent punishment of offenders. Rather, they perceived their major function to be that of securing compliance with the standards of safety, health and welfare required and thereby achieving the ends at which the legislation is directed.

A similar preoccupation with the 'ends' of law-enforcement has been observed in other agencies of this kind and has received some theoretical attention from Edwin M. Lemert (19) and F. E. Hartung (20). In the present context, however, its significance lies primarily in its profound effect upon the way in which inspectors selected appropriate modes of action in specific situations. Concerned with securing the offender's compliance rather than his punishment, they tended to choose methods of enforcement as much for their functional efficiency in attaining this objective as for their appropriateness as punitive responses. There was, moreover, substantial agreement among them that in normal circumstances regular inspections, repeated check-visits, formal communications and occasional threats together constituted the most efficient means to this end.

This belief in the efficacy of maintaining consistent pressure upon employers has been endemic in the Inspectorate since its inception (21). Well-founded or not, it is a cultural tradition which induces resistance to anything defined as an interference with the routine process of inspecting factories and following up matters which give rise to special concern. The fact that the inspectors in the District tended to view the prosecution of offenders as one potential intrusion of this kind is crucial to an understanding of the data which have been presented. To them, the additional time and paper-work inevitably involved in such action rendered it a method of enforcement to be used sparingly and, in the words of one of their superiors, 'as a tool of inspection'. This latter phrase accurately portrays the functional role which legal proceedings were perceived to play in relation to the enforcement process as a whole; whether utilised for their predicted effect upon an individual occupier or upon other employers in the area, they were seen as a means to an end rather than an end in themselves.

Despite a paramount interest in the outcome of their action rather than its retributive justification, the inspectors clearly did not regard the offender's past record as completely irrelevant to the decision-making process. Disregard of warnings, previous convictions and lack of 'progress' over prolonged periods all received frequent and explicit mention in reports which required or invited statements in support of any action proposed. But the relevance of these kinds of information seems to have derived largely from their perceived value as predictors of an occupier's likely response and therefore from their usefulness as indicators of the type of enforcement required to secure compliance in particular circumstances. As such they formed part of a more general but no less relevant syndrome comprising the employer's general attitude to the requirements of the law.

Nebulous as it may seem, the 'attitude of the occupier to his obligations' is formally recognised in the Inspectorate's standing instructions as a factor which may legitimately be taken into account when allocating the amount of time to be spent with particular firms. In the files which were examined, references to such attitudes commonly took the form of summary descriptions which categorised firms variously as 'good', 'bad', 'co-operative' or more pointedly, as 'putting production first' or 'regarding legal requirements as trivialities'. It was when a firm's previous history was interpreted as an indication of its unsatisfactory attitudes rather than its adverse economic position or otherwise extenuating circumstances that severe enforcement was most likely to ensue. Thus, for example, while previous warnings were cited in connection with almost all of the prosecutions which were taken during the period, many occupiers who violated the law in an identical respect on more than one occasion were not subjected to this action.

It would seem then that informal rules governing the general attitudes of occupiers and the promptness of their response to pressure from the Inspectorate played a crucial part in the determination of appropriate enforcement decisions. Relatively serious offences escaped severe action when these rules were not breached; comparatively minor ones could provoke legal proceedings when they were. That the methods adopted by the Inspectorate to secure compliance could depend as much upon an employer's position in respect of these unwritten 'constitutive norms' as upon the substantive nature of his offences against the Factories Act is apparent in the following extract from one prosecution report:

'This firm seems to regard legal requirements as trivialities and therefore proceedings are proposed in respect of all (the) cases. Whilst conditions in the factory are generally satisfactory, it is felt the management need a sharp reminder to shake them out of their 'can't care' attitude.'

This aspect of the background to the data already presented has important ramifications for the continuing debate about the absolute liability of offenders under the Factories Act. Giving rise to quite justifiable jurisprudential concern, the dangers inherent in the application of this principle appear to be somewhat mitigated in practice by virtue of the Inspectorate's prosecution policy. The importance which is attached to the offender's responsiveness and general demeanour could be said to approximate to an operational requirement of negligence as the basis of criminal liability (22). A firm's inattention to circumstances and consequences is more obviously blameworthy after receipt of explicit instructions from the Inspectorate. With regard to the wider issue, it should be remembered that the genesis of violation may frequently lie at this level of generality. Reluctance to allocate financial resources, to interrupt production lines or to institute efficacious organisational changes often constitute the real sources of violation but would be very difficult to prove in court. By taking these factors into account the Inspectorate perhaps retains some amorphous notion of corporate mens rea even though the concept has been allowed to disappear from 'the law in books'.

From the more theoretical and interpretative perspective which is the main concern of this paper, the germane conclusion emerging from the fore-going examination of enforcement in its immediate context is the explanatory inadequacy of Sutherland's argument in its crudest form. The Inspectorate's extensive use of non-threatening, administrative procedures and its correspondingly infrequent recourse to action in the courts derive from patterned beliefs about the function of an inspector and about how this may best be performed in normal circumstances. In view of their longevity it is possible that these beliefs owe their historical origins to a systematic bias which favoured employers as an occupational group invested with high social status; but their survival into the present day need not imply its continued operation. By dint of early institutionalisation into the department's way of thinking they may have outlived their original motivation and derived sustenance from processes of cultural transmission down through generations of inspectors. While bearing some resemblance to the constellation of attitudes and assumptions that Sutherland claimed as characteristic of agencies dealing with white-collar

203

criminals, these beliefs certainly cannot be traced today to the immediate motivational sources which he appears to have regarded as both crucial and self-evident. The explanatory pretensions implicit in his theory are most likely to be vindicated within a historical analysis of the enforcement of factory legislation. Applied to the contemporary scene they comprise an emotive description of outcomes rather than an adequate explanation for their occurrence.

Not least among the criticisms which can be levelled against students of white-collar crime with the notable exception of Aubert (23), is their failure to locate the subject inside a wider framework of social change. The importance of such a setting for an analysis of the enforcement of factory legislation is paramount. The Factories Acts originated as a legislative response to conflicts concomitant with the new forms of social organisation which were engendered by the Industrial Revolution. Their enforcement, like their subsequent history, has had to contend with the continual emergence of new situations resulting from uninterrupted innovation. The dangers of collision between divergent interests having survived largely undiminished, the Inspectorate's task comprises the implementation of dominant values in these situations without stifling progress on the one hand or leaving the conflict to resolve itself in social disarray on the other. Thus, many of the files which were examined in the course of this survey revealed the Department to be steering a middle if not altogether ambivalent course with regard to new machinery and techniques, committed neither to a policy which might have rendered experimentation unattractive in the eyes of manufacturers nor to one which abandoned employees to the mercies of untrammelled industrial progress.

Further complications arise from the continuous impact of techno-logical and other kinds of change upon the substantive content of norms governing already existing situations. Long-established and hitherto acceptable industrial processes may be discovered to involve previously unrecognised risks to health; more frequently, new methods of safe-guarding against risks all too well known may be devised. During this research several instances were encountered in which the inspectors applied substantial enforcement pressure in an effort to secure improve-ment in safeguards which had previously been introduced by the 'offenders' at the Department's own request. In others their evident concern was to persuade occupiers to abandon or modify processes which though not explicitly proscribed were nonetheless deemed hazardous. Through the assiduous pursuit of changeable and changing standards, the inspectors were as much concerned with controlling and inducing orderly change as with the prevention of deviation and the maintenance of an industrial status quo.

One immediate implication of the reciprocal relationship between the enforcement of this legislation and processes of social change is that the

204

'crimes' of the factory-occupier may not be comparable with those of the more traditional criminal. Although alteration in the normative requirements imposed by laws relating to 'ordinary' crimes is by no means uncommon, it is rarely if ever such a continuous process nor one so institutionalised at the enforcement level. A distinction must therefore be maintained between the social antecedents of the norms involved. Thieves, the penal system's closest equivalent to the alleged white-collar criminal, violate rules of conduct which, whatever their origin, are by now a traditional part of our culture; the factory-occupier seldom contravenes such rules even though he may break the criminal law. More important, since the agencies dealing with the two types of offender may differ substantially in their manifest and latent objectives, comparison of their enforcement practice − the sine qua non of any conclusion about the 'differential implementation' of laws relating to white-collar crime − may be of questionable validity.

Many features of the enforcement policy outlined in this paper are almost certainly not unique to the Factory Inspectorate. Indeed, they may well be just as characteristic of laws relating to business and professional behaviour as the almost exclusive application of such statutes to persons of upper socio-economic class. If such should be the case, the traditional view of white-collar crime stands in need of substantial modification. Examination of the background to the enforcement of factory legislation points not only to the path which such a reappraisal might follow but also to the subject's potential contribution to a more general sociology of law. If the social control of white-collar crime is characterised by a high degree of emphasis upon the generation of change, there is a pressing need to discover the factors which determine the direction which is taken. The empirical referents of this problem lie in the political processes surrounding legislation itself and in the development of value hierarchies and conflicts inside agencies of enforcement. No less pressing is the need to investigate how and under what circumstances the enforcement of law can best function as an instrument of social change. The efficiency of repressive criminal law in this respect is an issue upon which sociologists, like contemporary politicians, are by no means agreed.

1. G. B. Shaw 'Preface' in Sidney and Beatrice Webb English Prisons Under Local Government London, Longmans & Co. (1922)
2. E. H. Sutherland White Collar Crime New York, Holt, Rinehart & Winston (1949)
3. V. Aubert 'White-Collar Crime and Social Structure' American Journal of Sociology 58 (1952) pp. 263-71
4. P. W. Tappan 'Who is the Criminal' American Sociological Review 12 (1947) pp. 96-102. See also R. G. Caldwell 'A Re-examination of the Concept of White-Collar Crime' Federal Probation 22 (1958) pp. 30-36
5. V. Aubert op. cit.
6. See, for example, D. Chapman Sociology and the Stereotype of the Criminal London, Tavistock (1968)

7. E. H. Sutherland op. cit. p. 8
8. C. R. Jeffery 'The Structure of American Criminological Thinking' Journal of Criminal Law, Criminology and Police Science 46 (1956) pp. 658-72
9. Ibid. p. 669
10. R. L. Akers 'Problems in the Sociology of Deviance' Journal of Social Forces 47 (1968) pp. 455-65
11. Ibid. p. 456
12. V. Aubert op. cit. p. 264
13. Ibid. p. 265
14. C. R. Jeffery op. cit. p. 666 traces this tendency to one particular brand of positivism: 'The Positivists refuse to recognise that what is criminal is determined by legislation. They refuse to apply the scientific principles of determinism to the study of the law.'
15. R. W. C. Taylor The Factory System and the Factory Act London, Methuen (1894) p. 33
16. H. M. Chief Inspector of Factories Annual Report London, H.M.S.O. (1967) Cmnd. 3745
17. B. L. Hutchins and A. Harrison A History of Factory Legislation London, King & Son (1911); M. W. Thomas The Early Factory Legislation Leigh-on-Sea, Thames Bank (1948)
18. For purposes of this research, a 'firm' was defined as all premises in the district which were under occupation by one employer
19. E. M. Lemert Human Deviance, Social Problems and Social Control Englewood Cliffs, Prentice-Hall (1967) Chap. 1
20. F. E. Hartung 'White-Collar Offences in the Wholesale Meat Industry in Detroit' American Journal of Sociology 56 (1950) pp. 25-34
21. See, for example, Inspector Howell's report for the last quarter of 1836 in which he stated the opinion that 'frequent visiting is equally efficacious with convictions in producing obedience to the law'. Parl. Papers (1837) XXXI p. 107
22. For a fuller discussion of the use of these socially rather than legally relevant criteria see W. G. Carson 'Some Sociological Aspects of Strict Liability and the Enforcement of Factory Legislation' Modern Law Review 33 (4) (1970) pp. 396-412
23. V. Aubert op. cit.

A Sociological Analysis of the Law of Vagrancy

by William J. Chambliss
Reprinted from Social Problems Vol. 12
(Summer 1964) pp. 67-77

With the outstanding exception of Jerome Hall's analysis of theft (1) there has been a severe shortage of sociologically relevant analyses of the relationship between particular laws and the social setting in which these laws emerge, are interpreted, and take form. The paucity of such studies is somewhat surprising in view of widespread agreement that such studies are not only desirable but absolutely essential to the development of a mature sociology of law (2). A fruitful method of establishing the direction and pattern of this mutual influence is to systematically analyze particular legal categories, to observe the changes which take place in the categories and to explain how these changes are themselves related to and stimulate changes in the society. This paper is an attempt to provide such an analysis of the law of vagrancy in English Law.

Legal Innovation: The Emergence of the Law of Vagrancy in England

There is general agreement among legal scholars that the first full fledged vagrancy statute was passed in England in 1349. As is generally the case with legislative innovations, however, this statute was preceded by earlier laws which established a climate favorable to such change. The most significant forerunner to the 1349 vagrancy statute was in 1274 when it was provided:

'Because that abbies and houses of religion have been overcharged and sore grieved, by the resort of great men and other, so that their goods have not been sufficient for themselves, whereby they have been greatly hindered and impoverished, that they cannot maintain themselves, nor such charity as they have been accustomed to do; it is provided, that none shall come to eat or lodge in any house of religion, or any other's foundation than of his own, at the costs of the house, unless he be required by the governor of the house before his coming hither. (3)

Unlike the vagrancy statutes this statute does not intend to curtail the movement of persons from one place to another, but is solely designed to provide the religious houses with some financial relief from the burden of providing food and shelter to travelers.

The philosophy that the religious houses were to give alms to the poor and to the sick and feeble was, however, to undergo drastic change in the next fifty years. The result of this changed attitude was the establishment of the first vagrancy statute in 1349 which made it a crime to give alms to any who were unemployed while being of sound mind and body. To wit:

'Because that many valiant beggars, as long as they may live of begging, do refuse to labor, giving themselves to idleness and vice, and sometimes to theft and other abominations; it is ordained, that none, upon pain of imprisonment shall, under the colour of pity or alms, give anything to such which may labour, or presume to favour them towards their desires; so that thereby they may be compelled to labour for their necessary living.'(4)

It was further provided by this statute that:

'. . . every man and woman, of what condition he be, free or bond, able in body, and within the age of threescore years, not living in

207

merchandize nor exercising any craft, nor having of his own whereon to live, nor proper land whereon to occupy himself, and not serving any other, if he in convenient service (his estate considered) be required to serve, shall be bounded to serve him which shall him require ... And if any refuse, he shall on conviction by two true men, ... be commited to gaol till he find surety to serve.

And if any workman or servant, of what estate or condition he be, retained in any man's service, do depart from the said service without reasonable cause or license, before the term agreed on, he shall have pain of imprisonment.' (5)

There was also in this statute the stipulation that the workers should receive a standard wage. In 1351 this statute was strengthened by the stipulation:

'An none shall go out of the town where he dwelled in winter, to serve the summer, if he may serve in the same town.' (6)

By 34 Ed 3 (1360) the punishment for these acts became imprisonment for fifteen days and if they 'do not justify themselves by the end of that time, to be sent to gaol till they do'.

A change in official policy so drastic as this did not, of course, occur simply as a matter of whim. The vagrancy statutes emerged as a result of changes in other parts of the social structure. The prime-mover for this legislative innovation was the Black Death which struck England about 1348. Among the many disastrous consequences this had upon the social structure was the fact that it decimated the labor force. It is estimated that by the time the pestilence had run its course at least fifty per cent of the population of England had died from the plague. This decimation of the labor force would necessitate rather drastic innovations in any society but its impact was heightened in England where, at this time, the economy was highly dependent upon a ready supply of cheap labor.

Even before the pestilence, however, the availability of an adequate supply of cheap labor was becoming a problem for the landowners. The crusades and various wars had made money necessary to the lords and, as a result, the lord frequently agreed to sell the serfs their freedom in order to obtain the needed funds. The serfs, for their part, were desirous of obtaining their freedom (by 'fair means' or 'foul') because the larger towns which were becoming more industrialized during this period could offer the serf greater personal freedom as well as a higher standard of living. This process is nicely summarized by Bradshaw:

'By the middle of the 14th century the outward uniformity of the manorial system had become in practice considerably varied ... for the peasant had begun to drift to the towns and it was unlikely that the

208

old village life in its unpleasant aspects should not be resented. Moreover the constant wars against France and Scotland were fought mainly with mercenaries after Henry III's time and most villages contributed to the new armies. The bolder serfs either joined the armies or fled to the towns, and even in the villages the free men who held by villein tenure were as eager to commute their services as the serfs were to escape. Only the amount of 'free' labor available enabled the lord to work his demense in many places.' (7)

And he says regarding the effect of the Black Death:

'... in 1348 the Black Death reached England and the vast mortality that ensued destroyed that reserve of labour which alone had made the manorial system even nominally possible.' (8)

The immediate result of these events was of course no surprise: wages for the 'free' man rose considerably and this increased, on the one hand, the landowners problems and, on the other hand, the plight of the unfree tenant. For although wages increased for the personally free laborers, it of course did not necessarily add to the standard of living of the serf, if anything it made his position worse because the landowner would be hard pressed to pay for the personally free labor which he needed and would thus find it more and more difficult to maintain the standard of living for the serf which he had heretofore supplied. Thus the serf had no alternative but flight if he chose to better his position. Furthermore, flight generally meant both freedom and better conditions since the possibility of work in the new weaving industry was great and the chance of being caught small (9).

It was under these conditions that we find the first vagrancy statutes emerging. There is little question but that these statutes were designed for one express purpose: to force laborers (whether personally free or unfree) to accept employment at a low wage in order to insure the landowner an adequate supply of labor at a price he could afford to pay. Caleb Foote concurs with this interpretation when he notes:

'The anti-migratory policy behind vagrancy legislation began as an essential complement of the wage stabilization legislation which accompanied the break-up of feudalism and the depopulation caused by the Black Death. By the Statutes of Labourers in 1349-1351, every ablebodied person without other means of support was required to work for wages fixed at the level preceding the Black Death; it was unlawful to accept more, or to refuse an offer to work, or to flee from one county to another to avoid offers of work or to seek higher wages, or to give alms to able-bodied beggars who refused to work.' (10)

In short, as Foote says in another place, this was an 'attempt to make the vagrancy statutes a substitute for serfdom' (11). This same conclusion is equally apparent from the wording of the statute where it is stated:

'Because great part of the people, and especially of workmen and servants, late died in pestilence; many seeing the necessity of masters, and great scarcity of servants, will not serve without excessive wages, and some rather willing to beg in idleness than by labour to get their living: it is ordained, that every man and woman, of what condition he be, free or bond, able in body and within the age of threescore years, not living in merchandize, (etc.) be required to serve. . .'

The innovation in the law, then, was a direct result of the afore-mentioned changes which had occurred in the social setting. In this case these changes were located for the most part in the economic institution of the society. The vagrancy laws were designed to alleviate a condition defined by the lawmakers as undesirable. The solution was to attempt to force a reversal, as it were, of a social process which was well underway; that is, to curtail mobility of laborers in such a way that labor would not become a commodity for which the landowners would have to compete.

Statutory Dormancy: A Legal Vestige.

In time, of course, the curtailment of the geographical mobility of laborers was no longer requisite. One might well expect that when the function served by the statute was no longer an important one for the society, the statutes would be eliminated from the law. In fact, this has not occurred. The vagrancy statutes have remained in effect since 1349. Furthermore, they were taken over by the colonies and have remained in effect in the United States as well.

The substance of the vagrancy statutes changed very little for some time after the first ones in 1349-1351 although there was a tendency to make punishments more harsh than originally. For example, in 1360 it was provided that violators of the statute should be imprisoned for fifteen days (12) and in 1388 the punishment was to put the offender in the stocks and to keep him there until 'he find surety to return to his service' (13). That there was still, at this time, the intention of providing the landowner with labor is apparent from the fact that this statute provides:

'. . . and he or she which use to labour at the plough and cart, or other labour and service of husbandry, till they be of the age of 12 years, from thenceforth shall abide at the same labour without being put to any misery or handicraft: and any covenant of apprenticeship to the contrary shall be void.' (14)

210

The next alteration in the statutes occurs in 1495 and is restricted to an increase in punishment. Here it is provided that vagrants shall be 'set in stocks, there to remain by the space of three days and three nights, and there to have none other sustenance but bread and water; and after the said three days and nights, to be had out and set at large, and then to be commanded to avoid the town' (15).

The tendency to increase the severity of punishment during this period seems to be the result of a general tendency to make finer distinctions in the criminal law. During this period the vagrancy statutes appear to have been fairly inconsequential in either their effect as a control mechanism or as a generally enforced statute (16). The processes of social change in the culture generally and the trend away from serfdom and into a 'free' economy obviated the utility of these statutes. The result was not unexpected. The judiciary did not apply the law and the legislators did not take it upon themselves to change the law. In short, we have here a period of dormancy in which the statute is neither applied nor altered significantly.

A Shift in Focal Concern

Following the squelching of the Peasant's Revolt in 1381, the services of the serfs to the lord '. . . tended to become less and less exacted, although in certain forms they lingered on till the seventeenth century . . . By the sixteenth century few knew that there were any bondmen in England . . . and in 1575 Queen Elizabeth listened to the prayers of almost the last serfs in England . . . and granted them manumission' (17).

In view of this change we would expect corresponding changes in the vagrancy laws. Beginning with the lessening of punishment in the statute of 1503 we find these changes. However, instead of remaining dormant (or becoming more so) or being negated altogether, the vagrancy statutes experienced a shift in focal concern. With this shift the statutes served a new and equally important function for the social order of England. The first statute which indicates this change was in 1530. In this statute (22 H.8.c. 12 1530) it was stated:

> 'If any person, being whole and mighty in body, and able to labour, be taken in begging, or be vagrant and can give no reckoning how he lawfully gets his living; . . . and all other idle persons going about, some of them using divers and subtle crafty and unlawful games and plays, and some of them feigning themselves to have knowledge of . . . crafty sciences . . . shall be punished as provided.'

What is most significant about this statute is the shift from an earlier concern with laborers to a concern with *criminal* activities. To be sure, the

211

stipulation of persons "being whole and mighty in body, and able to labour, be taken in begging, or be vagrant" sounds very much like the concerns of the earlier statutes. Some important differences are apparent however when the rest of the statute includes those who ". . . can give no reckoning how he lawfully gets his living"; "some of them using divers subtil and unlawful games and plays." This is the first statute which specifically focuses upon these kinds of criteria for adjudging someone a vagrant.

It is significant that in this statute the severity of punishment is increased so as to be greater not only than provided by the 1503 statute but the punishment is more severe than that which had been provided by *any* of the pre-1503 statutes as well. For someone who is merely idle and gives no reckoning of how he makes his living the offender shall be:

'. . . had to the next market town, or other place where they [the constables] shall think most convenient, and there to be tied to the end of a cart naked, and to be beaten with whips throughout the same market town or other place, till his body be bloody by reason of such whipping.' (18)

But, for those who use 'divers and subtil crafty and unlawful games and plays,' etc., the punishment is '. . . whipping at two days together in manner aforesaid' (19). For the second offence, such persons are:

'. . . scourged two days, and the third day to be put upon the pillory from nine of the clock till eleven before noon of the same day and to have one of his ears cut off.' (20)

And if he offend the third time '. . . to have like punishment with whipping, standing on the pillory and to have his other ear cut off'.

This statute (1) makes a distinction between types of offenders and applies the more severe punishment to those who are clearly engaged in "criminal" activities, (2) mentions a specific concern with categories of "unlawful" behaviour, and (3) applies a type of punishment (cutting off the ear) which is generally reserved for offenders who are defined as likely to be a fairly serious criminal.

Only five years later we find for the first time that the punishment of death is applied to the crime of vagrancy. We also note a change in terminology in the statute:

'. . . and if any ruffians . . . after having been once apprehended . . . shall wander, loiter, or idle use themselves and play the vagabonds . . . shall be eftfoons not only whipped again, but shall have the gristle of his right ear clean cut off. And if he shall again offend, he shall be committed to gaol till the next sessions; and being there convicted upon indictment, he shall have judgment to suffer pains and execution of death, as a felon, as an enemy of the commonwealth.' (21)

It is significant that the statute now makes persons who repeat the crime of vagrancy a felon. During this period then, the focal concern of the vagrancy statutes becomes a concern for the control of felons and is no longer primarily concerned with the movement of laborers.

These statutory changes were a direct response to changes taking place in England's social structure during this period. We have already pointed out that feudalism was decaying rapidly. Concomitant with the breakup of feudalism was an increased emphasis upon commerce and industry. The commercial emphasis in England at the turn of the sixteenth century is of particular importance in the development of vagrancy laws. With commercialism came considerable traffic bearing valuable items. Where there were 169 important merchants in the middle of the fourteenth century, there were 3,000 merchants engaged in foreign trade alone at the beginning of the sixteenth century (22). England became highly dependent upon commerce for its economic support. Italians conducted a great deal of the commerce of England during this early period and were held in low repute by the populace. As a result, they were subject to attacks by citizens and, more important, were frequently robbed of their goods while transporting them. 'The general insecurity of the times made any transportation hazardous. The special risks to which the alien merchant was subjected gave rise to the royal practice of issuing formally executed covenants of safe conduct through the realm.' (23).

Such a situation not only called for the enforcement of existing laws but also called for the creation of new laws which would facilitate the control of persons preying upon merchants transporting goods. The vagrancy statutes were revived in order to fulfill just such a purpose. Persons who had committed no serious felony but who were suspected of being capable of doing so could be apprehended and incapacitated through the application of vagrancy laws once these laws were refocused so as to include '... any ruffians ... [who] shall wander, loiter, or idle use themselves and play the vagabonds ...' (24)

The new focal concern is continued in 1 Ed. 6. c. 3 (1547) and in fact is made more general so as to include:

'Whoever man or woman, being not lame, impotent, or so aged or diseased that he or she cannot work, not having whereon to live, shall be lurking in any house, or loitering or idle wandering by the highway side, or in streets, cities, towns, or villages, not applying themselves to some honest labour, and so continuing for three days; or running away from their work; every such person shall be taken for a vagabond. And ... upon conviction of two witnesses ... the same loiterer (shall) be

213

marked with a hot iron in the breast with the letter V, and adjudged him to the person bringing him, to be his slave for two years . . .'

Should the vagabond run away, upon conviction, he was to be branded by a hot iron with the letter S on the forehead and to be thenceforth declared a slave forever. And in 1571 there is modification of the punishment to be inflicted, whereby the offender is to be 'branded on the chest with the letter V' (for vagabond). And, if he is convicted the second time, the brand is to be made on the forehead. It is worth noting here that this method of punishment, which first appeared in 1530 and is repeated here with somewhat more force, is also an indication of a change in the type of person to whom the law is intended to apply. For it is likely that nothing so permanent as branding would be applied to someone who was wandering but looking for work, or at worst merely idle and not particularly dangerous *per se*. On the other hand, it could well be applied to someone who was likely to be engaged in other criminal activities in connection with being 'vagrant'.

By 1571 in the statute of 14 Ed. c. 5 the shift in focal concern is fully developed:

'All rogues, vagabonds, and sturdy beggars shall . . . be committed to the common gaol . . . he shall be grievously whipped, and burnt thro' the gristle of the right ear with a hot iron of the compass of an inch about; . . . And for the second offense, he shall be adjudged a felon, unless some person will take him for two years in to his service. And for the third offense, he shall be adjudged guilty of felony without benefit of clergy.'

And there is included a long list of persons who fall within the statute: 'proctors, procurators, idle persons going about using subtil, crafty and unlawful games or plays; and some of them feigning themselves to have knowledge of . . . absurd sciences . . . and all fencers, bearwards, common players in interludes, and minstrels . . . all juglers, pedlars, tinkers, petty chapmen . . . and all counterfeiters of licenses, passports and users of the same'. The major significance of this statute is that it includes all the previously defined offenders and adds some more. Significantly, those added are more clearly criminal types, counterfeiters, for example. It is also significant that there is the following qualification of this statute: 'Provided also, that this act shall not extend to cookers, or harvest folks, that travel for harvest work, corn or hay'.

That the changes in this statute were seen as significant is indicated by the following statement which appears in the statute:

'And whereas by reason of this act, the common gaols of every shire are like to be greatly pestered with more number of prisoners than heretofore hath been, for that the said vagabonds and other lewd persons before recited shall upon their apprehension be committed to the said gaols; it is enacted ...' (25)

And a provision is made for giving more money for maintaining the gaols. This seems to add credence to the notion that this statute was seen as being significantly more general than those previously.

It is also of importance to note that this is the first time the term *rogue* has been used to refer to persons included in the vagrancy statutes. It seems, *a priori*, that a 'rogue' is a different social type than is a 'vagrant' or a 'vagabond'; the latter terms implying something more equivalent to the idea of a 'tramp' whereas the former (rogue) seems to imply a more disorderly and potentially dangerous person.

The emphasis upon the criminalistic aspect of vagrants continues in Chapter 17 of the same statute:

'Whereas divers *licentious* persons wander up and down in all parts of the realm, to countenance their *wicked behavior*; and do continually assemble themselves armed in the highways, and elsewhere in troops, *to the great terror* of her majesty's true subjects, *the impeachment of her laws*, and the disturbance of the peace and tranquility of the realm; and whereas many outrages are daily committed by these dissolute persons, and more are likely to ensue if speedy remedy be not provided.' (Italics added)

With minor variations (e.g., offering a reward for the capture of a vagrant) the statutes remain essentially of this nature until 1743. In 1743 there was once more an expansion of the types of persons included such that 'all persons going about as patent gatherers, or gatherers of alms, under pretense of loss by fire or other casualty; or going about as collectors for prisons, gaols, or hospitals; all persons playing or betting at any unlawful games; and all persons who run away and leave their wives or children ... all persons wandering abroad, and lodging in ale-houses, barns, outhouses, or in the open air, not giving good account of themselves,' were types of offenders added to those already included.

By 1743 the vagrancy statutes had apparently been sufficiently reconstructed by the shifts of concern so as to be once more a useful instrument in the creation of social solidarity. This function has apparently continued down to the present day in England. The changes from 1743 to the present have been all in the direction of clarifying or expanding the categories covered but little has been introduced to change either the meaning or the impact of this branch of the law.

We can summarize this shift in focal concern by quoting from Halsbury. He has noted that in the vagrancy statutes:

'... elaborate provision is made for the relief and incidental control of destitute wayfarers. These latter, however, form but a small portion of the offenders aimed at by what are known as the Vagrancy Laws, ... many offenders who are in no ordinary sense of the word vagrants, have been brought under the laws relating to vagrancy, and the great number of the offenses coming within the operation of these laws have little or no relation to the subject of poor relief, but are more properly directed towards the prevention of crime, the preservation of good order, and the promotion of social economy.' (26)

Before leaving this section it is perhaps pertinent to make a qualifying remark. We have emphasized throughout how the vagrancy statutes underwent a shift in focal concern as the social setting changed. The shift in focal concern is not meant to imply that the later focus of the statutes represents a completely new law. It will be recalled that even in the first vagrancy statute there was reference to those who 'do refuse labor, giving themselves to idleness and vice and sometimes to theft and other abominations'. Thus the possibility of criminal activities resulting from persons who refuse to labor was recognized even in the earliest statute. The fact remains, however, that the major emphasis in this statute and in the statutes which followed the first one was always upon the 'refusal to labor' or 'begging'. The 'criminalistic' aspect of such persons was relatively unimportant. Later, as we have shown, the criminalistic potential becomes of paramount importance. The thread runs back to the earliest statute but the reason for the statutes' existence as well as the focal concern of the statutes is quite different in 1743 than it was in 1349.

Discussion

The foregoing analysis of the vagrancy laws has demonstrated that these laws were a legislative innovation which reflected the socially perceived necessity of providing an abundance of cheap labor to landowners during a period when serfdom was breaking down and when the pool of available labor was depleted. With the eventual breakup of feudalism the need for such laws eventually disappeared and the increased dependence of the economy upon industry and commerce rendered the former use of the vagrancy statutes unnecessary. As a result, for a substantial period the vagrancy statutes were dormant, undergoing only minor changes and, presumably, being applied infrequently. Finally, the vagrancy laws were subjected to considerable alteration through a shift in the focal concern of the statutes. Whereas in their inception the laws focused upon the 'idle' and 'those refusing to labor' after the turn of the sixteenth century and emphasis came to be upon 'rogues', 'vagabonds', and others who were suspected of being engaged in criminal activities. During this period the

216

focus was particularly upon 'roadmen' who preyed upon citizens who transported goods from one place to another. The increased importance of commerce to England during this period made it necessary that some protection be given persons engaged in this enterprise and the vagrancy statutes provided one source for such protection by re-focusing the acts to be included under these statutes.

Comparing the results of this analysis with the findings of Hall's study of theft we see a good deal of correspondence. Of major importance is the fact that both analyses demonstrate the truth of Hall's assertion that: 'The functioning of courts is significantly related to concomitant cultural needs, and this applies to the law of procedure as well as to substantive law' (27).

Our analysis of the vagrancy laws also indicates that when changed social conditions create a perceived need for legal changes, these alterations will be effected through the revision and refocusing of existing statutes. This process was demonstrated in Hall's analysis of theft as well as in our analysis of vagrancy. In the case of vagrancy, the laws were dormant when the focal concern of the laws was shifted so as to provide control over potential criminals. In the case of theft the laws were re-interpreted (interestingly, by the courts and not by the legislature) so as to include persons who were transporting goods for a merchant but who absconded with the contents of the packages transported.

It also seems probable that when the social conditions change and previously useful laws are no longer useful there will be long periods when these laws will remain dormant. It is less likely that they will be officially negated. During this period of dormancy it is the judiciary which has principal responsibility for *not* applying the statutes. It is possible that one finds statutes being negated only when the judiciary stubbornly applies laws which do not have substantial public support. An example of such laws in contemporary times would be the 'Blue Laws'. Most states still have laws prohibiting the sale of retail goods on Sunday yet these laws are rarely applied. The laws are very likely to remain but to be dormant unless a recalcitrant judge or a vocal minority of the population insist that the laws be applied. When this happens we can anticipate that the statutes will be negated (28). Should there arise a perceived need to curtail retail selling under some special circumstances, then it is likely that these laws will undergo a shift in focal concern much like the shift which characterized the vagrancy laws. Lacking such application the laws will simply remain dormant except for rare instances where they will be negated.

This analysis of the vagrancy statutes (and Hall's analysis of theft as well) has demonstrated the importance of 'vested interest' groups in the emergence and/or alteration of laws. The vagrancy laws emerged in order to provide the powerful landowners with a ready supply of cheap labor. When this was no longer seen as necessary, and particularly when the landowners were no longer dependent upon cheap labor nor were they a powerful interest group in the society, the laws became dormant. Finally a

217

new interest group emerged and was seen as being of great importance to the society and the laws were then altered so as to afford some protection to this group. These findings are thus in agreement with Weber's contention that 'status groups' determine the content of the law (29). The findings are inconsistent, on the other hand, with the perception of the law as simply a reflection of 'public opinion' as is sometimes found in the literature (30). We should be cautious in concluding, however, that either of these positions are necessarily correct. The careful analysis of other laws, and especially of laws which do not focus so specifically upon the 'criminal', are necessary before this question can be finally answered.

In conclusion, it is hoped that future analyses of changes within the legal structure will be able to benefit from this study by virtue of (1) the data provided and (2) the utilization of a set of concepts (innovation, dormancy, concern and negation) which have proved useful in the analysis of the vagrancy law. Such analyses should provide us with more substantial grounds for rejecting or accepting as generally valid the description of some of the processes which appear to characterize changes in the legal system.

1. Hall, J., Theft, Law and Society Bobbs-Merrill, 1939. See also, Alfred R. Lindesmith, 'Federal Law and Drug Addiction,' Social Problems Vol. 7, No. 1, 1959, p. 48
2. See, for example, Rose, A., 'Some Suggestions for Research in the Sociology of Law,' Social Problems Vol. 9, No. 3, 1962, pp. 281-283, and Geis, G., 'Sociology, Criminology, and Criminal Law,' Social Problems Vol. 7, No. 1, 1959, pp. 40-47
3. 3 Ed. 1. c. 1   4. 35 Ed. 1. c. 1
5. 23 Ed. 3.   6. 25 Ed. 3 (1351)
7. Bradshaw, F., A Social History of England, p. 54
8. Ibid.   9. Ibid., p. 57
10. Foote, C., 'Vagrancy Type Law and Its Administration,' Univ. of Pennsylvania Law Review (104), 1956, p. 615
11. Ibid.   12. 34 Ed. 3 (1360)
13. 12 R. 2 (1388)   14. Ibid.
15. 11 H. & C. 2 (1495)
16. As evidenced for this note the expectation that '. . . the common gaols of every shire are likely to be greatly pestered with more numbers of prisoners than heretofore . . .' when the statutes were changed by the statute of 14 Ed. c. 5 (1571)
17. Bradshaw, op. cit., p. 61   18. 22 H. 8. c. 12 (1530)
19. Ibid.   20. Ibid.
21. 27 H. 8. c. 25 (1535)   22. Hall, op. cit., p. 21
23. Ibid., p. 23   24. 27 H. 8. c. 25 (1535)
25. 14 Ed. c. 5. (1571)
26. Earl of Halsbury, The Laws of England, Butterworth & Co., Bell Yard, Temple Bar, 1912, pp. 606-607.
27. Hall, op. cit., p. XII
28. Negation, in this instance, is most likely to come about by the repeal of the statute. More generally, however, negation may occur in several ways including the declaration of a statute as unconstitutional. This later mechanism has been used even for laws which have been 'on the books' for long periods of time.

Repeal is probably the most common, although not the only, procedure by which a law is negated.

29. M. Rheinstein, Max Weber on Law in Economy and Society, Harvard University Press, 1954
30. Friedman, N., Law in a Changing Society, Berkeley and Los Angeles: University of California Press, 1959

The Deviance-Amplifying System *by L. T. Wilkins*
Reprinted from Social Deviance London, Tavistock (1964) pp. 87-94

It is possible that some societies, for some reason, find it necessary to treat deviance with extreme intolerance, and others are able to accommodate greater degrees of deviance, and, *as a result of such tolerance, experience less serious deviance*. It seems that it is possible for a society to operate in such a way that its social-sanctions systems become devalued. If such a feedback mechanism is in operation, the system within which it is applied tends towards instability. If a small initial stimulus generates a response, part of which response becomes a further stimulus, a highly critical and powerful servo-mechanism results. Such a feedback mechanism is at least implicit in the theoretical work of Kitsuse and Dietrick. (1) Re-examination of Sutherland's theory of differential association led Kitsuse and Dietrick to modify it in the following way:

(i) The individual learns the values of the delinquent subculture through his participation in gangs which embody that subculture.
(ii) The motivations of individuals for participation in gangs are varied.
(iii) The malicious, non-utilitarian, and negativistic behaviour which is learned through participation in the subculture is met by formal negative sanctions, rejection, and limitation of access to prestigeful status within the middle-class system.
(iv) Thus, participation in the delinquent subculture creates similar problems for all its participants.
(v) The participants' response to the barriers raised to exclude them from status in the middle-class system ... is a hostile rejection of the standards of "respectable" society and an emphasis upon status within the delinquent gang.
(vi) The hostile rejection response reinforces the malicious, non-utilitarian, and negativistic norms of the subculture.

The links in this circular chain may be described as a 'positive feedback loop'. While such a loop continues the situation will continue to get further and further out of control. The point of entry into such a system which may result in modification of the loop does not have any significance in terms of the outcome. It may be easier to enter at one point rather than another, but ideally the modification required is to change the loop into a negative feedback so that the system tends towards a desirable stability. It will be noted that, like Cloward and Ohlin, Kitsuse and Dietrick limit their model to gang behaviour, though such restrictions seem to be unnecessary if their theory is extended to a general theory of deviance.

Progressions, Good and Bad

The definitions of deviant behaviour relate to the information and cultural experiences of the individuals making the definitions. Both communities of saints and communities of criminals would define certain behaviour as lying outside the limits of tolerance of that particular culture. If the definitions of deviance lead to the removal from the experience of 'normal' people of certain deviant persons, the future definitions of deviance will not include the experience relating to those so removed. Moreover, if the action against deviants is such that they are not retained within the general system of values and controls, the new group created by the definition, as well as the residual group, will tend to construct new values and controls. Not only will the parent population cease to include within its experience the information relevant to the deviant, but the deviants may cease to have information regarding normal behaviour. This mechanism relates to the loop proposed by Kitsuse and Dietrick.

In terms of a model based on the calculus of probabilities, the situation does not remain static. The sector which is cut off by the definition does not remain attached to the general distribution. The transition from one distribution to different distributions may be related to the theories of 'reference groups', and in terms of the present model is as illustrated in Figure 1.

Let us first consider deviations at the left-hand cut-off point which have been associated in these illustrations with the 'sinful' or 'criminal' end of the scales. It will be possible to show similar mechanisms which operate at the right-hand cut-off point, and to generalize the theory at a later stage.

The modification of the information available within the truncated sections of the distributions will generate forces which will force the two distributions apart. The norms of the distributions cut off will no longer be the same as the norms of the distributions from which identification has been severed (i.e. the parent distributions). That is to say, instead of a centripetal force towards the general (parent) norm of the culture, the norms of the truncated parts of the distribution will reveal characteristics of a centrifugal force. This is, of course, another way of expressing the effect of the 'positive feedback loop'.

220

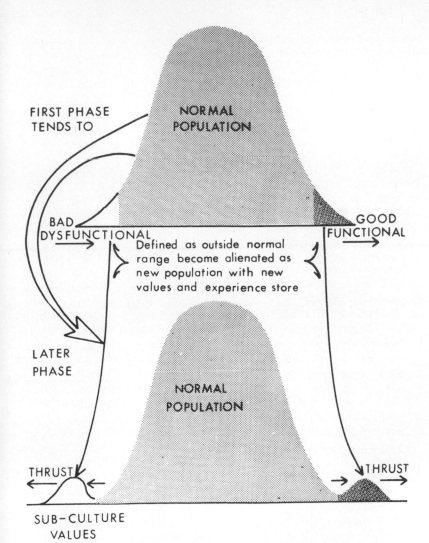

FIRST PHASE
TENDS TO

NORMAL
POPULATION

BAD
DYSFUNCTIONAL

GOOD
FUNCTIONAL

Defined as outside normal
range become alienated as
new population with new
values and experience store

LATER
PHASE

NORMAL
POPULATION

THRUST

THRUST

SUB-CULTURE
VALUES

FIGURE 1.   Evolution of sub-cultural and deviant social systems

Using Kitsuse and Dietrick's style of presentation as in the preceding section, the following feedback system may be proposed:

Less tolerance leads to →
> more acts being defined as crimes
> leads to →
> more action against criminals
> leads to →

221

more alienation of deviants
leads to →
more crime by deviant groups
leads to →
less tolerance of deviants by conforming groups
and round again ↱

The General Model

It is now possible to take some general postulates and attempt to relate them together into a complex theory. The following postulates may be stated:

1. People tend to behave with respect to situations and things as they perceive them to be.
2. Distinctions between what is legitimate and what is illegitimate are made culturally.
3. Legitimate and illegitimate opportunities can be distinguished, and the *balance* between the two types of opportunity presents an important variable.
4. If the balance between legitimate and illegitimate opportunities remains constant, the amount of crime will tend to vary according to the total number of opportunities. Hence it follows that the disturbance of the balance will modify the crime rate, if the rate is considered in relation to the opportunity structure.
5. Since perceptions influence behaviour, the definitions (perceptions) of the culture have an influence upon the members of the culture and the sub-cultures as perceived and defined by the culture itself.
6. Human decision-making skill (information processing) is influenced not only by the nature of the information, but by the 'channel' through which it is received.
7. Information which is perceived as irrelevant (orthogonal) to the dimension of action is treated as no information.
8. Systems in which information regarding the functioning of the system is fed back into the system present different characteristics from systems where such feedback information is lacking or is minimal.
9. People do not play 'expected values', thus actual odds do not explain behaviour; even perceived expected values may not provide a sufficient basis for prediction of behaviour since small probabilities are not treated in terms of pay-off maximization.
10. Norms are set for the culture, but different sections of a culture will experience greater or lesser difficulties in achieving success within the norms.

222

The above set of postulates cannot be related together in any simple unidirectional cause → effect model. The model proposed may be described as a deviation-amplifying system. The type of model proposed is well stated by Magoroh Maruyama (2). As he says, 'The law of causality may now be revised to state A SMALL INITIAL DEVIATION WHICH IS WITHIN THE RANGE OF HIGH PROBABILITY MAY DEVELOP INTO A DEVIATION OF A VERY LOW PROBABILITY or (more precisely) into a deviation which is very improbable within the framework of probabilistic unidirectional causality.' Models based on deviation-amplifying systems have been found to be necessary to explain economic behaviour, and it is not surprising, nor does it represent a high degree of originality, to propose similar models for other forms of satisfaction-seeking human behaviour.

The implications of the deviation-amplifying system are far-reaching; as Maruyama says, 'these models are not in keeping with the sacred law of causality in the classical philosophy (which) stated that similar conditions produce similar effects'. It is now possible to demonstrate that in some cases similar conditions may result in dissimilar products.

Applying the general dynamic model and the postulates stated above to the particular problem of crime, the following system may be proposed:

(a) Certain types of information, in relation to certain systems, lead to more acts being defined as deviant.

(b) The individuals involved in the acts so defined are 'cut off' from the values of the parent system by the very process of definition.

(c) The defining act provides an information set for the individuals concerned and they begin to perceive themselves as deviant. (Perhaps the main way in which any person gets to know what sort of person he is is through feedback from other persons.)

(d) The action taken by society and the resulting self-perception of the individuals defined as deviant, lead to the isolation and alienation of the specified individuals.

(e) This provides the first part of a deviation-amplifying system. The definition of society leads to the development of the self-perception as 'deviant' on the part of the 'outliers' (outlaws), and it is hardly to be expected that people who are excluded by a system will continue to regard themselves as part of it.

(f) The deviant groups will tend to develop their own values which may run counter to the values of the parent system, the system which defined them as 'outliers'.

(g) The increased deviance demonstrated by the deviant groups (resulting from the deviation-amplifying effect of the self-perception, which in turn may have derived from the defining acts of society) results in more forceful action by the conforming groups against the nonconformists.

(h) Thus information about the behaviour of the nonconformists (i.e. as (f) above) received by the conforming groups leads to more acts being defined as deviant, or to more stringent action against the 'outliers'; and thus the whole system (a)–(g) can itself continue round and round again in an amplifying circuit.

This type of model need not be regarded as too surprising. A similar situation explains the relationship between confidence and prices on the Stock Market. If this type of model is a fair representation of the social system in relation to deviant behaviour, some interesting predictions can be made from the theory. In particular, if a model of this kind applies, it is not necessary to show that the individual parts have a large effect on any detail of the system; the important feature of this type of model is that it represents an unstable system. Small initial differences, perhaps even due to chance variations in the network, can build up into quite large forces. A number of mutual causal processes can be identified in other fields of science where the initial stimulus was extremely small, and possibly randomly generated, but where the final results were of very considerable importance.

It is possible to examine this model in relation to some differences in criminal behaviour which have not been satisfactorily explained by the simple unidirectional cause → effect model. The majority of students of the problem of drug addiction have expressed interest in the fact that Britain has no real problem in this area whereas it represents a very considerable problem in the United States and in some other countries.

Many observers from the United States have studied the system of drug addiction and narcotics control in England. Although different observers from America were in England at the same time and discussed with the same people, their views differ regarding what was observed. Some writers have reported that they could find no differences between the British and the United States systems of control, others have found what they believe to be major differences. It would appear that the perception of systems of control differs between observers who are, in fact, observing the same thing and taking similar evidence. Some have claimed that the different systems of control in the two countries could explain the difference in the incidence of addiction, others have claimed that since there are no differences, or none of any significance, the different patterns of addiction cannot be due to any differences in the systems of control. It may be that these conflicting views by experts are capable of resolution through the theory proposed. Perhaps the following summary statements indicate a satisfactory model for this problem:

(a) the perception ('image') of the use of drugs in England differs from that in the United States;
(b) the perception of the addict differs;

224

(c) the perception of the police differs;

(d) small differences in the control system, or even in the perception of the control system, could generate large differences in the perception of addiction, which could amplify the effects of the official controls;

(e) less action is defined as 'crime' in Britain, and as a result, or in addition, fewer people are defined as 'criminal', whatever the objective differences may be;

(f) the *balance* between legitimate and illegitimate means for obtaining drugs in the two countries differs;

(g) the 'information set' (or folklore — it does not have to be true!) regarding the official control system and the function of drugs, both culturally and in the sub-cultures of the two countries, differs;

(h) a different perception of a situation will give rise to behaviour which differs, since behaviour tends to be consistent with perception.

If this model is a sound one, it would be possible for the situation in England to change rapidly and radically owing only to minor changes in the balance of factors. Which factors are critical in an unstable (feedback) situation of this kind is not a particularly meaningful question — any change in the situation may change the outcome throughout the whole field. It is possible, or even probable, that any attempt to tighten up the British regulations with a view to making a minor problem even less of a problem may be a disturbance of the generating system of perceptions which could produce a more serious problem.

If complex models of this kind do in fact explain types of human behaviour which are disapproved of by society, social action to remedy a perceived 'evil' (dysfunctional behaviour) could take place at many points, but any action is likely to misfire and to result in the opposite effect to that which the action is desired to achieve.

If people are excluded by the system they are not likely to feel themselves to be part of it. This is the same argument as is made in theories of alienation and anomie. It would appear that the sanctions applied by a society to its sub-cultures may appear to them to be so extreme that they are alienated from the general values system of that society. The rejection of a deviant, may act as an information set modifying his own tolerance through his experience of the culture (that is his 'store'). If a society truncates its normal distribution at low values of standard deviations it will tend to reduce the cohesiveness of its own social order. Lack of tolerance for behaviour which is not completely *intolerable* may defeat its own ends, not only through the devaluation of sanctions, but by inducing a self-definition of deviance, where such a definition is not justified in terms of the social dysfunction of the behaviour.

1. J. I. Kitsuse and D. C. Dietrick 'Delinquent Boys: a Critique' American Sociological Review 24 (1959) pp. 213 ff.

2. M. Maruyama Mimeo paper circulated by Research Department of the Department of Corrections, Sacramento, California (1962)

Mods, Rockers and the Rest: Community Reactions to Juvenile Delinquency by Stanley Cohen
Reprinted from The Howard Journal *(12) London, 1967 pp. 121-130*

This paper deals with one part of a research project being carried out within a certain theoretical framework in criminology and the broader field of the sociology of deviance. To understand why certain aspects of the subject matter — the Mods and Rockers phenomenon — are being considered rather than others, it is necessary to provide a brief statement of this framework.

Theoretical Framework

The main purpose of the research project is to investigate social reaction to deviant behaviour. The rationale behind this approach was first set out in a strangely neglected textbook by Lemert (1) and systematized more recently by Becker (2). This approach views deviance as a transactional process, the result of interaction between the person who commits an act and those who respond to it. Social reaction to deviance, the crucial variable in this approach, is largely ignored in conventional research in criminology and social deviance. In the field of juvenile delinquency, for example, the bulk of research is directed towards the taxonomic tabulation of the delinquents' traits (or attitudes, or values) in an attempt to see how delinquents differ from non-delinquents (3). On this basis causal theories are constructed. But the deviant act is not, or not only, deviant *per se*, it has to be defined and treated as such by the community. Social problems are what people think they are — there is an objective and verifiable situation, but also a subjective awareness of it and a definition by certain people that the situation is inimical to their interests and that something should be done about it (4). The damage to art treasures by floods is a 'problem' to those whose commercial or aesthetic values are tied up with the preservation of art treasures. If this group of people didn't exist, there would be no problem. In the same way, the delinquent is a problem, but a problem *for someone*.

So when Becker writes that society creates deviance, he does not mean this in the conventional sense of there being social factors in the individual's situation which prompt his action, but that '. . . social groups

226

create deviance by making the rules whose infractions constitute deviance, and by applying these rules to particular persons and labelling them as outsiders.' From this point of view, deviance is not a quality of the act the person commits, but rather a consequence of the application by others of rules and sanctions to an 'offender' (5). The audience, not the actor, is the crucial variable.

One effect of community reaction is to confirm the deviant in his self-identity. When the community reacts negatively to a person's deviation from valued norms, he tends to define his situation largely in terms of the reaction. He takes on a new self-concept, identifies himself in a new light and even begins to act like the stereotype of him. James Baldwin has vividly described the position of many Negroes in these terms: he notes how his father '... was defeated long before he died because ... he really believed what white people said about him' and warned his nephew: 'You can only be destroyed by believing that you really are what the white world calls a nigger' (6).

This reaction sequence sets into operation what Wilkins calls a 'deviation-amplifying system' (7) and the present research is aimed at observing the workings of this sort of system. The sequence would run something like this:

1. Initial deviation from valued norms, leading to:
2. Punitive reaction by the community (which may lead to the segregation of groups and marking them as deviant):
3. Development of a deviant self-identity and behaviour appropriate to this identity:
4. Further punitive reaction, etc.

Although it is not within the scope of this lecture to develop the theme, it should be pointed out that this sort of analysis is not just a manipulation of theoretical models. As Wilkins himself has made very clear, the implications for social policy, in the fields of both treatment and prevention, are considerable. Schur has recently used this type of model to examine the impact of public policy on abortion, homosexuality and drug addiction (8). He shows, for example, how policy based often upon vital misconceptions about the nature of the deviant behaviour, may be expressed in legal prescriptions. This 'criminalization' of deviance then forces the individual into reinforcing a criminal self-image that creates problems for himself and society at large. The classic example, of course, is the creation of the addict sub-culture as partly at least a consequence of the public stereotype (the 'dope fiend') and repressive legislation. In the context of compulsory hospitalization, treatment may just reinforce the self-image.

The Present Study

Deviance is not a 'thing' which can be observed and studied. The term is a conceptual category and all we have are types of behaviour that have been classified as deviant. For research purposes we have to choose one of these types and juvenile delinquency is simply one such type that can be studied. Again though, juvenile delinquency is not a concrete enough category for this type of study — the term is a legal definition and not a behavioural syndrome. So, for reasons including its topical importance as a subject in its own right, the unit of study for this section of the project was narrowed down to what is classifiable (for want of a less emotive word) as 'hooliganism'. The Mods and Rockers phenomenon of the last three years, particularly in the form it took of disturbances and so-called riots at English seaside resorts over bank holiday weekends, provides an archetypal example of this behaviour.

Because we are using the transactional framework to explore certain aspects of the community reaction, the study is necessarily self limiting. It does not attempt to provide a comprehensive account of the whole phenomenon e.g. in historical terms or in terms of sub-cultural theory.

Method

In an exploratory study of this nature there are few guidelines on which method to use for collecting data. In the event almost all possible methods were tried. These included:— content analysis of all press cuttings covering the period Easter 1964—August 1966 (national as well as relevant local press); 65 interviews carried out with a quota sample of spectators on the Brighton sea-front during Whitsun 1965; various other interviews with local figures, e.g. newspaper editors, local government officials, hotel proprietors, M.P.'s etc.; and personal observation of crowd behaviour, police action and court hearings. (The final research report will also use data from 140 intensive interviews carried out in a London Borough on the more general topic of attitudes to delinquency.)

The Initial Deviation

Clacton is an East Coast resort not particularly well known for the range of amusements it provides for its younger visitors. Easter 1963 was worse than usual — it was cold and wet, in fact the coldest Easter Sunday for eighty years. The shopkeepers and the stall-owners were irritated by the lack of business and the young people milling around had their own irritation fanned by rumours of cafe owners and barmen refusing to serve some of them. A few groups started roughing around and for the first time the Mods and Rockers factions, a division at that time only vaguely in the air, started separating out. Those on bikes and scooters roared up and down, windows were broken, some beach huts were wrecked, one boy fired a starting pistol in the air. The vast number of young people crowding the streets, the noise, everyone's general irritation and the often panicky actions of an unprepared and undermanned police force, made the two days seem rather frightening.

One of the most significant features about Clacton is that there appear to have been present a number of what the police would call 'trouble-makers' — mainly Rockers from the East End or small East Anglian villages. Contrasted with the fringe supporters, these are the same hard core who in race riots and other crowd situations are predisposed to take the initiative and to respond violently to what is perceived as police provocation. All the 24 boys charged in the Clacton court claimed that they had been the unlucky ones, that they had been picked out at random. Yet 23 out of the 24 had previous convictions — the police's chances of picking out 23 previous offenders at random out of a crowd of say a thousand, is one in a couple of million.

As we shall show, many aspects of the Mods and Rockers have parallels in the class of phenomena known as mass delusion. These studies (9) show that the first stage is invariably a real event — the delusion or hysteria is created because the initial event is reported in such a way as to set in motion a cumulative sequence which serves to fulfill the expectations created by the earlier events. In terms of our model this is an amplifying process.

The Process of Amplification

One of the most important elements in the reaction to deviance is the growth of a generalised set of beliefs to explain the behaviour. Once the first stage of reporting is past, the community feels the need to make sense of what has occurred — this is especially the case when the event is perceived as a dislocation of the smooth running of things: the killing of a policeman, a political assassination, a natural disaster. People look for explanations, self-styled experts proclaim favourite theories, stereotypes are confirmed or new ones are created, words acquire a symbolic meaning — 'Aberfan', 'Dallas', 'Braybrook Street', 'Clacton'.

In the case of deviancy, these generalised beliefs invariably involve spurious attribution; all sorts of traits are attributed to the deviant and, on the basis of little or no evidence, a whole set of misconceptions arise. Let us give a few examples of some of these elements.

'Violence and Damage' — it was widely believed that the Mods and Rockers caused widespread damage and were involved in violent assaults on each other or 'innocent holidaymakers'. In fact the amount of damage

229

done was not excessive — in the three year period there were less than ten cases of malicious damage — in Hastings, August 1964, for example, one of the 'big' events, there were only four charges of malicious damage out of 64 arrests.

During Whitsun 1964, although there were 54 arrests in Bournemouth the damage was £100, in Brighton with 76 arrests the damage was £400, in Margate with 64 arrests the damage was £250. Compare these figures to the *real* cost to the resorts which was in extra police charges: the four successive bank holidays between Easter 1965 and Easter 1966 cost the Brighton Council an extra £13,000. The amount of serious violence similarly was negligible — only one tenth of the original Clacton offenders were charged with offences involving violence. In Margate, Whitsun 1964, supposedly the most violent week-end, where according to the *Daily Express* (19/5/64) 'The 1964 boys smeared the traditional postcard scene with blood and violence', there were two not very serious stabbings and one man dropped onto a flower bed. The typical offence was using threatening behaviour or obstructing the police. Leaving aside the obvious inconvenience caused to adults by crowds of youths milling about on the pavements and beach, few innocent holidaymakers were the victims of violence — the targets were members of a rival group or, more often, the police.

'Loss of trade' — it was widely believed that the troubles scared potential visitors away and the resorts suffered financially. The evidence for this is at best dubious. Papers quoted figures from Brighton for Whitsun 1964 showing that the number of deck-chairs hired had dropped by 8,000 on the previous year's week-end. This drop was attributed to the effects of the Mods and Rockers. Analyses of other figures, however, show that the total number of visitors was probably more — the reason why fewer deckchairs were hired was that Whit Monday was one of the coldest for decades — the temperature had dropped overnight by 14° F. and the beaches were virtually deserted. Interviews and observation suggest that if anything, the Mods and Rockers attracted some visitors and by the end of 1965 certainly, the happenings were part of the Brighton scene — the pier, whelks and the Mods and Rockers could all be taken in on a day trip.

'Affluent Youth' — attitudes and opinions are often shaped and bolstered up by legends and myths. One of the most recurrent of the Mods and Rockers myths was the one about the boy who told the Margate magistrates that he would pay his £75 fine with a cheque. This myth was frequently used to justify the image of the Mods and Rockers as classless, affluent, and scooter or moter-bike owners. The story was in itself true enough — what few papers bothered to publish and what they all knew, was that the boy's offer was a pathetic gesture of bravado. He later admitted that not only did he not have the £75 cheque but did not even have a bank account and had never signed a cheque in his life. The

230

affluence image has very little factual basis. The Clacton offenders had on them an average of 15/- for the whole bank holiday week-end. The best off was a window cleaner earning £15 a week, but more typical were a market assistant earning £7 10s. and a 17-year-old clerk earning £5 14s. The average take home pay in a sample of offenders from Margate, Whitsun 1964, was £11 per week. The classless image is also none too accurate — the typical Rocker was an unskilled manual worker, the typical Mod a semi-skilled manual worker (10). In all cases, the majority of young people present hitched or came down by train or coach. The scooter and motor-bike riders were a minority, albeit a noisy and ubiquitous minority.

A detailed analysis of a number of other such images, shows that a large component of the deviation is, in Lemert's term, 'putative': 'The putative deviation is that portion of the societal definition of the deviant which has no foundation in his objective behaviour. (11) Why is this sort of belief system important?

In the first place the sterotypes implied in the putative deviation serve to sensitize the community to any sign of incipient deviance. A previously ambiguous situation which may have been 'written off' as a Saturday night brawl now becomes re-interpreted as a 'Mods and Rockers clash'. In the weeks following the first two or three major happenings, a number of such incidents were reported from widely scattered localities. Minor scuffles and fights and increased police vigilance were reported by the Press under such headings as 'Mods and Rockers Strike Again'. There were also numerous false alarms — after Whitsun 1964 for example, the police in Stamford Hill after answering a false alarm stated that 'people are a bit jumpy after the trouble on the coast'. This type of sensitization which turns non-events into events, is exactly the same process noted by students of mass delusion. In a state of hypersuggestibility following the reporting of a 'Mad Bomber' or a 'Phantom Anaesthetist' or a 'Sex Fiend On The Loose' ambiguous events are re-interpreted to fit into the belief. This is made easier when there is a composite stereotype available with readily identifiable symbols such as clothes. To the residents of Brighton, any boy between fourteen and twenty wearing a fur-collared anorak was a Mod. At the end of one Bank Holiday the police stood at the station putting back on the trains all 'suspicious looking' arrivals who could not prove that they were local residents.

Another way in which beliefs are important in amplifying deviance is that they serve to legitimate the action of society's agents of control. *If* you are dealing with a group that is vicious, destructive, causing your community a financial loss, and symbolically repudiating your cherished values, then you are justified to respond punitively. *If*, moreover, this is an affluent horde of scooter-riders, then 'fines won't touch them' and you have to propose confiscation of their scooters, forced labour camps, corporal punishment, turning the fire hoses on them. By the logic of their own definitions, the agents of control have to escalate the measures they

231

take and propose to take to deal with the problem. So by Easter 1965 the magistrates in Brighton were employing the highly dubious practice of remanding young people in custody as a form of extra-legal punishment. Bail was refused not on the merits of the individual case but as a matter of principle — the ostensible reason given by the magistrates for remand as being to enable the police to make enquiries, was not in fact the reason given in court when bail was opposed. The police opposed bail on the grounds that if the boys were allowed to go free justice would not be done and that the public would not be protected. On the flimsiest evidence a boy, who by the police's own account had done nothing more than refuse to 'move along', would be certified as an 'unruly person', refused bail and remanded in custody in an adult prison — in some cases for up to three weeks. A test case of this sort when taken before a Judge in Chambers resulted in the immediate release of a 16-year-old boy from prison on bail. Although precise data is difficult to obtain, at least 20 cases have been traced of successful appeals on the grounds of wrongful arrests or disproportionately high sentences. There is no doubt that in certain cases, admittedly under conditions of extreme physical and psychological strain and under direct provocation, arrests were made quite arbitrarily and with unnecessary violence. In one instance, arrested youths were observed being pushed through a gauntlet of police punches before literally being thrown into the van.

Informal agents of social control also took up extreme positions. On the initiative of a group of senior aldermen and councillors, the Brighton Council overwhelmingly passed a resolution calling for the setting up of compulsory labour camps for Mods and Rockers. A group of Great Yarmouth businessmen and hotel-keepers set up a Safeguard Committee which seriously debated a scheme of setting up road blocks outside the town to prevent any invasion.

We have discussed three types of processes identifiable in the reaction: the growth of generalised beliefs, which contain a putative element, the sensitization to deviance and the escalation of methods of social control. To evaluate the effects of the reaction on the self image we would need a more complicated type of research design than has been used here — a longitudinal study of the impact of community reaction on young people's self concepts. At present we can only use the overt behaviour as the dependent variable and assume that this behaviour is consonant with the actors' self image.

In the first place, as we have seen, the behaviour was often 'created' because of community sensitization. The atmosphere of expectancy present at the seaside resorts resulted in incidents being created out of nothing.

Two boys stopped to watch a very drunk old tramp dancing about on the beach. They started throwing pennies at his feet. Within 45 seconds there were at least a hundred people gathered round and in 60 seconds

232

the police were there. I turned my back on the crowd to watch the spectators gathering on the promenade above and by the time I turned back, two policemen were leading a boy away from the crowd.

(*Notes*, Brighton, Easter 1965).

Incidents such as these were created by sensitivity on the part of both audience and actors. There was a sense among the young people that they had to play to the gallery; the literal gallery of the adults lining the railing as at a bullfight, and the photographers running around from one event to the other; and the metaphorical gallery of the consumers of the mass media who had read in their morning papers 'Seaside Resorts Prepare for the Hooligans' Invasion'. The control agents, especially the police, created deviance not only in the sense of provoking the more labile members of the crowd into losing their tempers, but in Becker's sense of making the rules whose infraction constituted deviance. So, for example, certain areas were designated in advance as 'trouble spots'. If a number of youths were congregating in one of these trouble spots even for legitimate reasons (such as sheltering from the rain) they could be moved along, because policy was to keep these spots free. If one refused to move along he could be arrested and charged with wilful obstruction. (Under Sec. 51(3) Police Act 1964.)

Another significant effect of the reaction was, in Tannenbaum's phrase, the 'dramatisation of evil'. The adult reaction was not only negative — it could hardly have been otherwise — but it was hostile in the melodramatic sense. There was the famous speech by a Margate magistrate about his town being '... polluted by hordes of hooligans ... these long-haired mentally unstable petty little hoodlums, these sawdust Caesars who can only find courage like rats hunting in packs'; there were the newspaper headlines about 'vermin'; there was the show of force on the spot — police dogs, horses, walkie talkies, water board vans converted into squad cars; there were scenes like the police ceremoniously marching a group of youths through a street lined with spectators.

One way in which this hostility was reacted to was by returning it in kind. In the first series of events, the crowd, with the exception of the hard core referred to earlier, maintained fairly good humoured relations with the police. Attacks were disrespectful gestures such as knocking of helmets rather than malicious. In the 1966 incidents, the atmosphere was more tense. The lines had hardened:

A policeman walked quite peacefully between two rows of boys near the aquarium. Some of them started whistling the Z-car theme and one shouted out 'Sprachen the Deutsch Constable'?

— (*Notes*, Brighton, Easter 1966).

Another way in which the conflict was hardened was between the two groups themselves. Although the Mods and Rockers represent two very

233

different consumer styles – the Mods the more glossy fashion-conscious teenager, the Rockers the tougher, reactionary tradition – the antagonism between the two groups is not very deep, they have much more in common, particularly their working class membership. There was initially nothing like the gang rivalry supposed to characterise the American type of conflict gang caricatured in West Side Story, in fact there was nothing like a gang. Commercial and media exploitation of the Mod-Rocker difference, and misguided attempts to explain the whole situation of unrest in terms of this difference, hardened the barriers. The groups were merely loose collectivities or crowds within which there was occasionally some more structured grouping based on territorial loyalty. e.g. 'The Walthamstow Boys', 'The Lot From Eltham'. Constant repetition of the gang image made these collectivities see themselves as gangs and behave in a gang fashion. Yablonsky has noted the same process in his study of delinquent gangs as near groups (12).

The Role of the Mass Media

Without being able to consider here all the mechanisms through which the reaction was amplified, it is necessary to comment on the most important of these, the mass media. One must remember that in mass society one's view of deviance is usually second hand. In the hypothetical village community one might have been able to react to the village idiot in terms of first-hand impressions. In mass society images arrive already processed – policymakers can and do make decisions about say delinquents or drug addicts on the basis of the most crude and misleading images. In the case of the Mods and Rockers the media were responsible to a large extent for the putative deviance. An analysis, for example, of the House of Commons debate on 'Juvenile Delinquency and Hooliganism' (27th April 1964) shows the extent to which the images and stereotypes provided by the media were the basis for theories and policy proposals.

It is not just that the newspapers exaggerated the amount of behaviour – this is more or less inevitable. Estimates in any crowd situation such as a political rally or sporting event are notoriously inaccurate. What was more important was the manner of presentation – the sensational headlines, the interviews with dramatic characters and subtle techniques well known to war correspondents, such as reporting the same incident twice. Another effective technique was the misleading juxtaposition of headlines – on at least three occasions headlines such as 'Mod Found Dead in Sea', 'Boy Falls to Death from Cliff' were used as sub-headings in Mods and Rockers reports. In every case the deaths had no connection at all with the disturbances and were pure accidents.

The chief roles of the media seem to have been in transmitting the stereotypes and creating an expectancy before each event that something was going to happen. This last role was particularly taken by the local press which highlighted reports about local traders arming themselves with tear gas, citizens forming vigilante patrols, etc.

Differential Reaction

It is, of course, a fallacy to think of the mass media influencing a purely passive audience. Communication is responded to selectively, and the sort of questions we would like to answer are:— to what extent were the stereotypes and images absorbed by the community? How did the reaction crystallize into attitudes and opinions (e.g. about causes and solutions)? How were these attitudes affected by variables such as social class, education, political membership? Why did the reaction take the form it did?

The final research report will attempt to answer these questions. A preliminary analysis of the data from the Brighton sample only, suggests that the following type of generalisations might emerge:—

1. The reaction of the general public is less intense and less stereotypical than the reaction reflected in the mass media.

2. Local residents in the areas affected are more punitive than out of town visitors and the public in general.

3. Little difference between the Labour and Conservative groups were found. Except at the extreme of authoritarianism, political preference does not correlate with attitudes to delinquency.

4. The two most frequent single causes given for the Mods and Rockers events are 'boredom' and 'too much money'.

5. A dimension such as 'punitiveness' is too gross to measure attitudes to deviant behaviour. Certain groups, particularly working class and upper class, can at the same time be 'tolerant' of the behaviour and also devise the most punitive solutions for dealing with the behaviour when it is perceived as 'going too far'. The middle class less often make this distinction.

Conclusion

It must be emphasised again that as this is an analysis of the ways in which social reaction impinges upon the genesis and amplification of deviance, little has been said about the behaviour itself. This does not mean that one is trying to deny an objective reality or even less trying to present the Mods and Rockers as innocent victims of conspiracy and discrimination. Social forces work in far more subtle ways. Although people *were* inconvenienced or hurt, and there were fights and vandalism, there is at the very least enough evidence to suggest that the development of this behaviour was not independent of the reaction it provoked. Can one go further and say that the transactional theory is proved?

Clearly the present study is not a complete validation. For one thing, the crucial variable of the deviant self identity has not been measured and it might be a defect of the theory that this type of variable is peculiarly difficult to operationalise. There are problems in the model immediately apparent — for example why does the Wilkins-type of amplification sequence ever stop? Theoretically something like the Teddy Boy movement should have carried on growing. We know that this did not happen and there are already signs that the Mods and Rockers are going the same way. There are obviously factors 'outside' the model to account for these changes. Another problem is why not everybody exposed to the same definitions develops the appropriate self-image.

Until such questions are answered, we can only conclude that transactional theory provides a potentially useful framework for studying deviance. In the case of the Mods and Rockers at least, it gives an additional dimension to any other causal explanation.

1. Lemert, E. M.: Social Pathology, (London: McGraw Hill 1951).
2. Becker, H. S.: Outsiders, Studies in the Sociology of Deviance, (New York: Free Press, 1963).
3. Deutcher, I.: 'Some Relevant Directions for Research in Juvenile Delinquency', in Rose, A. R. (Ed.) Human Behaviour and Social Processes, (London: Routledge and Kegan Paul, 1962) pp. 468–481
4. Fuller, R. C., and Meyers, R. R.: 'Some Aspects of a Theory of Social Problems', Amer. Sociol. Rev. 6, (February 1941), pp. 24-32
5. Becker: op. cit. p. 9
6. Baldwin, J.: The Fire Next Time, (Penguin, 1964) p. 13
7. Wilkins, L.: Social Deviance, (London, Tavistock, 1964). See also the preceding paper in this book
8. Schur, E. M.: Crimes Without Victims, Deviant Behaviour and Public Policy, (New Jersey: Prentice Hall, 1965)
9. Johnson, D. M.: 'The Phantom Anaesthetist of Mattoon', Journal of Abnormal and Social Psychology, 40, (1945) pp. 175-186 etc.
10. Barker, P. and Little, A.: 'The Margate Offenders: A Survey', New Society, Vol. 4, No. 96, (30th July 1964), pp. 6-10
11. Lemert: op. cit. p. 56
12. Yablonsky, L.: The Violent Gang, (New York: Collier Macmillan, 1962).

Juvenile Delinquency and the School by C. M. Phillipson

This paper discusses some neglected aspects of the relationship between patterns of delinquency and the educational system. Evidence is presented from a variety of sources which suggests that analysis of the relationship between educational processes and juvenile delinquency could contribute to our understanding of the development of delinquent careers.*

Reference to the educational system by sociologists interested in delinquency emerged with the development of sub-cultural interpretations of delinquency. Differing interpretations of the role of the school have been proposed by sociologists working within the sub-cultural tradition but most of these interpretations remain hypothetical and do not rest on empirical research. Moreover the kinds of hypotheses proposed draw attention to a few highly selected features of school and the educational system; this restricted focus stems largely from the limited range of analytical questions considered within subcultural perspectives (1). Because these authors' considerations of the role of the school are peripheral to their main arguments their interpretations of its role in relation to delinquency typically seem to be geared to fitting in logically with the main tenets of their theories; their hypothetical interpretations of the school are designed to buttress the internal logic of their arguments. This would seem to account in part for the very different orientations to the school presented, for example, in the work of Cohen, Cloward and Ohlin, Miller, and Downes, none of whom made any empirical study of educational processes.

For Cohen delinquency is a 'reaction formation' response of lower working class boys to their status problems which arise from their failure to succeed in terms of the school's 'middle class measuring rod'; Cloward and Ohlin emphasise the role of the educational system in providing opportunities for legitimate occupational success, and consider the relationship between the distribution of inadequate educational opportunities and patterns of delinquency. By ignoring the school Miller suggests by default that it has little or no effect on the working class boys who are responsible for a large proportion of official delinquency. Downes, in analysing the relevance of American sub-cultural theories to the English situation, argues that the bottom stratum of secondary school boys have realistically low occupational aspirations and rapidly become dissociated from the school, viewing its activities as irrelevant to their futures.

Apart from the overall theoretical and methodological difficulties of the sub-cultural approach (2) there is one particular difficulty which it raises that is relevant in the present context. The American sub-cultural theorists' main interest has been in conceptualising the relationship between patterns of delinquency and particular features of American society and they have been concerned only marginally with general social processes such as, becoming deviant, social control, or stigmatisation (3). Thus, whilst at the most abstract level the concept of sub-culture may be useful for understanding some forms of delinquency in societies other than

* I am indebted to Michael Power of the Social Medicine Research Unit and Alan Segal of Goldsmiths' College for their valuable comments on an earlier draft of this paper.

America, the particular concepts and the contents of the theories developed by American authors seem to be highly culturally specific; they were generated to understand delinquency in American society. However there are such major structural differences between America and other industrial societies that it would seem unlikely that the American sub-cultural theories could explain delinquency in other societies. There are major economic, political, ethnic, legal, penal and educational differences between America and, for example, England; these structural differences reflect clear differences in the very area of central importance to the sub-cultural approach — norms and values. It is therefore hardly surprising that Downes found little English evidence to support the blanket transfer of any of the American sub-cultural theories to the English situation (4). The cultural specificity of American writing is a general problem which becomes especially relevant in considering particular institutional spheres such as the educational system.

American writing on delinquency in its occasional references to the school and education has understandably emphasised substantive features of the American educational system which differ considerably from those of the English system, for example, in terms of its political organisation, content, access to higher education, and social status of the teacher (5). Even when the school has been considered in any detail by delinquency theorists their discussions have been limited to the concerns of the sub-cultural tradition, especially to the hypothesised discontinuity in values between social class or status groups. Certainly the kinds of questions raised by the writers in the more inclusive deviance perspective (6), concerning, for example, the social definitions of deviance, rule enforcement processes, and the development of deviant careers, have been largely ignored by sub-cultural writers both in their general formulations and in their occasional references to the school.

A further common feature of sociologists' consideration of the role of the school in relation to delinquency is the assumption of constancy. This assumption of constancy seems to operate at three levels: firstly, apart from Macdonald's study of self-reported delinquency (7), there has been no suggestion that structural differences within the educational system may affect the generation of delinquency. In this country, for example, one question concerning the structure of secondary education would be to ask whether within a homogeneous working class community official delinquents come in the same proportions from different strata of the educational system (secondary modern schools, grammar schools) or are drawn disproportionately from one kind of school? Secondly, the possibility of the differential contribution to a community's delinquency of schools within the same stratum has been overlooked. Finally, the assumption of constancy has been reinforced at the level of the value system supposedly mediated by the school; stemming largely from the work of Cohen there has been an unquestioned assumption that all schools

238

mediate a common value system. As Downes puts it: 'it might be argued that the school ... is a universal institution: whereas types of schools vary widely in the types of skill they seek to impart, they display a high degree of consensus on the value system they both seek to impose and deploy as criteria' (8).

Throughout the literature the reference is to 'the school' rather than to particular schools; sociologists seem to be operating with highly abstract models of the school which rest on their intuitive hunches about what the schools are really like. Although they pay lip service to the school's importance their implicit assumption seems to be that its influence is constant in relation to pupils' and teachers' experiences of it. Presenting discussions of 'the' school in these abstract terms, as if it were a constant influence, implies that all boys from similar social backgrounds experience all schools in similar ways. If Cohen's discussion is taken as typifying the sub-cultural writers' approach, his argument implies that the school is simply a forum in which working class boys are faced with middle class curricula and values and that any random sample of working class boys would experience any school in a working class community in an identical way. The implicit suggestion is that all schools are sufficiently alike to produce a standardised response from their pupils. The idea that there may be considerable differences between overtly similar schools, that some schools may facilitate and others hinder the drift into delinquency, does not seem to have occurred to writers on delinquency.

Operating with a highly abstract model of the school is convenient analytically because it allows one to make assumptions about what schools are 'really' like and precludes the raising of awkward questions about the aetiology of delinquency the answers to which might disturb neat theoretical formulations. Thus the main limitations of existing formulations about delinquency which refer to or make assumptions about school life are, firstly, the narrow range of questions which they pose about the school's role, and secondly, the abstract model of the school as a constant organisational setting with which they operate. The result is a series of varying hypothetical interpretations of the school's role. Empirical evidence and hypotheses from various sources and levels of analysis are now presented which suggest that the influence of the school is very far from constant and that a widening of the interpretive frame of reference in relation to schools may contribute to the understanding of the dynamics of delinquency.

At the commonsense level of understanding there are two background factors which provide grounds for re-considering the role of the school. Firstly there is the fact that the official peak age for indictable offences (9) is 14, the year before leaving school, and when the school leaving age was raised from 14 to 15 so did the official age peak for indictable offences rise from 13 to 14; in spite of the valid sociological criticisms of the use of the official criminal statistics as measures of the parameters of actual illegal behaviour in a community (10) this association between the official peak age for indictable offences and school leaving age has not been satisfactorily explained or explained away. In effect, as Power has shown, there seem to be two groups of offenders in the juvenile age range: on the one hand, there are secondary schoolboys who steal and they account for the indictable age peak at 14; on the other hand, there are the older schoolboys and young workers who become increasingly involved in a range of offences, such as offences of minor violence, aggression and traffic offences. So that while new cases of stealing decrease fairly rapidly after 14, the total for all offences continues to rise. Secondly, commonsense attitudes towards schools in any given community call into question the assumption of constancy; schools of the same type in the same neighbourhood acquire different qualitative reputations amongst parents, children, and teachers. These judgements are likely to stem from a wide range of sources and may have little relation to the actual educational performance of the schools measured in terms of, say, examination results; nor may these public reputations have anything to do with delinquency but commonsense perceptions do suggest that overtly similar schools provide their members with qualitatively different experiences. Thus at the commonsense level of understanding two perceptions, concerning the official peak age for delinquency and differential reputations of overtly similar schools, provide the background for an analysis of delinquency and educational processes.

Evidence from a continuing study of the juvenile court population in one homogeneous inner urban working class London borough provides the foundation for a range of hypotheses concerning the relationship between schools and patterns of delinquency (11). Since 1958 basic data has been collected by the Social Medicine Research Unit of the Medical Research Council on all children resident in the borough who have appeared before a juvenile court anywhere for offences almost always committed off school premises and out of school hours; included in this data are school attended and home address.

One general finding of the study was that, in terms of official prevalence, one boy in every four resident in the borough made at least one court appearance as a juvenile. When this figure of official prevalence is placed in the context of all the studies of self-reported delinquency, both in America and England, it can be seen that delinquency is an essentially normal activity for boys in the borough (12). The findings about the schools are limited to male juveniles. Secondary school population figures were obtained for each year since 1958 thus enabling the computation of annual delinquency rates for all secondary modern schools in the borough; at the commencement of the study there were twenty such schools (13). Enumeration district delinquency rates for the 301 census enumeration districts in the borough were also calculated by relating home addresses of the official delinquents to census population data for the enumeration districts (14).

Firstly, the character of the schools' delinquency rates suggests that the notion of constancy, implicit in the previous delinquency literature is a myth; Tables 1 and 2 show that there was gross variation in delinquency rates between the twenty schools and that these differences were remarkably consistent over a six year period (a period during which the school population had turned over completely); the high rate schools had consistently high rates throughout the period while only a few boys from the low rate schools appeared before the courts over the six years. The annual computation of these school rates has continued for the reduced number of schools since 1964 and the consistent pattern of gross variation between the thirteen remaining schools has persisted. Table 1 gives the incidence rates for the schools and shows that the range in the annual average of boys making a first court appearance is very wide. The differences between the schools are even more marked when all court appearances are included; this can be seen from Table 2 where school rates

TABLE 1 First Appearances Before The Courts (Cases Proven) 1958-64		TABLE 2 Annual Average of all Cases Proven Before The Courts 1958-64	
Secondary schools in the borough	Annual average 'delinquency rate' per 100 boys aged 11 – 14	Secondary Schools in the borough	Annual average 'delinquency rate' per 100 boys aged 11 – 14
J	0.7	J	0.9
B	1.2	B	1.9
R	1.5	R	2.1
N	1.9	N	2.6
D	2.1	D	3.2
P	2.3	G	5.2
G	2.8	P	5.7
L	3.3	S	6.1
F	3.5	E	7.2
S	3.6	T	7.7
E	3.8	F	7.8
C	4.0	H	8.5
T	4.1	U	8.8
H	4.3	O	9.2
U	4.4	W	9.8
O	4.4	C	10.0
W	4.8	L	10.4
A	5.7	A	13.8
Q	6.4	Q	16.6
M	7.8	M	19.0
All	3.4	All	7.2

Annual average number of boys in these schools = 4,691
Annual average number of first offenders (Case proven) = 160

for all cases proven are shown (this includes those boys who appear several times in one year or in more than one year). In fact the situation was one in which a majority of the borough's official delinquents went to a minority of its schools (15).

These wide variations in incidence and appearance rates were not related in any consistent way to differences in the more obvious overt characteristics of the schools and thus cannot be explained in terms of them; the differences were unrelated to school size, to the sex or ethnic composition of the school, to the 'local authority' or 'voluntary' management status of the schools, to the age and type of the school buildings, or to other processes of selection (16). The differences were also unrelated to the character of the intake into the secondary schools at the age of 11; there were two aspects to this. Firstly, the overall ability mix of the entry to each school at the age of 11 (that is whether the school selected given proportions of children of different ability gradings or was unselective) did not differentiate between schools with different delinquency rates. Secondly, when one year's intake from the feeder primary schools of one secondary school was analysed the primary schools showed no ability to pick out the future delinquents: there were adverse comments by the head on half the boys who later became officially delinquent and nothing on the remaining half; moreover there was no difference in the verbal reasoning and arithmetic scores between the future delinquents and non-delinquents. Quite apart from the fact that very few children have become officially delinquent before transfer to secondary school it was clear that the primary schools were not selecting out the potential delinquents and directing them to particular schools; thus the secondary school selection decisions of parents, primary school heads, and secondary school heads, and the criteria on which they were based were unrelated to the schools' delinquency rates.

Finally there was no known variation in local police practices that could have contributed to, let alone have accounted for, these differences in school rates. Certainly official statistics and court populations are the result of selective social control processes and cannot be taken as indices of the quantity and quality of delinquency in the community; nevertheless careful analysis of official data may reveal patterns which are too consistent to ignore and which at the same time are unrelated to the processes of law enforcement and official statistic construction. In the present case there is neither empirical evidence nor a logical explanation to support the argument that the regularities of the data on schools and delinquency were mere epiphenomena of official social control processes.

However the key argument which would refute the hypothesis that aspects of school life differentially facilitate the drift into delinquency concerns the role of the schools' catchment areas. The obvious question is, do the schools with high rates draw their pupils and their official delinquents disproportionately from high rate neighbourhoods and the low rate schools vice versa? Is the school rate simply a reflection of a surrounding officially highly delinquent sub-culture? To answer this question meant separating out the effects of neighbourhood and school, to see if school rates were at all independent of catchment area rates.

The delinquency rates for the enumeration districts showed even greater variation in incidence and appearance rates than the schools; thus over an eight year period (1958–1965) some districts had an annual average first court appearance rate of over 12% while others had rates of less that 1%. However the interesting feature of this data concerned the variation in enumeration district rates within the socially homogeneous borough; the variation in delinquency rates between enumeration districts within the borough was as gross as the variation between whole zones or social areas found by the American delinquency ecologists. These within-borough differences in a socially homogeneous area, like the data on the schools, reinforce the suggestion that there is a considerable gap between American theories about delinquency and the English evidence. Two methods were used to relate the variation in school delinquency rates to the variation in enumeration district rates.

Five schools were chosen which covered the full range of delinquency. Each school's population for one year (1964-1965) was taken and every boy in the school, officially delinquent and officially non-delinquent, was given the delinquency rate of the enumeration district in which he lived. Table 3 shows the results of the first method. The enumeration districts were divided into two groups, a high and a low group, according to their delinquency rates; every boy in each of the five schools was then classified according to whether he lived in a high or a low rate district. Column 2 in the Table gives the 'total prevalence' (the proportion of boys in the school in 1964-65 who had ever been officially delinquent). This proportion is then given for those boys living in high and those in low rate enumeration districts; it can be seen that, within any one school, there is little difference in the delinquency rates of boys living in high and those in low districts. If school rate had been a mere reflection of the catchment districts' rates one would have found that for each school the proportion of delinquents living in high delinquency districts was much higher than the proportion of those living in low rate districts; in fact there is no significant difference in the proportions between the two groups.

The alternative method is shown in Table 4. The population of each of the five schools was divided into two groups, the officially delinquent and the officially non-delinquent. The Weighted Mean Delinquency Rates for the enumeration districts where the two groups lived were then calculated; this was done by assigning to each boy the actual rate of the district where he lived, summing these rates for each group, and then obtaining the average rate for each group by dividing by the number of boys in the two groups. The Table shows that the high delinquency rate schools did not

TABLE 3 Relation of Delinquency Rates to Districts
Served by the Schools: Method 1

Secondary schools in the borough	'Delinquency rate' Prevalence in 1964-65 per 100 boys aged 11-14 Resident in		
	All Districts	"High" Delinquency Districts	"Low" Delinquency Districts
	%	%	%
B	3	3	4
D	4	6	3
K	7	9	5
C	11	13	9
Q	25	25	25
Average in these schools	8	10	6

No. of boys in these schools = 1,717
No. of the boys 'ever delinquent' = 141

TABLE 4 Relation of Delinquency Rates to Districts
Served by the Schools: Method 2

	Secondary Schools in the borough				
	Q	C	K	D	B
Proportion of boys 11 − 14 "ever delinquent"	25	11	7	4	3
W.M.D.R. for E.D.'s where delinquents live	8.2	9.7	9.1	8.7	8.9
W.M.D.R. for E.D.'s where non-delinquents live	9.6	8.4	8.0	7.7	7.1

W.M.D.R. = Weighted Mean Delinquency Rate
E.D. = Enumeration District

draw their pupils from enumeration districts with higher delinquency rates than the low rate delinquency schools; in fact, quite against expectation, in the highest rate school (Q) the Weighted Mean Delinquency Rates for enumeration districts where non-delinquents lived was actually higher than

244

that for the districts where the official delinquents were resident. Thus the conclusion is that the variation between schools in delinquency rates is not accounted for by variation in the district rates. Some schools apparently protect their pupils from delinquency while others may put them at risk of it. In the remainder of this paper empirical evidence from other sources and hypotheses derived from personal observation in the schools themselves are used to suggest some of the issues which research following up these findings might consider (17).

The overall problem of interpretation raised by these findings would seem to be this: given that every school is unique, are there any typical features of these schools which are consistently related to their pattern of delinquency rates? How could some schools provide a framework which inhibits the delinquent response and others one which encourages it? This general question immediately raises the issue of the various levels of analysis at which the findings might be followed up; complementary data from several levels of analysis would seem essential for any adequate interpretation. Thus, for example, data would be required at the level of the relationship between the school and the community (for example in terms of the differential allocation of resources between schools), at the level of the school as a highly structured social organisation, at the various levels of interaction within the school, and at the level of the typical social meanings attached to school life by the participants in it. No attempt is made in the following discussion to provide a comprehensive coverage of all the possibly relevant issues at each level of analysis; the present selection of issues is dependent upon existing evidence and ideas from other studies and on personal observation.

As noted earlier, previous references to the school in the literature on delinquency have been confined to the most general questions about the relationship between the school and the wider community, as in the discussions of Cohen, and Cloward and Ohlin. For this reason these more general questions are passed over here in favour of focussing on those aspects of school life which have largely been ignored by writers on delinquency. However it is worth noting in passing one aspect of the relationship between schools and the wider political community. The Plowden Committee's recommendations concerning positive discrimination in favour of educational priority areas at the primary school level (18) suggests that there is increasing recognition that many primary schools have been deprived of adequate resources; that the same deprivation has occurred at the secondary level seems a logical extension of Plowden's thinking and analysis. There is thus public and official acceptance that there are large differences between areas in the standards of educational provision; it requires only a small leap to recognise that these large differences occur not only between areas but between schools in the same area (19). These differences are likely to be subtly related to both local and national issues of educational policy.

However if the aim is to understand the differences in delinquency rates between an apparently homogeneous group of schools more specific analyses are required. In particular it would seem relevant to examine those features of school organisation which may crucially affect the patterns of interaction and the styles of action which emerge within a school and which may influence teachers' and pupils' definitions of their situations. One way of approaching this is to view the school as a social organisation in which social identities are created and are sustained, and to examine the social processes through which these occur; in this context the emergence of one particular kind of identity, the delinquent identity, would seem to be important (20). What are the features of school organisation which can differ considerably between schools and that might initially encourage the delinquent response and subsequently the emergence of a delinquent identity?

The school is organised around the point of teacher-pupil interaction and is judged and evaluated in terms of the outcome of this interaction. An analytical distinction can be made between two broad areas of influence of teachers on pupils (21). Firstly, there are the 'academic' or 'pedagogic' goals of the school, the imparting of quantities of knowledge and techniques of learning. There is more or less agreement over what these ends are even though there is disagreement over the means for achieving them. The character of these pedagogic ends and the techniques used in trying to achieve them in different strata of the educational system (for example grammar, technical, secondary modern, comprehensive) opens up or closes off future opportunities for the pupils and is of obvious importance to pupils' perceptions of their post-school future. Secondly, there are the non-academic values (for example moral and political values) which are mediated by teachers both intentionally and unintentionally; little agreement exists among teachers over the non-academic ends or means of education. There is confusion among them about the 'right' position to adopt and the appropriate extent of their influence over a wide range of such issues. This ambivalence and uncertainty does not necessarily lessen their influence in relation to these issues but it does suggest that it is likely to take on an arbitrary and chance character which is more open to a range of subtle pressures than the more stable pedagogic values. Variable features of school organisation which impinge on the teaching situation may influence in unintended directions the ways in which these non-academic issues are handled in different schools. The point is that both the pedagogic and non-pedagogic values of the school and the ways they are handled may be related to delinquency; but the pedagogic, being both more stable and more or less common to all parts of a given stratum of the educational system are more likely to exert a relatively constant influence in terms, for example, of the way they may structure pupils' future life-styles. This constant kind of influence would seem to be nearer that implied by Cohen, Cloward and Ohlin, and Downes in their discussion of the relation between the school, the educational system, and delinquency. Where there is a uniform and national system of education, as in England, it is these constant features which both link the individual pupil to the wider political community and its decisions, and also give him a set of experiences which are typical for a large segment of the school population. However the more variable handling of the non-pedagogic values may be equally important in its effects on various aspects of pupils' school careers; any given school would seem to acquire what Webb calls its 'tone' (22) largely from its handling of the non-academic aspects of the educational process. The reputation of the school in the local community would seem to rest more on the overt factors, such as the boys' dress and behaviour outside the school, than from its academic record, which may be both non-existent and irrelevant in many inner-urban communities. Non-academic criteria clearly enter into teachers' definitions of pupils' characters, of the discipline problem, or into their commitment to non-classroom school activities, and it is in these and other areas that teachers' personal values may impinge in various ways on pupils' delinquencies.

The analytical problem is to locate those aspects of school life which influence teachers' and pupils' typical definitions of their interaction situations so as to encourage delinquent responses by pupils not only inside but more especially outside the bounds of the school. The following suggestions concerning some of these possible influences are limited to selected features of the formal structure of the school and some aspects of teachers' definitions of their situations (23).

At the institutional level there appear to be several aspects of school which structure the patterns of staff-pupil interaction. A general hypothesis is that high staff turnover and absenteeism rates contribute to certain definitions of the school situation by teachers and pupils. A high staff turnover means that pupils are regularly faced with different authority figures who make different and often conflicting demands upon them; the lack of steady, stable relationships will tend to result in a confusion among pupils about how to respond in similar situations to a constant flow of different teachers. A regular turnover of teachers provides a setting for the growth of cynicism among pupils about the worth of their school; one result may be a steady decline in the evaluation by pupils both of the school and of themselves. It becomes clear to them that the school, and by extension themselves, are not rated highly by the succession of teachers who pass through. This 'low institutional pride', shared by both pupils and teachers, creates a climate for both rebellion and dissociation from the school as an institution. Various types of delinquent acts, inside and outside the school, such as minor vandalism, truancy or theft, may partly reflect this rebellion. The expectation would therefore be that schools with high turnover rates would have higher delinquency rates than those with low rates of turnover.

The sociological literature on formal organisations contains a few

247

references to turnover of personnel and its effect on internal organisational relationships; there is, however, some supportive evidence for this turnover hypothesis from two other sources. Firstly as part of a subsequent study of the Inner London Education Authority's welfare services carried out by the Social Research Unit of Bedford College (24), I undertook a study of 42 primary schools to illustrate a method for defining schools in need of priority treatment for welfare services. Data were collected for each school on two groups of factors: a series of indices of staff turnover were computed and these were correlated with a group of 'problem' indices which were taken as an estimate of the welfare problems faced by the schools (25). Several kinds of correlation coefficients were computed, for example, each factor with every other factor, and the group of staff turnover indices with the group of problem indices; the results showed that there were positive relationships between the turnover indices and the problem indices. Primary schools which had high staff turnover were typically the schools which possessed the greatest welfare problems (26). As this analysis was carried out on primary schools only it obviously could not include any data on delinquency. This finding may be seen then as tentative support for the high turnover/high delinquency hypothesis; if the group of welfare problems was stretched to include school delinquency rates it is possible that this type of analysis at the secondary school level would produce similar results.

A second source of generally supportive evidence comes from two studies of mental hospitals. Wulbert, in a study of inmate behaviour in a ward of a mental hospital (27), suggested that 'low inmate pride' (the avoidance of identification with inmate status) underlay dimensions of collective behaviour in the ward. He found that a period of disorder in which patients' deviance increased sharply (assaults, elopement, destruction, and refusals) was preceded by an unusually high turnover of staff and patients. Whilst his concept of 'low inmate pride' is not directly transferable to the school setting in the form in which he conceptualised it, his findings lend support to the high turnover hypothesis. Similarly, Stanton and Schwartz in their earlier study of a mental hospital noted that collective disturbances on the ward were typically preceded by a period of partial disorganisation among the staff (28).

There is evidence to support the investigation of the relationship between delinquency rates and other aspects of the formal school organisation. Hargreaves in his valuable study of the social relations in 'Lumley' school (29), an inner-urban secondary modern, describes two features of school organisation which are relevant in the present context, streaming and the curriculum. Some of Hargreaves' most interesting findings relate to the effects of streaming on the boys in the school and especially its effect on the development of different peer groups within the school. He showed that there was a strong gradient across the four streams in the fourth year in the percentage of boys with at least one court appearance (in 4A — 3% and in 4D 55%) and posited the emergence of two distinct sub-cultures in the school; these two sub-cultures, a conforming and a 'delinquescent' sub-culture (whose attitudes were negative in terms of the school's values) emerged during the third and fourth years partly as a response to the streaming system. The boys who present discipline problems were consistently demoted through the streams during their school careers; this system of transfer between streams led to a convergence of boys with similar orientations in the same stream. Hargreaves notes that there was no homogeneity of I.Q. within the streams, so that several boys who started their secondary school careers in the top streams, through successive demotions had ended up in the C and D streams by the fourth year. This sub-cultural polarisation effect of the streaming system was reinforced firstly, by the structure of the time-table which led to different opportunities for interaction between upper and lower stream boys and the consequent development of negative stereotypes between the two halves of the streaming system, and secondly by the tendency of teachers to favour and reward high stream boys at the expense of their peers in the low streams. Hargreaves' data on responses to streaming lends some support to Cohen's 'negative polarity' hypothesis (30).

A related aspect of formal organisation, the curriculum, is discussed both by Hargreaves and by Stinchcombe in his study, 'Rebellion in a High School' (31), and is of relevance to understanding the negative or delinquent responses of boys to school. In the English education system examination results are the proffered carrot, the prime motivating device, but low stream boys see these as irrelevant to their perceived futures (32). Hargreaves argues that one of the principle reasons for the progressive retardation and development of a delinquescent sub-culture among the low stream boys is the fact that they are unlikely to be motivated to work hard at school because they cannot see any useful or tangible reward for their labours. This is often reflected in teachers' behaviour towards low stream boys; they expect little of the boys who subsequently come to adapt to this reduced expectation with a lowered level of aspiration and self-evaluation. Further evidence on this is provided by Stinchcombe; using data from an elaborate questionnaire study in one American high school he suggests that rebellion (truancy and disruptive class behaviour) is strongly and consistently related to attitudes of 'expressive alienation' (a term taken from Cohen) from school values and activities. Such alienation is partly a result of the disjunctive articulation between the curriculum and the labour market for many of the pupils. This problem is likely to be exacerbated by the conflicting definitions of the aims of the school held by pupils and teachers; a study of young school leavers found that there were very big differences between pupils and heads in what they thought were the the school's most important objectives. The most important school objectives for the boys concerned the teaching of things connected with their future employment, while these received very low priority among the heads for whom the most important objectives were concerned with personality and character (33).

Using a similar argument to that of Hargreaves in relation to the perceived future which schoolchildren see for themselves, Stinchcombe makes the point that the school cannot promise much because the society cannot promise much. Schools are peculiarly dependent on images of the future as motivating devices and the rewards they can offer for adherence to school values are purely symbolic. For those boys not heading for the kind of adulthood approved by the school and enshrined in the curriculum, the main symbols of development towards adulthood (e.g. masculinity) are symbols not controlled by the formal organisation of the school. Sugarman's data on secondary school boys' attachment to youth culture values complements Stinchcombe's findings. He found that poor conduct ratings of the boys in school were strongly related to their commitment to the 'teenage role' and to a youth culture which rejected conformity to the school's values (34). Further areas of investigation would thus be the relationship between streaming, curriculum organisation and content and differential rates of delinquency between schools.

Personal observation in the schools of the delinquency study suggests that it may be possible to develop a typology of teachers according to their motivational patterns. It seemed that different kinds of teachers predominated in the different schools and that the balance between these types of teachers in any given school impinged directly on the character of teacher-pupil interaction. The balance of types was inevitably related to the pattern of teacher turnover. A crude classification according to the teacher's overall orientation to education suggests that there are at least five types of teacher to be found in inner urban schools: firstly, there are long-stay teachers who have a high degree of pupil involvement and who are committed to teaching in such areas. Secondly, there is a group of young, inexperienced teachers at a crucial career stage whose initial teaching experience may well influence their decisions to stay in or leave such areas. Thirdly, there is a group of long-stay teachers who lack the 'pupil involvement' of the first group but who remain in such areas out of apathy or because they lack qualifications for advancement elsewhere; they may even achieve a degree of upward occupational mobility in these areas, because of the lack of competition, which they could not achieve elsewhere, so that there may be a positive incentive to remain in the area. Fourthly, there are 'subject-oriented' teachers who are comparatively rare in inner urban areas because their academic interests are unlikely to be met. Fifthly there are the supply teachers, many of whom, although lacking both pupil and subject involvement, may stay for extended periods in such schools because of the shortage of teachers; supply teachers are really stop-gaps and this is reflected in many teachers' view of them as 'child minders'.

This is obviously not an exhaustive typology and typologies based on other criteria could be developed (35); however, the hypothesis here is both that these groups of teachers are not scattered randomly between the schools and also that the different combinations and concentrations of types will be related to the differential distribution of delinquency between schools. For example, a high turnover school, almost by definition, will have a preponderance of types two and five; another school might have a fairly stable but predominantly apathetic staff and so on. Clearly an ideal balance between types cannot be put forward, but it seems likely that some concentrations of types will have deleterious effects on the character of teacher-pupil relationships, perhaps contributing to pupils' 'expressive alienation', while others may create conditions for stable and creative relationships.

A further point about the two related structural characteristics, turnover and the balance of teacher types, is that they are both likely to be self-propagating. Whatever the sources of high turnover (for example, the chance departure of three or four long-stay teachers at the same time) once started, the spiral of instability is hard to stop, for new teachers, particularly young and inexperienced teachers, tend to take their cues from the definitions of the teaching situation already in existence in a school. It may be very difficult for a young teacher to reject the informal values and attitudes of the staff room; if these attitudes encourage a steady flow of teachers through the institution the new teacher may rapidly opt to join the exodus.

Finally at the level of interaction between teachers and between teachers and pupils within the school there are two aspects of the teachers' social meaning structures (36) which are relevant to an understanding of the relationship between school and delinquency. One concerns the social processes through which certain meanings emerge and the other some aspects of the substantive content of teachers' social meaning structures (37).

The school provides a useful setting in which to investigate the 'labelling process' (38) in relation to the development of delinquent careers. Cicourel and Kitsuse (39) point out that the school can be viewed as producing a variety of adolescent careers, such as 'academic', 'clinical', or 'delinquent' careers, the sociological problem being to understand the processes and their consequences for adolescents' school careers by which adolescents 'come to be defined and classified as social types' (40). The variety of adolescent school careers are reflected in various school rates, such as, the drop-out rate, the college attendance rate, the truancy rate, and in this context we can include the delinquency rate, although surprisingly this is not referred to by Cicourel and Kitsuse; these rates can be viewed as summary indices of a range of organisationally produced adolescent careers. In their discussion of the process of social typing of delinquent careers in the school, Cicourel and Kitsuse concentrate on the 'interpretive rules utilised by the organisational personnel who decide

251

what forms of behaviour and what kinds of evidence warrant actions which define individuals as deviant within the system' (41). The development of delinquent careers and the imputations of delinquent identities to pupils by teachers in the school may be critically influenced by information received by the school from outside sources; information brought to the school's attention by the court, the police, social workers, or local residents may subtly re-orient teachers' perceptions of the boy. The generalised symbolic value of a deviant label like 'delinquent' and its stereotypical character may lead school personnel (and others) to reconstruct the biography of a boy so that his delinquency becomes 'understandable' or is seen as reflecting what the boy had 'essentially' been like all the time (42).

A complementary aspect of the labelling process and imputations of deviant identity, which is not discussed by Cicourel and Kitsuse but study of which is essential for understanding the development of delinquent and deviant careers, is the response of the boy to the labelling process. If a long-term delinquent career reflects some self-imputations of a delinquent identity by a boy, do these self-imputations have their sources in typically recurring situations? Sociologists have so far tended to emphasise the formal stages of penal processing (for example, the court appearance or institutionalisation) as the significant steps in the development of a deviant identity (43); however, it may be equally as important to study the consequences for self-concept of social typing, stereotyping, and stigmatisation in less formal and public interaction settings, such as the classroom, the headmaster's study, the peer group, or the family. Study of the social processes through which delinquent careers are generated and sustained and of the social meanings of a delinquent identity within the school could clarify the differential distribution of delinquency rates between schools.

Informal discussion with teachers and observation in the schools suggests that there are aspects of teachers' perceptions of delinquency as a problem which are likely to reinforce the pattern of delinquency between schools. In particular the character of their attitudes towards and their knowledge of delinquency in general, in the local community, and in their own school in particular are of relevance. Firstly, even taking the official criminal statistics as a criterion, their level of information about delinquency was low; they typically shared the common public misconceptions about the main parameters of criminal and delinquent activities, that is, of the prevalence and scale of different offences (for example the tendency to exaggerate the amount of violent crime). As a consequence they knew little about the actual character of delinquency within the community in which they taught and how it compared to other communities; they had only the scantiest knowledge about, for example, the number of local children making court appearances. This ignorance is, of course, shared with most of the population for there is no reliable local

252

information available on such issues. Reflecting this general pattern of misinformation, and most important in this context, they knew little about the prevalence of official delinquency in either their own school or in the other local schools; they certainly knew nothing of the gross differences in rates between schools. Interestingly this actual lack of knowledge frequently went hand in hand with a firm belief among teachers that they had a very good knowledge of the delinquents in their own school (44).

This misinformation about the local pattern of delinquency had consequences for the way teachers defined the problem in their school. Because they had no yardstick against which to set their own experience and no accurate knowledge of the situation, whatever the actual rate of delinquency in their school, they typically defined the situation as normal; whether the school had a very high, an average, or a very low rate, the teachers, knowing nothing of these differences, had no reason to define the situation as anything other than absolutely normal. Levels of delinquency were typically defined as 'exactly what one would expect in a school (or neighbourhood) like this'. Their typical beliefs about the aetiology of delinquency complemented and reinforced this definition of normality; the home, the family, and 'bad company' were some of the mono-causal scapegoats used by teachers to account for delinquency. As these scapegoats invariably lay beyond the school walls, so all responsibility for the 'problem' of delinquency could be placed elsewhere, usually on parents, police, social workers, or the juvenile court. Very few teachers saw the school as in any way a contributor to the patterns of delinquency and as a result responsibility for action in relation to the problem was conveniently placed elsewhere. Thus the definition of normality, when wedded to the ideas of responsibility, seemed to lead to an acceptance of the delinquency status quo and a claim by teachers that no new action or re-appraisal of the school's role in relation to the problem was required. These selected aspects of the meanings attached by teachers to delinquency seem likely to re-inforce the delinquency-fostering situations in the high-rate schools.

There were other aspects of teachers' reactions to delinquency in the schools which are worth further investigation. Several sociologists have referred to the 'institutional immunity' to law enforcement offered by some organisational settings (45). The school is a prime example of one such organisation; many delinquent acts take place within schools which never come to the attention of officials outside the school (for example theft, vandalism, insulting behaviour, and minor forms of violence). Schools prefer to deal with internal delinquency themselves and only on very rare occasions do they call in the police to deal with an offence committed within the school. This seems to reflect a curious reversal of attitude, usually on the part of headmasters: whilst the overall causes of and responsibility for delinquency were typically attributed to external

253

agents, when internal delinquencies occurred the school invariably assumed responsibility for action. This could have been for a variety of reasons, such as guarding the public reputation of the school or even because the school felt that although not responsible it could deal with the problem more effectively than other agents. These responses and the consequent institutional immunity of the schools creates a double standard of enforcement of which pupils are well aware; offences open to prosecution outside can be committed with relative impunity within the school. Whilst the pattern of internal handling of cases was common to the schools there was considerable variation between them in the kinds of disciplinary responses and punishments used in dealing with internal delinquencies.

The comparative isolation of the school from those agents who have external responsibility for delinquency, especially social work agencies, may contribute to this 'go-it-alone' approach of the school to delinquency; the rarity of contact between the school and social welfare organisations and their frequent mutual antagonism seems to reflect misunderstandings and prejudices of both sides about the other's role. Certainly a common stereotype of social work held by teachers is rooted in nineteenth century conceptions of social work as a combination of the provision of moral uplift and free shoes.

In conclusion, the suggestion is that the school situation appears to be a strategic setting in which to examine some aspects of the development of delinquent careers. Evidence has been presented which suggests both that the assumption of constancy of the schools' influence and the abstract model of the school which are found in the literature on delinquency are myths and that the character of a given school may contribute to the quantity and quality of delinquent activities of its pupils. These myths are reinforced by the commonsense understandings and perceptions of the teachers in the schools, their perceptions of the problem and their definition of the situation as normal perpetuate the very structures and processes which appear to be contributing to the creation of delinquent identities and careers. If we are to understand the processes through which these differential responses between schools occur, analysis at several complementary levels seems necessary; the typical social meanings attached to school experiences by the participants must be placed in the context of both the structural characteristics of the schools and also the articulation between the school and the surrounding political culture.

1. The main contributors to the sub-cultural 'school' are, A. Cohen Delinquent Boys New York, Free Press (1955); R. Cloward and L. Ohlin Delinquency and Opportunity New York, Free Press, (1960); and W. B. Miller 'Lower Class Culture as a Generating Milieu of Gang Delinquency' Journal of Social Issues 14 (3) (1958) pp. 5-19. For valuable critiques of the sub-cultural approach see, D. Matza Delinquency and Drift New York, John Wiley & Sons Inc. (1964); A. V. Cicourel The Social Organisation of Juvenile Justice New York, John Wiley & Sons Inc. (1968); J. F. Short and F. L. Strodbeck Group Process and Gang Delinquency

Chicago, University of Chicago Press (1965); D. M. Downes The Delinquent Solution London, Routledge & Kegan Paul (1966). See also the preceding section of this book. There has been a considerable amount of prescriptive writing by sociologists on the role of the school in relation to delinquency: see for example W. Kvaraceus Juvenile Delinquency and the School New York, World Book Company (1945) and The Dynamics of Delinquency New York, Merrill Books (1966); R. M. Maciver The Prevention and Control of Delinquency New York, Atherton (1966) Chap 11. For the most comprehensive summary of the existing American sociological literature on the school and delinquency, both analytical and prescriptive, see W. E. Schafer and K. Polk 'Delinquency and the Schools' Taskforce Report: Juvenile Delinquency and Youth Crime Washington, Presidents' Commission on Law Enforcement and Administration of Justice (1967) Appendix M pp. 222-277

2. See Matza op cit. and Cicourel op. cit.

3. Analysis of these processes can be found in the work of those authors writing within the broader deviance perspective; for example, H. Becker Outsiders New York, Free Press (1963) and (ed) The Other Side New York, Free Press (1964); E. Lemert Social Pathology New York, McGraw-Hill (1951), and Human Deviance, Social Problems and Social Control Englewood Cliffs, Prentice-Hall Inc. (1967); K. Erickson Wayward Puritans New York, John Wiley & Sons Inc. (1966); D. Matza Becoming Deviant Englewood Cliffs, Prentice-Hall (1969) and J. Lofland Deviance and Identity Englewood Cliffs, Prentice-Hall (1969)

4. See Downes op. cit.

5. On one aspect of the differences see R. H. Turner's comparison of selection in the English and American educational systems: R. H. Turner, 'Sponsored and Contest Mobility and the School System' in A. H. Halsey, Jean Floud, and C. Arnold Anderson Education, Economy and Society New York, Free Press (1961) Chap. 12

6. See footnote 3

7. Macdonald, in a study of the admitted delinquencies of secondary school boys, found that the type of school (Grammar or Secondary Modern) was independently associated with admission rates for some offences; there was a greater tendency for Secondary Modern boys to admit to some offences. Moreover, she found that middle class children at Secondary Modern schools admitted to more delinquency than their counterparts at grammar schools, implying that the type of school had an independent effect on admission to delinquencies. She suggested that the Secondary Modern as a type acted to increase the same offences for which working class children had already 'shown some affinity' (p. 109). She did not suggest, however, that there might be large differences between Secondary Moderns in their delinquency producing propensity; in fact her suggestion is that the effect of type of school is for the most part an extension of the effect of social class L. Macdonald Social Class and Delinquency London, Faber & Faber (1969)

8. Downes op. cit. p. 60

9. Criminologists invariably speak of 14 as being the peak age for official crime *in general*; in fact, as M. J. Power has shown, it is only the peak age for indictable offences and when non-indictable offences are added the peak age moves out of the juvenile age range. It is thus quite misleading to speak of 14 as the peak age for all official crime. The age peak at 14 is accounted for almost entirely by minor indictable theft offences. See M. J. Power 'Trends in Juvenile Delinquency' The Times London (9th August 1962)

10. See especially A. V. Cicourel and J. I. Kitsuse 'A Note on the Use of Official Statistics' Social Problems 11 (1963) p. 131

11. For earlier brief presentations of these findings see C. M. Phillipson 'Juvenile Delinquency and the School' The Teacher's World London, (28th June 1966) and M. J. Power, M. R. Alderson, C. M. Phillipson, E. Shoenberg, J. N. Morris,

'Delinquent Schools?' New Society London, (19th October 1967) p. 542

12. These self-reporting studies suggest that the official statistics do register the main trends of delinquent activity. For example, Belsen in a very carefully designed study found not only that about 50% of boys in his sample admitted to acts for which they could be brought to court but also that there was a direct relationship between frequency of admitted stealing and likelihood of being caught: W. Belsen The Extent of Stealing by London Boys and Some of its Causes London, Survey Research Centre, L.S.E. (1969). For comparative American material see M. Gold Status Forces in Delinquent Boys Ann Arbor, The University of Michigan (1963)

13. The delinquency rates for the few independent grammar schools in the borough were negligible; the twenty secondary schools between them took 85% of the borough's boys aged 11-14 inclusive. Educational re-organisation in the twelve years since 1958 has reduced the number of non-grammar schools to thirteen; some of these are designated as comprehensive schools although the independent grammar schools remain in the borough

14. Ennumeration districts, unlike American census tracts, are geographically and socially arbitrary units which contain an average population of 600

15. The only other published comparative data comes from a study in the West Riding; Clegg and Megson obtained data on court appearances by pupils of thirty schools during a three-year period. A similar pattern of variation in school delinquency rates was found. These rates were related to socio-economic indices of the schools' environments, to divisional education officers' assessments of the schools, and to the schools' use of corporal punishment; the results were somewhat inconclusive but suggested that delinquency was least in those schools where 'corporal punishment was used sparingly'. A. Clegg and G. Megson Children in Distress Penguin Education Special, London, Penguin Books (1968) Chap. 10

16. For example, the pattern of parental choice in relation to secondary schools had no relation to delinquency; schools with both very high and very low rates of delinquency had a very high proportion of parental first choices. See also the New Society article by Power et al. op. cit. p. 542

17. We had hoped to test some of these hypotheses in the schools for which we had delinquency rates. However, the Inner London Education Authority prevented us from taking research any further by refusing us access to either the schools or to any documentary data about them. There is a certain irony in the fact that the very organisations and personnel whose ostensible goal is the advancement of knowledge both prevented the follow-up of these findings and refused to recognise their validity in spite of their obvious relevance to the problems faced by the schools

18. 'Children and Their Primary Schools' Report of the Central Advisory Council for Education Vol. 1 London, Her Majesty's Stationery Office (1967) paragraphs 131-177

19. Further support for this and the rejection of the assumption of constancy is contained in evidence from the Plowden Report: 400 H.M. Inspectors rated the country's 20,000 Primary Schools on a nine-point scale from 'outstanding' to 'bad/gross incompetence'; over one-seventh of all Primary Schools were placed in the bottom three categories of the scale. This official depiction of the gross variation in the quality of Primary Schools lends support to the hypothesis of similar variation at the secondary level. 'Children and their Primary Schools' op. cit. Vol. 1 Part 4, paragraphs 267-276

20. The argument is obviously not that the school is the only, or even the most important, setting for the creation of a delinquent identity, but rather that it is an important and neglected one

21. For an interesting alternative formulation of these two areas of influence and their relationships to social control within the school, see Bernstein's discussion of 'instrumental' and 'expressive' culture and their transmission by the school. B.

Bernstein et al. 'Ritual in Education' in J. Huxley (ed) 'A discussion of ritual-
isation in animals and man' Philosophical Transactions of the Royal Society of
London Series B. 251 London, (1966) p. 772

22. John Webb 'The Sociology of a School' British Journal of Sociology XIII (3)
London, (September 1962) pp. 264-272

23. The school can also be analysed from the point of view of the pupils, for
example, as a setting in which peer groups emerge and delinquent activities are
planned; see, for example, R. Lambert The Hothouse Society London, Weidenfeld
& Nicolson (1969). Similarly, the nature of informal staff relationships, their
harmony or disharmony, would seem to be related to the 'tone of the school'; the
headmaster likewise can exert great influence on many aspects of school life.
However, no evidence from other sources suggests any clear relationship between
any of these and the occurrence of delinquency and no clear hypotheses emerged
from personal observation. The most useful source of ideas for the analysis of
within-school processes is W. Waller The Sociology of Teaching New York, John
Wiley & Sons Inc. (1965) in which Waller views the school as a 'despotism in a
perilous state of equilibrium' and describes the processes by which this is
maintained and disrupted.

24. See M. Jefferys, B. M. Bryant, S. W. Guttmacher, and C. M. Phillipson The Social
Welfare Services of the I.L.E.A.: 1965-66 London, I.L.E.A. (1967)

25. The problem indices were: percentage of pupils receiving free school dinners,
percentage of parents absent from routine school medical examinations,
percentage of pupil turnover, and an index of the heads' estimates of the
prevalence of selected health and welfare problems among the pupils

26. For example, the correlation coefficient between annual staff turnover and the
percentage of pupils on free dinners was + .606; the relationship between the two
groups of factors was + .335; both were significant.

27. R. Wulbert 'Inmate Pride in Total Institutions' American Journal of Scoiology
71, (July 1965) p. 5

28. A. H. Stanton and M. S. Schwartz The Mental Hospital London, Tavistock (1954)
p. 395

29. D. H. Hargreaves Social Relations in a Secondary School London, Routledge &
Kegan Paul (1967). See also the paper by the same author in the preceding section
of this book.

30. Macdonald's data on the relation between streaming and admitted delinquencies
lends further support to Hargreaves' findings, op. cit. pp. 110 f.

31. A. Stinchcombe Rebellion in a High School Chicago, Quadrangle Books (1964).

32. W. H. Taylor, in The Secondary Modern School London, Faber & Faber (1963),
also discusses the ways in which secondary modern schools tried to ape the
grammar schools with inadequate resources and shows how there was a steady
move towards the incorporation of formal examinations in secondary modern
schools' curricula. J. Partridge, in Middle School London, Gollancz (1966),
similarly presents a depressing picture of the irrelevance of the school's activities
to a large group of pupils

33. R. Morton-Williams and S. Finch Enquiry I London, Schools Council, Her
Majesty's Stationery Office (1968) pp. 33 and 42

34. B. Sugarman 'Involvement in Youth Culture, Academic Achievement and
Conformity to School' British Journal of Sociology XVIII (2) (June 1967) p. 151

35. For a more elaborate discussion of teacher types and stereotypes, and alternative
criteria for a typology, see Waller op. cit., Chaps. 22 and 23

36. The term 'social meaning structure' is taken from the writing of A. Schutz; see
especially, A. Schutz Collected Papers Vol. 2. The Hague, Martinus Nijhoff
(1964). For sociologists in the social phenomenological tradition analysis of the
actors' typical social meaning sometimes is essential for valid sociological
explanation

257

37. Waller's analysis of teachers' and pupils' definitions of the situation is very relevant to an understanding of teachers' social meaning structures: op. cit. Chap. 18

38. For general discussions of labelling theory see Becker op. cit. Lemert op. cit., and Matza op. cit.

39. (a) A. V. Cicourel and J. I. Kitsuse 'The Social Organisation of the High School and Deviant Adolescent Careers' in E. Rubington and M. S. Weinberg (eds) Deviance: the Interactionist Perspective New York, Macmillan (1968) and (b) A. V. Cicourel and J. I. Kitsuse The Educational Decision Makers Indianapolis, Bobbs Merrill (1963).

40. Rubington and Weinberg op. cit. p. 126

41. Cicourel and Kitsuse (a) op. cit. p. 133

42. For a discussion of this process in relation to stereotypes of mental illness see T. J. Scheff Being Mentally Ill Chicago, Aldine Books (1966) pp. 64-83

43. See, for example, H. Garfinkel, 'Conditions of successful Degradation Ceremonies' American Journal of Sociology 61 (March 1956) pp. 420-24; F. Tannenbaum Crime and the Community New York, Columbia University (1938); E. Goffman Asylums New York, Doubleday Anchor (1961).

44. This delusion may partly have resulted from the fact that officially the school is supposed to be informed about all court appearances and should provide the juvenile court with a school report on each child before the courts; however, due to pressure on the courts and the speed with which many cases are dealt, school reports are obtained for only a proportion of all court cases (60% in the one school in which this was investigated). Even when the school is informed it is at the discretion of the head whether to disclose the information to other teachers; in the schools observed there seemed to be big differences between heads in the way they used this discretion

45. D. Chapman Sociology and the Stereotype of the Criminal London, Tavistock (1968); J. P. Martin Offenders as Employees London, Heinemann (1962)